GERDIEN JONKER, VALÉRIE AMIRAUX (EDS.)
POLITICS OF VISIBILITY
Young Muslims in European Public Spaces

[transcript]

© 2006 transcript Verlag, Bielefeld
Coverlayout: Kordula Röckenhaus, Bielefeld
Cover illustration: Patrick Zachmann, Voting Muslim representatives in France. Paris, April 2003; © 2006 Magnum Photos/Ag. Focus
Typeset by: Andrea Gruttmann, Bielefeld
Printed by: Majuskel Medienproduktion, Wetzlar
ISBN 3-89942-506-5

Distributed in North America by:

Transaction Publishers
New Brunswick (U.S.A.) and London (U.K.)

Transaction Publishers	Tel.: (732) 445-2280
Rutgers University	Fax: (732) 445-3138
35 Berrue Circle	for orders (U.S. only):
Piscataway, NJ 08854	toll free 888-999-6778

TABLE OF CONTENTS

Appendix

ACKNOWLEDGMENTS

This volume results from three years of collective brainstorming. We had two occasions to meet and discuss the work in progress. Our first meeting took place at the Centre Marc Bloch in Berlin on December 7, 2003. It was followed by an evening of discussion with some representatives of local Muslim associations, which provided the opportunity of open and intense exchange on different matters concerning Muslims in Europe. A second meeting took place at the Institut d'études de l'Islam et des sociétés du monde musulman (IISMM) in Paris on July 5, 2004. We thank the Heinrich Böll Stiftung and Aliyeh Yegane (Berlin), the Centre Marc Bloch, and the IISMM for making these meetings possible.

We also thank the contributors for having accepted to play the collective game from the beginning to the end and for helping to create the open and friendly atmosphere that was so constructive for our work. It showed us that collective scientific projects can be accomplished on a trustful basis and without stress. This approach also implied that the contributors accepted that we work with them on the different drafts of their texts, without considering our suggestions and discussions intrusive. For this trust, we express our heartfelt thanks.

With the exception of one, none of the authors is a native English speaker. Ginger A. Diekmann, the copyeditor of this volume, saved us time and energy, helping us to make the volume come into existence. And to make our "looks and sounds like English" actually become English. Finally, we express our gratitude to Karin Werner, director of the Global Local Islam Series at transcript, for welcoming our volume in her publication series.

During the research and in the final stages of the writing, three babies successively made their way into the world, somewhat disrupting the schedule. Their existence sometimes turned our endeavours into something closely resembling an equal opportunity adventure. Our final thanks therefore must go to Salomé (February 2004), Chloé (April 2004), and Daphne (October 2005) for helping us to prove that it can be done.

Gerdien Jonker and Valérie Amiraux

Valérie Amiraux & Gerdien Jonker

INTRODUCTION: TALKING ABOUT VISIBILITY – ACTORS, POLITICS, FORMS OF ENGAGEMENT

This volume started as several scholarly enterprises on the periphery of an international conference. Perhaps dissatisfaction with the meeting in question was at the root of its initiation, but more decisive, certainly, was that the right people happened to meet at the right time. The group that gathered together had not met before in this particular configuration. There were established academics and junior academics from different disciplines and with different scholarly backgrounds. Some had published extensively, whereas others were still working on their dissertation. What they shared was an awareness of a quickly growing gap in the field of Muslim visibility in Europe through the emergence of a heterogeneous and—to all appearances—very resourceful group of newcomers in the public arena. And a wish to make these voices available to a larger audience.

Mapping the Field of Muslim Visibility in Europe

In 2003, when we began the data collection that builds the basis of this book, policymakers and important segments of the media in many parts of Europe had been putting pressure on local Islamic organizations, accusing them of covering up fundamentalist sympathies and networks and of siding with terrorists. Translated into different discourses and practices, this trend spread throughout Europe. As a side effect of 9/11 and the Madrid bombings, the Islamic tradition was once again publicly charged of not being compatible with Western values such as democracy and human rights. Suspicion had taken root that, when all was said and done, Islam fostered principles that justified terrorism. Allegations of the incompatibility of Islamic and European values became stronger and more frequent, re-inviting public discussion about the loyalties of Muslim European citizens to democratic values. Almost everywhere in Europe, the public sought information about the scriptural basis of this religion, and sales of the Quran and related exegesis increased accordingly, sometimes creating the conditions for "public moral panics" that fed the general perception of Islam as an internal threat, in particular in countries where liberal multiculturalism had been the policy of choice (Werbner 2004, 452). A situation arose in which migrants from Muslim countries and their offspring were stigmatized as Muslims—regardless of their degree of religious involvement or Muslim identification—and treated as a potential danger.

Coinciding with this development was the emergence of a very heterogeneous group of young people which was publicly redefining what it meant to be a Muslim in Europe, as individuals or as members of a collective. Young people not only were taking the place of the older generation in almost all of the "old" Muslim associations across Europe—reflecting a generational shift in leadership in most of the European host countries. In addition, we noted that new youth groups were forming and organizing across the boundaries of nationality. Moreover, many actors made their entry on local and national stages who were not part of an organization and did not stress their religious belonging, but who nevertheless insisted on acting and speaking as a Muslim. What seemed to connect all these actors was their search for public recognition of a distinct identity that they themselves labeled "Muslim." They also shared a desire to be treated not as second-class citizens but as full citizens. In other words, a group of young people had made its entry on the European public stage, and it had laid claim to its own definitions over and against the political labels with which it saw itself confronted.

The countries in which we traced this group of people were Great Britain, the Netherlands, Belgium, France, Germany, Switzerland, and Italy; the urban settings included Berlin, Antwerp, Rotterdam, Bradford, Paris and its suburbs, and Carrara and Macerata in Italy. The scale of the initiatives we examined included the cleaning of a neighborhood park (Berlin), the repainting of a local train station (Macerata), the defense of Islam on talk shows (France, the Netherlands, Great Britain), the organization of exhibitions on Islamic history and Muslims (Antwerp, Paris), and interfaith encounters (Italy, Great Britain). Political careers and activism popped up just about everywhere. In addition to these actors, we also searched for radicals, from hard-to-reach youth to the jihadis who were so persistently evoked in the media. From our collective findings it appeared that, within the Muslim populations of Europe, the latter represented an obscure domain, one that was avoided in public and very rarely commented upon to outsiders. Terrorists, or so it appeared to us, are the eternal absentees. Whenever possible, we have tried to locate their relationship within the larger context in order to convey the voice of these marginal actors.

Our common research question, however, aimed at encompassing a far larger group. Without excluding the phenomenon of terrorists, it intended to map the whole field of Muslim visibility. Over the last two years we explored the available space for action that is open to self-described Muslims in European Union (EU) member states. When a minority group hitherto hidden from view suddenly becomes public, and migrant communities turn into public actors that are labeled Muslim from the outside, what is the sanctioned space in which they may act? How, in which specific arenas, and with what intensity are they allowed to act in terms of their own definitions in the European public sphere? Where are the limits and who defines these limits?

The answers we have come up with are not a recital of *halal* and *haram*, of the religiously allowed and the forbidden, although these may exert their influence in some cases. Rather, through the different chapters of this volume the reader will get to know the grey zones of interaction between groups, communities, and individuals on the one hand, and self-described Muslims and majority society on the other. All kinds of (in-)visibilities take shape in these grey areas. The contributions in this volume examine, from different perspectives and on various scales, the processes that transform these grey zones into accepted spaces for discourse, dialogue, and actions.

Forms of Differentiation

In the articulation of Muslim visibilities, two opposite forces seem to be at work: pressure from without and pressure from within. We consider their existence side by side without overemphasizing the impact of terrorism and the ensuing security measures on Muslim populations. If they had an impact at all, it may well be that violent action in the name of Islam urged other Muslims to create counterimages and to come to the rescue—if not the recreation—of the Islamic tradition. We instead focus our attention on a cluster of developments that occurred more or less in the same time span in the seven countries presented in this volume but that seem to have very different roots.

On closer inspection, three developments especially turned out to be reactions to the stigma of "Muslim" imputed from outside the Muslim community. First, over the last few years many local religious communities have withdrawn from whatever exchange they had been entertaining with majority society. Once pressed into the defensive, they ceased to participate in public events that addressed Islam or the Muslim minorities in Europe. Thus, numerous intermediaries, study circles, roundtables, boards, advisory committees, and hearings lost their Muslim participants. The first differentiation thus entails a distancing from non-Muslim society (Jonker, Fadil, Amiraux, Abdel-Samad).

Not necessarily connected to this development was the exit of the old generation of mosque founders and the entry of a new generation that was born or socialized in Europe. The newcomers set about the task of formulating an Islam of their own, which sometimes differed radically from the traditional and defensive ideas of their parents. Most of these reformulations are now oriented towards Europe; nonetheless, they do differ very much from one other. What they share is a notable distance from the parent generation. The second differentiation, therefore, is that between the generations (Frisina, Jonker, Fadil).

The security-related pressures set into motion a process of internal differentiation aimed at distancing oneself from external stigmatization. This process involved distinguishing oneself, with all available means, as the more

11

cultured, the more religious, and the most secular, as better educated and less primitive than one's neighbors. All over Europe, Iranians and Turks distanced themselves from "Arabs," as did Bosnians from Turks, Lebanese from Palestinians, Sufi-oriented groups from Islamist ones, and secular Palestinians from their religious compatriots. In some contexts, the distinction between secular groups and religious groups led to a clear articulation of one's political values within the context of settlement. In other contexts, it led to redefinitions of what Islam in Europe is about. It urged definitions of a "real Islam" as well as attempts to identify who "belongs" and who does not (Fadil, Boender, Amiraux, Frisina, Yurdakul). The third differentiation therefore gravitates towards claims of representation and power.

In the emerging display of Muslim visibility in Europe captured in this volume, Muslim democrats face Muslims who question democratic structures, and zealots and missionaries challenge believers who insist on private, intimate religiousness. There are radical activists who join with intermediaries looking for compromises, and secular liberals who keep their distance from the rule-abiding orthodox. The reader will encounter hate preachers as well as imams who manage to network in civil society, hard-to-reach youths, and partners in interfaith discussion groups. Angry young students have been given a voice, as have content believers with a high spiritual mission in secular society. All of these groups and individuals compete with each other in the articulation of what it means to be a Muslim in Europe. The competition is not always conscious and in some cases may also be the result of public policies. Hidden from view are the faceless young men who contemplate, prepare, and/or execute mass murder. Over recent years their actions have managed to attract the bulk of media attention and throw a shadow on all other forms of Muslim claims-making. One aim of this volume is to clearly show that the articulation of Muslim difference in Europe takes on many other forms.

Performances on Public Stages

Once these coexisting and extremely diverse modalities of being a Muslim had been observed and documented, the question of their interpretation and the choice of the relevant framework for analysis came to the fore. The central difficulty that we faced when collectively preparing this volume was the identification of both a common conceptual "language" and a common analytical approach to apply to our respective work. In purely descriptive terms, what we were facing in our various research contexts were combinations of strategies to go public that were presented in roughly the same period (2003–2005), both on national and on local stages. The ultimate decision to bring our work together under an analytical "public" umbrella came naturally after the first discussions, when we sat down together and started describing aspects of the ethnographic observations that we had made.

The strength of this volume lies precisely in the different types of qualitative data that were accumulated through fieldwork by its contributors. An emphasis on this qualitative dimension is central to the study of Muslims in Europe. It illustrates that it is possible to write a theoretically informed piece that is empirically grounded but nonetheless relevant to a broader context of political sociology and the sociology of religion (Madsen et al. 2002; Modood 2005). Ethnographic descriptions are present in all of the chapters of this volume, though they do not address similar samples. This method allowed the authors to illustrate in a concrete manner the multiple and complex modalities through which Muslims are engaged as Muslims in their various contexts. Nadia Fadil, in her analysis of the Union of Mosque and Islamic Organisations of Antwerp, concentrates on how individual members of this group relate their personal conception of being a Muslim to practices of citizenship. Valérie Amiraux addresses similar questions while giving the floor to Muslims who do not belong to associations. Philip Lewis provides snapshots based on conversations with imams whom he characterizes as educated, and also describes these individuals in their routine activities. Welmoet Boender focuses on the incorporation of Dutch imams through the institutionalization of Rotterdam-based religious training. In these contributions, the authors needed to master both the semantics of their discussion partners and their location in a network of meanings that is produced by others (e.g., the state, other Muslims). Gerdien Jonker's contribution specifically focuses on the elaboration of distinct discourses by competing Muslim associations which see themselves as confronted with the same security-inspired stigmata.

The use of ethnographic data enabled the authors to underline both the subjective dimension of the formation of public engagement and the coexistence of competing narratives in a public sphere. It also helped them to do justice to a nonutilitarian reading of the way in which Muslims—with different skills and different objectives—make their way to participative citizenship. From this qualitative field approach emerged a study of normal "in-the-making" experiences of Muslims in Europe. Our approach illustrates the gap that exists between the ideological bias with which policymakers and large segments of the media observe Muslims in Europe, and the pragmatic analysis of individuals' practices and actions that is prevalent in the social sciences. Unlike the former, our data also encompass subjective experiences of justice and injustice, trust and mistrust.

The notion of public space helped us to select our different fields while heeding at least two dimensions: Public space was, first of all, the space in which social actors played a public role and presented themselves to others. In a way, this is the sensorial, perceptive dimension of public space, the one that gives all participants the opportunity to consider otherness and to confront it in physical space (on bodily practices, see Göle 1997; Arthur 1999). This concept of public space also applies to Muslims who discover their internal plurality through the options they have within their respective European contexts. Public space also appeared to be the site for elaborating on common values and projects; in this sense, it was a nonmaterial space utilized to define the conditions of living together. Some would say that public space has a visible and an invisible side. What are Muslims entitled to do? And what is explicitly prohibited in non-Muslim European societies? It is clear that going public is unavoidably linked—both for collectives and for individuals—to the opportunities offered by the specific context and the institutional landscape.

While analyzing our findings, another aspect of public space became important for our work. This was the theatrical dimension, in which public space becomes a "stage" on which people play "roles" (Goffman 1971, 1980). As shown throughout this volume, individuals and groups compete on this stage for the ownership of definitions concerning the nature of being Muslim and the meaning of Islam. The discussions of good versus bad Muslims, of pure and impure, can be related to this notion of an image that should be presented to various types of audiences. Pnina Werbner, who in her most recent work elaborated on the impact of 9/11 on performative ability, described the pre-9/11 Pakistani community thus:

"In the past, British Pakistani Muslims had always been a vocal minority, demanding equal citizenship rights and never being afraid to speak their minds even if their opinions—support for the Iranian fatwa against Rushdie [...]—were out of line with British popular sentiments. They felt sufficiently secure in the UK to express their political opinions, however contentious, without fear. Indeed, in their own public arenas, in the diasporic public sphere they had created for themselves [...], Manchester Muslims articulated familiar visions of apocalyptic battles between Islam and the West, especially the USA, source of all evil." (Werbner 2004, 463)

Local public arenas offered them the opportunity to perform, as theater actors would do, in front of audiences that did not systematically share the same views. In return, the audience discussed and made comments, criticized and supported, denounced or identified with the actors on stage (on the use of Goffman's backstage and front stage in ethnographic work, see Eliasoph 1998). The same dynamics occur in European contexts when certain normative issues are discussed (e.g., wearing the veil).

Competition of necessity engenders a public setting, a space for representation or a front stage, in which actors appear, leaving a public impression or confronting policymakers. Public space offers them an open space, but one with certain constraints within which the players must respect the rules of the game. Unlike individuals, Muslim organizations in Europe no longer can ignore these rules. After forty years of sometimes invisible, sometimes distinct cohabitation, all now respond to post-9/11 policy-making, both on a national and on a European level.

Policymakers who define the "Muslim problem" in public space also draw profiles of possible discussion partners and try to exclude those who do not fit their rules (Amiraux 2004; Jonker 2005). Sometimes actors perform before an audience in accordance with rules that have been laid down by others. The question thus presents itself: How is the performed message perceived and received by the public that observes the scene? What is its reaction to the performances on the public stage? Both supporters and dissenters may distrust the players. They may keep silent or express their support in public. They may continue to gossip in private or confront the speaker during pauses. In some of the contributions to this volume, the generation gap is expressed only through the comments of the older generation on the efforts of their successors. In other cases peers formulate criticisms, boards appoint and dismiss representatives, and religious communities grope for a consensus that brings together opposing views.

Of course, to work with the notion of public space is to tackle a complex and well-studied field (Gaonkar and Lee 2002; Cefaï and Pasquier 2003; Göle and Amman 2004). Its multiple significations mean that it cannot be applied as a universal tool to any and every situation. Our larger framework can be compared to the "deprivatization" process described in the comparative work of Jose Casanova (1994). However, our purpose was not restricted to the idea of an eruption of religious issues in the public sphere.[1] Some contributions address the formulation of grievances, the way in which self-described Muslims protest against the redefinition of their belief system as a public problem, and their endeavors to shape and undermine that process (Abdel-Samad, Frisina, Jonker). Others cover the constitution of the public arena itself and analyze the modes with which Islam and Muslims have been turned into a public problem (Amiraux, Fadil; cf. Gusfield 1981). Other authors address the genesis of whole new grammars resulting from the political stigmatization of Muslims as a potential threat for non-Muslim societies (Jonker; cf. Gusfield 1996). Some contributions also address the commitment of non-Muslims in supporting the cause of Muslims and the response of public authorities to this support (Lewis).

The relevance of the concept of public space for mapping our work can be summed up in a number of points. First, it helped us to pin down the local and national specificity of which all contributions give evidence on different levels. Though we were collectively aware of a dynamic of "Muslim coming out" in European public settings, we were also perfectly conscious of its path-dependency on context-specific opportunities. We are referring here to political and legal opportunities as well as cultural types of opportunities, all of which continue to differentiate in each context and delimit the way in which religion finds its public place. The case studies, even when they sometimes appear to be similar, thus were firmly anchored in national and/or urban trajectories, and historical national variables could be kept in focus. Moreover, specific tensions and opportunities that are rooted in national trajectories could been taken into consideration. The same goes for the

---

1   The process of making religious issues key public issues can be driven by state policy, a political party, or the establishment of institutions representing one religion, or it can occur through the circulation of opinions, ideas, and shared knowledge.

specific conditions that Muslims deal with in order to raise their voices in public. The contributors shared the view that individual contexts and history play a role in explaining the specific articulation to the political domain of one's commitment as a Muslim in public. The public sphere is not neutral, and, as the product of a specific history, it is embedded in a complex of influences that reflect the national political culture. Muslims have not always been actors in that historical process, but they are now demanding participation and equal treatment as citizens of these countries. Likewise, national and European religious histories have an impact on how this minority religion acquires public presence. As the contributions illustrate, the private/public relationship should therefore be understood as an interdependency rather than as a strict separation. In that context, the quest for equality and recognition is also the demand for a civil society that is open to religious pluralism, both for individuals and for groups (Modood 2005). European states no longer can consider Muslims to be citizens without opening public space to the recognition of others' ways of doing things according to religious belief.

Second, all of us dealt with a new type of actor: people who interact with society as Muslims and who are determined to make their voices heard, regardless of the actual domain of their initiative. Their commitment surfaced in expected as well as unexpected spheres of activity, from religious teaching to political activism, from music and Sufi discussion groups to art. We quickly recognized that underlying all the case studies was a form of communication and relationship to society in which one's self-definition as a Muslim was never questioned but simply affirmed. The meanings of this identification, however, appeared to be very different from one situation to the next. Our choice to frame Muslim commitment as public commitment was influenced by the extreme diversity of the actors discussed in the various chapters. An analysis in terms of public space enables one to cover collective, organized activities as well as individual ones. It does not restrict the field to organized forms of engagement, but instead opens it up to relatively isolated and anonymous forms of being engaged as a Muslim.

The millions of Muslims living in the EU are indeed a complex and heterogeneous population that includes migrants, converts, European citizens, foreigners, men and women, old and young, believers and nonbelievers, secular Muslims, traditionalists, and radicals. The majority of them do not identify with the small minority of Muslim association members. The studies that compose this volume therefore include a broad spectrum of Muslim actors; sometimes their only commonality is the skills and resources needed to go public. We spoke with religious experts, imams, male and female teachers, social workers, political actors, charismatic leaders, anonymous believers, and political activists. The channels in which they operated, their level of experience, and their motivation to go public differed. But they all shared a self-definition as Muslim when confronted with public situations.

Third, as mentioned earlier, we selected our interview partners at the crossroads of the internal process of becoming visible (i.e., Muslims making

Muslims visible) and the push from outside to pinpoint Muslim presence in Europe (i.e., Muslims as a security problem). The chorus that can be heard today in European public spaces includes religious voices (e.g., when imams publicly assess the normative validity of homosexual behavior), political voices (e.g., when Milli Görüş leaders claim the right to become accepted as a partner of the state), and civic voices (e.g., when Muslim representatives denounce bombings or condemn the hijacking of journalists in Iraq). Consequently, the volume highlights the variety of potential attitudes towards society, including exit, silence, and loyalty (Hirschman 1978). The multiple meanings that are given to the word "Muslim" in the currently tense environment allow for defensive and inimical reactions but also involve positive communication about one's position in society. Some contributions touch upon the innovative ways in which self-described Muslims react when confronted with situations that provoke the Islamic tradition—although their religious identification requires them to either justify their tradition or keep silent. In this respect, the shift from the older guardians of the Muslim faith to a younger generation has been essential and is common to all countries, regardless of their history of migration. It is above all younger Muslims who are creating distance from traditional institutions, elaborating new demands for recognition and for the representation of interests, and developing strategies to distinguish the Muslim community from the dominant representation of Muslims as enemies.

Fourth, the precise nature of belief and its limits were never at the center of our research. We even thought it abusive to suggest that fieldwork grounded on the observation of religious practice could facilitate our understanding of belief, which is, after all, anchored in individual experience. Moreover, such experience must first be voiced in order to exist as a social fact (Luhmann 2000). It is only when people declare their faith through language or bodily practices that one can start to assess the role that religion plays in their actions. Thus, the role of religious practice and values in the daily exercise of citizenship was taken into consideration only when our interview partners chose to negotiate "lifestyle choices among a diversity of options not necessarily congruent with collective religious sentiments" (Eickelman 2000, 120). When, however, the individual did not express religious sentiment, it was not for the observer to ascribe religion as a framework to explain what he or she saw.

Finally, we wanted to maintain a constant focus on the plurality of experiences that our fieldwork made visible. The performance and expression of difference are central to the constitution of a democratic dynamic public space that enables the meeting of different types of beliefs, belongings, identities, and representations of the world. "The public sphere is articulated as including people with different characteristics, and as requiring participants to be able to carry on conversations that are not strictly determined by private interests or identity" (Calhoun 2002, 165). Unlike policymakers, who barely discern between one Muslim and the next, the new Muslim actors discussed in this volume themselves discern between those who "belong" and "others." This differentiation resulted in the coexistence of clashing visibilities. The questions of what "real Islam" is and who the "real Muslims" are loomed large and continue to do so. This process inevitably leads to competition and the empowerment of the group that gains the most support.

The attitudes and statements described in this volume mirror the emerging "work in progress" among Muslims in Europe. Their newness, however, does not preclude the researcher from taking into account the needs and sensibilities of the parent generation, which was grappling with opposing interests and defensiveness long before the recent political claims-making came into view. Policymakers may set the scene for their appearance while trying to define ways in which Muslims are allowed to differ, strictly discerning between "good" and "bad." But caught in between hurt feelings and the political class's power of definition, the new Muslim actors work with emancipation concepts of their own. Their business is the creation of new methods that further the peaceful establishment of Islam in EU member states and open up space for them to elaborate on the meanings of being a Muslim in EU societies.

The Structure of This Volume

Based on unpublished data that have been collected in seven Western European countries between August 2003 and July 2005, the contributions take into consideration Muslim actors who in recent years have entered the public sphere of their country of residence. Some contributions focus on individual actors, whereas others examine a whole professional stratum (imams and imam training), a "young" organization, or young people in "old" organizations. All contributions describe the specifics of national and urban frameworks, forms of differentiation, and the choice of public arena. They address the different forms of claims-making, which are anchored in the specificity of national and local contexts, and, whenever possible, relate these to parallel patterns of development among Muslims elsewhere.

Valérie Amiraux (France) follows five average French citizens who do not engage in any association but who nonetheless claim the right to a private religious identity. She analyzes the ways in which these people relate to their self-identification as a Muslim while confronted with the fact that its legitimacy is denied in a public space that respects *laïcité* only. How can they speak both as a believer and as a citizen? Supported with very rich field notes, this chapter portrays five individuals who are committed to making their voices heard on the subject of being a Muslim within a society that has institutionalized patterns of hostility towards religiosity.

Nadia Fadil (Belgium) pursues a somewhat similar direction, though she takes a different angle in her description of a form of claims-making that is widely considered to be specific to the Islamic religious tradition—namely, how Muslims should behave as "good" Muslims. Having done extensive fieldwork in a local Antwerp association, she explores the link that young Muslim activists constantly describe in order to relate their religious identification to political action. According to Fadil, performance as an Islamic political subject is a constellation of attitudes, ranging from resistance to a quest for recognition, which provides us with alternative interpretations of the role of associations in the political socialization of Muslims in Europe.

Annalisa Frisina (Italy) opens up a window on the claims-making of a genuine (religious) Muslim citizenship and a likewise genuine (secular) European citizenship. Focusing on an association founded by the children of immigrants, Frisina observes the formation of an active and above all autonomous citizenship anchored in local and everyday policy initiatives, which aim at individual self-realization yet at the same time seek access to larger public debates on Italian politics.

Welmoet Boender (the Netherlands) studies how the emergence of a European Islamic authority could possibly become institutionalized. Her account brings to light the precarious claims of "import" and "homegrown" imams. She also describes the precarious situation of religious students in private Islamic vocational institutions who navigate their future role as mediators between religious communities and secular society—aptly summarized as "something of a minefield."

Gerdien Jonker (Germany) opens another minefield as she discusses religious responses to political measures. In her analysis, the asymmetry between the partners becomes especially clear. Whereas policymakers want to control the "threat" that Muslims in Germany present, Muslim communities lay claim to the ability to cure the German "illness" resulting from the secularization of European societies.

Gökçe Yurdakul (Germany), through her analysis of the headscarf debate in Germany, uncovers the intensive claims-making among the children of Turkish migrants in Germany about the way a woman should appear in the public sphere. Her chapter demonstrates the centrality of the tense ties binding secular and Islamist groups to the representation they have of their coexistence in a pluralistic non-Muslim society.

Philip Lewis (Great Britain) brings us back to interfaith channels and to the many inroads to partnerships which imams in this country contribute to in order to stabilize the "one nation, many faiths" ideology of British politics. Preachers have to answer to the demands of at least two sides, however, a tension that sometimes bears very strange fruits.

Hamad Abdel-Samad (Germany) analyzes the specific framework in which young Muslims in Germany become isolated from society, radicalize, or even opt for violence. His contribution accurately reflects the voices that demand respect, the power of self-definition, and inclusion, as opposed to the marginalization and nonrecognition that these interviewees usually experience. Abdel-Samad's account opens a window on choices: denouncement, resignation, anger, and outrage.

19

References

Amiraux, V. 2004. Les musulmans dans l'espace politique européen. La délicate expérience du pluralisme confessionnel. Vingtième siècle. Revue d'Histoire 82 (April–June): 119–130.

Arthur, L., ed. 1999. Religion, dress and the body. Oxford: Berg.

Calhoun, C. 2002. Imagining solidarity: Cosmopolitanism, constitutional patriotism, and the public sphere. Public Culture 14 (1): 147–171.

Casanova, J. 1994. Public religions in the modern world. Chicago: University of Chicago Press.

Cefaï, D., and D. Pasquier, eds. 2003. Les sens du public: Publics politiques, publics médiatiques. Paris: PUF.

Eickelman, D. F. 2000. Islam and the languages of modernity. Daedalus 129 (winter): 119–136.

Eliasoph, N. 1998. Avoiding politics: How Americans produce apathy in everyday life. Cambridge, UK: Cambridge University Press.

Gaonkar, D. P., and B. Lee, eds. 2002. Public Culture ["New Imaginaries" issue devoted to Islam in public space] 14 (1).

Goffman, E. 1971 [1959]. The presentation of self in everyday life. Harmondsworth, UK: Penguin Books.

———. 1980 [1963]. Behavior in public places: Notes on the social organization of social gatherings. Westport, CT: Greenwood Press.

Göle, N. 1997. The forbidden modern: Civilization and veiling. Ann Arbor, MI: University of Michigan Press.

Göle, N., and L. Amman, eds. 2004. Islam in Sicht. Der Auftritt von Muslimen im Öffentlichen Raum. Bielefeld, Germany: transcript.

Gusfield, J. 1981. The culture of public problems: Drinking-driving and the symbolic order. Chicago: University of Chicago Press.

———. 1996. Contested meanings: The construction of alcohol problems. Madison, WI: University of Wisconsin Press.

Hirschman, A. O. 1978 [1970]. Exit, voice, and loyalty: Responses to decline in firms, organizations, and states. Cambridge, MA: Harvard University Press.

Jonker, G. 2005. From foreign workers to "sleepers": Germany's discovery of its Muslim population. In European Muslims and the secular state, ed. J. Cesari and S. MacLoughlin, 113–126. London: Ashgate.

Luhmann, N. 2000. Die Religion der Gesellschaft. 2 vols. Frankfurt: Suhrkamp.

Madsen, R., W. Sullivan, A. Swidler, and S. Tipton, eds. 2002. Meaning and modernity: Religion, polity, and self. Berkeley: University of California Press.

Modood, T. 2005. Multicultural politics: Racism, ethnicity, and Muslims in Britain. Minneapolis: University of Minnesota Press.

Werbner, P. 2004. The predicament of diaspora and millennial Islam: Reflections on September 11, 2001. Ethnicities 4 (4): 451–476.

Valérie Amiraux

SPEAKING AS A MUSLIM: AVOIDING RELIGION IN FRENCH PUBLIC SPACE[1]

Introduction

Three main ways of studying Muslims living in France have developed in the French social science literature over the last two decades (Amiraux 2004; Cesari 1994). The first gives priority to a reading of the public regulation of religious pluralism and of Islam as *culte* (worship; Frégosi 1998; Basdevant-Gaudemet 1996; Galembert and Belbah 2005). A second approach focuses on observing the articulation of "being a Muslim" and acting as a citizen (Babès 1997; Tietze 2002; Venel 2004). The third, intermediary trend considers the living conditions of Muslims in France with respect to the impact of certain constraints (*la laïcité*) and the requirement that both Muslim individuals and Muslim groups adhere to the limits set by these republican principles (Roy 2005). Within this third segment of the social science literature, one also finds volumes focusing on the ways in which Muslims address specific living conditions, such as differences between generations (Khosrokhavar 1997), conditions in public institutions (Geisser and Mohsen-Finan 2001; Khosrok-havar 2004), and, last but not least, the headscarf controversies (Gaspard and Khosrokhavar 1995; Lorcerie 2005; Babès 2005; Nordmann 2004; Baubérot, Costa-Lascoux, and Bouzar 2004). In addition, recent developments in sociology and political science emphasize the emerging profiles of religious authorities and leadership in France and Europe, or activists' socialization, in particular among Salafi and Tabligh movements (Amghar 2005; Khedimellah 2001).

In these works, being a Muslim in France is no longer discussed as a migration issue but instead as an issue tied to the politics of citizenship. It is also conceived as an individual choice—emancipated from any type of coercion—not simply as an inheritance.[2] To identify as a Muslim does not imply an unchanging identity, and there are many ways to express these identifications. Most of the literature has concentrated on organized forms of religious

---

1   I would like to thank Daniel Cefaï, Gerdien Jonker, Anne-Sophie Lamine, and Daniel Sabbagh for their careful reading of first drafts of this chapter and their stimulating comments.

2   This development corresponds to what other studies of different populations of believers also identify as a major change, in Europe and beyond (see Laermans, Wilson, and Billiet 1998).

identification and practices (thus privileging fieldwork on associations, mosques, and institutions), on organized forms of religious life. The interviews that constitute the core of this empirical data have been conducted with persons embedded in practices of exclusion or in conflicts (e.g., the building of places of worship, access to education, the wearing of the veil, the choice of a representative institution for Muslims) or persons sharing similar associative commitments. However, the majority of these publications emphasize the need to distinguish between Muslims committed to a life of worship and the anonymous ones, those individuals one hardly ever meets because they do not make an argument of their religious belief. This chapter attempts to elaborate on this point. It broadens and constructively criticizes the French tradition of knowledge by asking the following questions: Do Muslims have a life independent of their belief and their supposed belonging to a religious community in the French context? To what extent do Muslims cease to be Muslims when they are not addressed as such?[3] In other words, do Muslims (both men and women) exist outside of worship, and what kind of life do they lead as everyday citizens?[4]

It became difficult to identify who and what is at stake when people—including social scientists, but also journalists, policymakers, and the general public—talk about Muslims in France. This chapter offers a very personal attempt to be more focused in this process of defining Muslims as objects and subjects of social science research. At the same time, it retains as core material the personal experiences and narratives of five individuals who all identified themselves as Muslim believers in their discussions with me. In general in this volume, the authors offer a transversal analysis of various European contexts on the basis of empirical findings revealing the different performances of individuals who define themselves as Islamic political subjects in multiple domains (e.g., training, preaching, political commitment). The contributions also present a multiplicity of voices anchored in specific experiences but strongly tied to each other in that they raise similar questions (e.g., access to public space, conditions of participation, control of visibility, production of authority).

To take into account anonymous voices means to find one's way to women who do not wear a headscarf, men who do not wear distinctive signs (like a beard or certain clothing), and people who do not speak under an Islamic label. It means trying to take into account the daily contingencies and individual trajectories, the fears, emotions, troubles, and concerns that may

---

3 This question follows up on the hypothesis that a public exists only by virtue of its being addressed and therefore must claim some degree of attention from its members (Warner 2002, 60–61).

4 How do Muslims live when they are not being examined by journalists, politicians, or social scientists? As Michael Warner (2002, 60) has argued, "Most social classes and groups are understood to encompass their members all the time, no matter what. A nation, for example, includes its members whether they are awake or asleep, sober or drunk, sane or deranged, alert or comatose."

motivate some Muslims to keep silent and others to speak out. During our face-to-face meetings, my discussion partners in France told me their personal stories and anecdotes; they spoke of their experiences, the tests they have been going through, and the situations in which they felt directly questioned about their personal beliefs about what it means to be a Muslim. This chapter is thus grounded in specific micro experiences that I learned about through exchanges with individuals.[5] I met them while doing fieldwork, but they were at the periphery of that research. We met either through a joint project supervised by others (Yasmina and Larbi) or when I asked for their expertise from previous research projects (Kenza, Morad, and Lila).[6] On other occasions, they asked me to help them publicize their work, to give expert advice, or just to partici-pate in events they were organizing. I found them as much as they found me. Through the course of these meetings we discussed various topics, and I came to know them better as individuals. I finally considered that their different trajectories might be presented in this chapter as illustrations of the different modalities of going public as a Muslim in French public space.[7] Of course, this material does not stand for the 3.5 to 7 million Muslims thought to be living in France.[8] It is a tiny, detailed sample that does not fit the usual definition of what a legitimate sample should consist of. They cannot be said

---

5   As Berger and Luckmann (1967, 43) have noted, the face-to-face situation makes the other's subjectivity available through "a maximum of symptoms. In the face-to-face situation, the other is fully real." It allows the sociologist to at least move away from the anonymity inherit in typifications.

6   Names have been changed for Kenza and Morad. Larbi, Lila, and Yasmina have given me permission to use their real names when referring to our discussions.

7   I had several meetings which each of them except for Lila, whom I met at public events and once individually for a long interview. Some of the quotations in this text come from taped interviews, others from notes that I was taking during in-formal conversation. The conditions for gathering the data thus justify consider-ing the encounters to be talks rather than formal interviews. I personally do not consider interviews to differ from conversations: both consist of meetings be-tween two persons. This perspective is one of the important legacies of ethnog-raphy, as compared with the more formal position of political science and soci-ology towards conducting interviews (see Althabe 1990).

8   Since 1872 the French census has not included questions on religious belief. Public statistics have never properly covered the issue of faith among migrants. Since the 1980s some private surveys have been published; they deal with "the Muslim opinion" on issues such as the Gulf War in 1991, the first veil contro-versies in 1989 and 1994, and, more recently, the attacks on the World Trade Center. For most of these surveys, these figures are based on the definition of a Muslim as a "person of Muslim culture," basically referring to the nationality of origin of the parents or grandparents. To make a long story short, when people wish to trace back Muslims in France, they ask for the "home country" of the first migrants or look at the family name (if you have an Arab name, there is a good probability that statistics will consider you a Muslim). Thus, these statistics do not reflect actual practices, which obviously vary according to age, country of origin, and social background.

to represent a specific type of activism, nor a typical profile of second- or third-generation Muslims.

On the basis of these five cases and in reference to the current framing of the public discourse on Muslims in France, this chapter invites the reader to consider the "swing to commitment" (Boltanski 1999) of Muslim individuals from the position of spectator to one of actor on a public stage. During our conversations, these five individuals mostly emphasized their desire to care about people rather than about politics (see Eliasoph 1998, 23–31). In France today, there is no French Muslim community, no unique voice speaking in the name of all Muslims in the country. The public discourse on them is, however, framed by dominant narratives that have emerged in particular since 9/11.[9] The chapter opens with an analysis of the way in which this written production contributed to defining the type of social trajectories that Muslims living in France are allowed to follow. In examining this aspect I refer to the growing number of biographies, testimonies, and narratives of suffering published recently, which have become true commercial successes. These personal histories published by men and women have become part of the public domain. They have defined patterns of attitudes and thereby helped to demarcate the boundaries separating good behaviors from bad ones. How do the five interviewees relate to this public image of their own community of belief? In the next section I discuss, on the basis of specific experiences of my five discussion partners, the way in which public speech by Muslims is grounded in the French context (Goffman 1981). As in the preceding section, it relates the production of discourses to the individual experiences of my interviewees: To what extent do they feel empathy with or reject this highly audible voice? How does it affect their own "coming out" as Muslims? In the section that follows, I elaborate on the notion of going public, as rooted in the life trajectories and narratives of my discussion partners.

Conditions of Speech for Muslim Citizens: Public Demands and Dominant Narratives

Who are these individuals with whom I have been talking for the past two years? Larbi is a local imam in the second biggest mosque in Paris. He is the only one I knew before the events of 9/11. Morad is a businessman involved in local political activities in a city north of Paris. I met him in early 2002 while conducting research on discrimination against Muslims in France. I then happened to meet him regularly as I was following the implementation of the Conseil Français du Culte Musulman (French Council for Muslim Worship;

---

9 In the French context, 9/11 opened space for public deliberation and discussion of Islam-related topics, in a positive as well as a negative sense. On the one hand, it became easier for Muslims to be heard in certain arenas; on the other, racist statements about Islam and Muslims are more explicit and easier to express than ever.

hereafter CFCM). I met Kenza during research on discrimination against Muslims in the European Union. She is trained as a sociologist. She worked for different nongovernmental organizations and public agencies in charge of "immigration affairs" before she started to work for a Catholic charity foundation, where she has been in charge of international affairs since mid-2004. Lila has been wearing a veil since Ramadan 2004, two weeks before I met her as she was organizing the press release of the work done by her association on Islamophobia in France. At that time she had just resigned from her position as a lawyer in order to work for this association fighting against Islamophobia. Last but not least, when I first met Yasmina in mid-2002, she had just completed her master's thesis in international relations. We collaborated on a public exhibition on Muslims in different world cities which took place in Paris from May to November of 2004[10] She is now working at a research institute that specializes in Islamic Studies.

This group of people does not constitute the usual sample for a social scientist working on Islam and Muslims in the European Union. Indeed, they do not belong to a common associative network. They do not know each other personally, even if they may sometimes visit the same places (e.g., Larbi's mosque) or attend the same conferences. They do not live in the same neighborhood, but all do reside in Paris or its immediate surroundings (*les banlieues* or *les quartiers*). They do not work together or send their kids to the same school. They share, however, two things. First, all are of Algerian descent and live in France. Second, they all told me that they identify as Muslims. The following text based on their personal accounts attempts to analyze the conditions framing the access to public speech for Muslim French citizens. What are they permitted to do? What type of narratives are they entitled to produce? To what extent do they behave as Muslims, and what is their perception of that behavior? What makes them speak and act as Muslims rather than keep silent? What is their position in the public realm? Who do they speak for? What do they say about their situation as Muslim French citizens?

Following Charles Taylor's suggestion that social imaginaries are what enable the practices of a society by making sense of them,[11] one can only be pessimistic about the dominant perceptions about and representations of Muslims held by non-Muslims in France. In the French context, "being a Muslim" is indeed framed by dominant narratives—some of them originating from Muslims[12]—which have slowly contributed to the sedimentation and reification of public perceptions of the "typical life of Muslims in France,"

---

10 "Musulmanes, Musulmans au Caire, à Téhéran, Istanbul, Paris, Dakar [...]" was organized and sponsored by the Parc de la Villette and placed under the scientific codirection of Olivier Roy and myself (see Amiraux and Roy 2004).
11 "Social imaginaries," according to Taylor (2002, 106), are "the way ordinary people 'imagine' their social surroundings [...]: it is carried in images, stories, legends."
12 On specific anti-Muslim discourses by Muslims, see Geisser, 2003.

feeding the generation of stereotypical representations of how Muslims think, sleep, eat, love, and look.[13]

As a matter of fact, anyone willing to improve his or her knowledge of Islam and Muslims in France is immediately faced with a difficult choice. One could start by reading newspapers and magazines, watching television, and buying academic books. One could also rely on the testimonies delivered, in the form of either novels or biography, by "French citizens of Arab and Muslim descent"—women, men, old, and young. To talk about Muslims in France implies that one is also dealing with the dominant typifications of Muslims in Western media coverage.[14] To generalize about types of Muslims (the extremist, the assimilated, the republican, the secular, etc.) implies that one is considering the actors without touching upon the persons.[15] At the same time, however, to take this distinction between types of Muslims as a starting point may facilitate discussion and reflection. Indeed, it provides one with an opportunity to speak to groups of persons that end up to being aggregated together on the basis of an external manifestation of what seems to be common to all of them. Ultimately, the public discourse circulating in the media is caught between the hammer of horrible and tragic storytelling and the anvil of religious moral propositions.

The publications that I have in mind are for the most part books and written statements published as life stories and then publicized through the appearance of the authors on television shows. These appearances and the proliferation of their stories in the press and media at large (Gamson 1998) arouse pity and eventually involve the spectator, compelling him or her to act (Boltanski 1999, 32). The messages and images address first and foremost non-Muslims. Between rumors and gossip, urban legend and invented stories, this uncontrolled public discourse on Islam has found an audience (Pew

---

13 There has been a tendency to make aesthetic comments about the beauty of good and bad Muslims, which I have described elsewhere as Neo-Orientalist (Amiraux 2005). Chaddhort Djavann, an Iranian living in France, was one of the few Muslim women interviewed by the Stasi commission, which was given the mandate by French President Jacques Chirac to write a report on laïcité in France. Most of the comments on her hearing only mentioned that "she [was] beautiful." Interestingly, the same comment always comes to the fore when Tariq Ramadan is being discussed, as if it would add to the suspicions of radicalism. Olivier Roy begins his last book by discussing Tariq Ramadan's beauty (2005, 1).

14 Typification here refers to the conventions determining what characteristics help to identify persons: "The social reality of everyday life is thus apprehended in a continuum of typifications, which are progressively anonymous as they are removed from the 'here and now' of the face-to-face situation" (Berger and Luckmann 1967, 47–48).

15 This is, for instance, how Nacira Guénif and Eric Macé analyzed the headscarf controversies in France. What did the headscarf say? What did it perform? By the end, the headscarf talked of individuals, but individuals were kept silent (Guénif and Macé 2004; Tarraud 2005).

Research Center 2005). In a climate in which the perceptions of Muslims in France remain largely negative, commentators assert that Muslims demand to keep a distinct way of life and remain separate from the mainstream. In this light, their alienation is seen as a direct result of the cultural isolation of some Islamic enclaves in the heart of Western Europe (Stokes 2005), of which young veiled women serve as the living embodiment. In a recent survey, 70 % of the French interviewed for a Pew Research report said that they feel concerned about the increasing sense of Islamic identity developed by Muslims living in France, and 59 % said that they think Muslims want to remain distinct. It is no surprise, then, that 78 % of the French respondents believe that banning Muslim headscarves was a good idea (Pew Research Center 2005).

A pattern of public discourse on the situation of Muslims has thus emerged more explicitly in the last five years. In addition to social science discourses, the dominance of individual experience in narratives is now accepted as representative in the public sphere. The proliferation of books based on individual testimonies reflects several changes in the way French citizens of Arab and/or Muslim descent have been asked or have decided to speak out about their own trajectories. The published personal stories I am referring to are, for instance, those by Samira Bellil (2002) on sexual violence and collective rape (*les tournantes*), Loubna Meliane (2003) on political commitment, Abd al Malik (2004) on conversion to "good" Islam, Farid Abdelkrim (2002) on his perception of the abusive French "model of integration," Razika Zitouni (2005) on her upward social mobility, and Lila and Alma Levy (2004) on their exclusion from public schools because of their headscarves. Personal history works in these cases as proof, a demonstration, a manifestation.

In the public debates on Islam that center on secular issues, the expert becomes marginal and the individual, having directly experienced personally difficult situations, becomes the referee.[16] Religion is never the only focus of these authors, but they present themselves as "originating" from a Muslim family or background, and thus as having a voice to be heard and the legitimacy to speak up. So even when not mentioning religion at all in their works, these authors nevertheless have contributed to the promotion of their lifestyles as particular modalities of being Muslim in France. A good illustration of this is the process that contributed to the emergence of two images of the enemy among Muslim women during the last veil controversy in 2003/2004, which led to the vote on legislation passed in March 2004. On the one hand, a young Muslim girl alienated by men and forced by older people (mostly men) to

---

16 A parallel can be drawn with studies focusing on, for instance, the way in which private and sensitive topics (in particular those dealing with sexual life, violence, and harassment), which nowadays constitute the standard on many television and radio shows, also can be considered to open access to speech to citizens who are normally excluded (e.g., gays and lesbians, women, blacks, and, more generally, all visible minorities). See Cardon, 1995; Gamson, 1998.

wear a headscarf. On the other hand, a young, beautiful, and sexy girl from a migrant family, denouncing the headscarf as a major threat to women's emancipation in France's suburbs.[17] Suddenly, after fifteen years of intense discussion and fluctuation between total silence and intensely passionate public drama, hundreds of girls wearing an Islamic headscarf became a public problem for the nation. A consensus quickly became clear among the usual host of political groups and talk shows: only a law could rescue the poor girls wearing a headscarf. Nothing in Samira Bellil's book relates to Islam. Nevertheless, journalists explicitly drew a link: "It is a history of collective rape, of *tournantes*. These mechanisms do not date back to yesterday, but are an archaic and miserable madness, based on machismo, Islam, immigration, and disoriented parents who disorient children."[18]

This art of storytelling is not based only on pathological and extreme situations; rather, it also presents "common experiences": episodes of normal life in the French peripheries which can be paralleled with other trajectories in similar settings. Kenza, one of my discussion partners, is in her forties. She refers to this literature as books that speak to white French citizens. It is a necessary path to information for those who do not live in these neighborhoods ("les quartiers"). "Real life is not what they think it is. But, after all, everything is politics: all these women who wrote about their lives, whether Meliane or Bellil, they ended up being used by politicians" (Kenza, informal discussion in a Paris coffee shop, June 2005).

It is everybody's daily life made available, and comparable, to others' lives. This aspect helps the broader audience to identify with and be touched by these stories. Indeed, the expression of intense and authentic suffering, such as that in Samira Bellil's book, appears to be a way to tell one's story while respecting diversity and accepting others' lifestyles. Her book played a key role in the generation of a dominant framework for understanding relations between boys and girls in specific urban ghettos. As pointed out by Dominique Mehl (2003), the accumulation of situations as diverse as possible and marked by extremes is one way to organize the liberalization of public space. Individuals come with their personal trajectories and cannot be judged on that basis.[19] The literature fixes the scenario of paradigmatic lives: it establishes the official representation of how one lives as a Muslim woman (with a migrant background) in France (Mucchielli 2005, 111). This representation enters the political realm if it is defined as "a struggle over people's

---

17 Vincent Geisser has a label for each of these figures: *beurette voilée* for the veiled girl, and *beurette libérée* for the good, emancipated Muslim French citizen. See http://lmsi.net/impression.php3?id_article=215.

18 "C'est une histoire de viol collectif, de tournantes. Ce sont des mécanismes qui ne datent pas d'hier, une folie archaïque et misérable, sur fond de machisme, d'islam, d'immigration et de parents déboussolés, déboussoleurs" (*Libération*, October 7, 2002; quoted in Mucchielli 2005, 26; my translation into English).

19 In the aftermath of the Iranian revolution, many women wrote books to testify about male oppression.

imaginations, a competition over the meaning of symbols" (Eickelman 2000, 123).

These books based on personal trajectories deal with issues that previously were not considered to be of interest to the public or were considered to be too private and intimate.[20] Their existence, however, opens up the Pandora's box of the role of symbolic figures and models to follow. "I am here to testify and this is for free. I don't want anybody to follow me," explains Abd al Malik (2004) in his autobiography. When a person gains social legitimacy by publishing his or her individual story, there can be no criticism of the narrative: the way an individual tells his or her story is never put into question, though the author can be criticized for his or her conclusions, the analysis of the story, and/or the eventual impact it had (Guénif and Macé 2004). Bellil's story became the symbol of women's daily tragic life for the entire nation.

The targeted audience includes different components, characterized by direct knowledge of similar experiences (the nominal addressees), possible empathy with the situation (the implied addressees), and general ignorance of the topic (the targeted public of circulation) (Warner 2002, 54). Public visibility in television talk shows and magazines of these (presumed) Muslims speaking for themselves results in a somewhat disruptive and invasive presence. It also has collateral effects; in the case of Bellil, for example, she was quickly associated with the movement led by Fadela Amara (Ni Putes Ni Soumises, or "Neither Whores Nor Submissives"), which in the same period organized a national march all around the country, which ended in Paris on March 8, 2003 (Amara 2003).[21] In this context, a movement such as Ni Putes Ni Soumises, of which Loubna Meliane is a member, also contributed to the emergence of a new aesthetic of what a good, young, emancipated, and republican Muslim French citizen should look like, and how she should conduct her sex life.

It is probably one of the least savory aspects of this recent French controversy over the headscarf that it was less concerned with religion or with belief than with the stigmatization of good and bad behavior, particularly as it

---

20 Some words can be pronounced in public, others cannot. In public situations such as conferences and interviews, a number of Muslim leaders would prefer to speak of the "NPNS" (using the initial letters) rather than of the "Ni Putes Ni Soumises," just to avoid saying the "bad words" of the association's name, which means "Neither Whores Nor Submissives."

21 Amara's book (2003) is to a great extent an autobiography, as well as a presentation of the movement. The Ni Putes Ni Soumises movement began in February 2003 after a young girl (19-year-old Sohane) was burned alive in Vitry sur Seine in her housing estate's garbage area. The movement started with a march by five girls and two boys, who for five weeks walked across France in order to denounce the terrible living conditions of women in the *quartiers*. Following this *Marche des femmes contre les ghettos et pour l'égalité*, the Ni Putes Ni Soumises have been engaged in different initiatives but were in particular extremely important in the debate surrounding the discussion of the law banning religious symbols from public schools.

pertained to the relationship between men and women. The idea that women might wear a headscarf because they believed in its meaning and its symbolism simply never arose. And this perception of it had a strong political impact. The uniform reading of the Islamic headscarf in terms of oppression, alienation, and male domination played a key role in shaping people's imaginations and increasing the consensus in favor of the ban. The competition over the meaning of symbols opposed the "good," emancipated Muslim women (under the somewhat neocolonial supervision of central feminist figures) and the dominated ones. By considering the headscarf a symbol of women's oppression, most of the French historical feminist leadership adopted a neocolonial attitude towards veiled Muslim girls: "If you don't know why you should take off your headscarf, I'll tell you." To some extent, Orientalist typifications became the hallmark of institutional French feminism on the headscarf issue: Women of Muslim descent are beautiful; the veiled ones should definitely be emancipated from patriarchal domination and be given autonomous management of their entire body. This neocolonial representation of what Muslim women should do for themselves even led to the idea that they may not be able to defend themselves.[22] Moreover, both Muslim men and women must confront the patriarchal attitude of the French state, which attempts to impose certain behavior and rules, as if Muslims in France are not able to decide for themselves what is best for them. "May we think on our own?" Morad once asked me in February of 2003, while he was still involved in the preparatory work that ended up with the election of the CFCM. His decision to join the members of the preparatory group for the CFCM stemmed from his desire to be physically present in a room where

"all representatives are addressing the minister as if we were still in the colonial period. They barely speak correct French, and they just go there to be in the pictures with President Chirac. They are not interested in being heard or listened to. They just want to be there. With their names on the official documents and the header of the minister."

Morad and Kenza belong to the same age cohort (in their forties). Morad came to France in the 1980s to study mathematics at a university. Kenza was born in France. Notwithstanding their different trajectories in the French political system, they share a cynical view of the way French public space produces leading figures with whom Muslims and the children of migrants should identify. They also share a very cautious attitude towards the way politicians view these public figures as potential to gain votes. Yasmina and Lila belong to the same age cohort (late twenties). Both were born in France. When they consider the dominant narratives in the media, they adopt a more tolerant attitude, a mixture of forgiveness and compassion. Like Larbi, the imam in the north of Paris, they do not contest the validity of the testimonies, and they

---

22 A good illustration is the *Elle* magazine launch of the petition addressed to President Chirac (see Tarraud 2005).

insist on the positive effect that the publication of such sufferings must have had on their victims. All five, however, distance themselves from the potential for identification and minimize their own potential for becoming a model for other Muslims. This is completely unlike the discourse of, for instance, Muslim student organizations such as Étudiants Musulmans de France (associated with the Union des Organisations Islamiques de France), which continue to insist on the importance of being a perfect Muslim, a "role model," a source of inspiration for younger Muslims, and not a source of criticism by non-Muslims.[23]

The nature of these testimonies affects its audience at different levels. Most important, it ceases to be impersonal. As Yasmina explained when speaking about her situation as a guide for groups and individuals visiting the La Villette exhibition on Muslims in different cities, the presence of a public imposes constraints on speech. She elaborated on her uneasiness as she was, on the one hand, working on the organization of the exhibition and, on the other hand, part of the exhibition (as a member of the Muslim community and as a participant in a video of the exhibition, in which she explains the meaning of being a Muslim in Paris today on a 4 x 4 m screen).[24] She felt like she was serving as a representative of something she never thought she would have to talk about outside of her circle of relatives and friends. As Taylor (2002) has argued, the way a public is addressed says much about the footing every participant to the interaction stands in with the addressees. As a matter of fact, Yasmina was also in a relationship with these strangers—not understood as wandering outsiders but as already belonging to her world, as a "normal feature of the social" (Warner 2002, 56). The call to publicly share one's views may be experienced as a moment of intense vulnerability or as an occasion for strongly defending positions. During the six months of the exhibition, Yasmina met "a great sample of the Muslim population living in France." She stated that she felt "a lot of emotions doing this job as a guide and mediator. For instance, a Muslim woman, a convert, came several times to visit and asked me to go with her on pilgrimage."

Actual situations of conflict were difficult and sometimes violent (not physically violent), though she immediately added that they were quite rare.[25] Most of the questions and intense discussions were related to women in Islam; this was the case for both Muslim and non-Muslim visitors who

---

23 This comment is based on different interviews conducted among students of the Étudiants Musulmans de France movements in Paris and Bordeaux between November 2004 and July 2005.

24 The exhibition began with television screens showing different Muslims in different contexts of the exhibit and explaining what it means to him or her to be a Muslim in the context in which he or she lives. The visitor could thus first listen to Yasmina on television and then meet her in the exhibition.

25 In all, 65,000 people visited the exhibition. Yasmina remembers not more than seven very tense situations.

"were all continuously asking me about the Quran: What does it say on the veil, on marriage, on sex, on adultery [...]. Oh, you cannot imagine how people, Muslims or not, think of the Quran. As if it were a recipe book! But on the other hand, it means they all are looking for more information and want to improve their knowledge. It forced me to get back to books and to prepare for all these questions. [...] In some situations, people came to ask me advice. I also had to respond to very aggressive Muslim boys who told me I was not a good Muslim because I was not wearing a headscarf."

When she started the job, Yasmina had a clear idea of how she would person- ally relate to her work:

"I thought, 'OK, I am a Muslim, but people do not need to know what I do as a Muslim.' In the course of my job, I felt more and more an urgent need to act and to commit myself to helping people improve knowledge of their religion and helping non-Muslims to stop reducing us to a community of fanatics."

In particular, she felt an urgent need for more information about and commu- nication with young men and women whom she saw as

"abandoned to the authority of incompetent so-called imams and who say stupid and untrue things. I remember this young guy, in his twenties. He came to me with very aggressive comments about my way of being a Muslim. He had seen me on the TV screen, and he accused me of giving a bad image of Muslim women. Again it was about me not wearing a headscarf."

After discussing the Quran and the hadith with him, Yasmina ended up talking about more personal matters:

"I told him directly: Don't you think you have a problem with your desire and your sexual attraction for women? You should do your *ijtihad* ... At the end of it, I thought, 'My goodness, mothers should really educate their sons about the way they look at women.'"

Because she was constantly asked, in particular by young men, to justify her behavior, the way she dressed, what she ate, her makeup, the imperative action appeared to Yasmina to be

"the next step in my life as a Muslim. It is as if I were told: OK now, act! Think of others instead of reading books and going alone to conferences. This job and the exhibition definitely changed my views on the situation and on my potential contribution to improving it."

Yasmina's experience expresses many things, but the most striking one is perhaps related to her discovery of the suffering and moral abandon of the persons who accused her of not properly behaving according to standards defined by local self-declared authorities. Albeit differently, Lila, trained as a lawyer, is also concerned about "racism and discrimination motivated by the fact that you are a Muslim." During her studies at law school, she decided to contribute professionally to the fight against discrimination in the framework of a small local association, the Collectif Contre l'Islamophobie en France,[26] which was created in 2003 in Saint Denis in the suburbs of Paris. Up to Ramadan 2004, she had not worn the headscarf.

"Indeed, ironically, I had no direct experience of discrimination caused by my belief in Islam. The only experience I had took place when I was still unveiled. I had just finished with a job interview in the 16th arrondissement of Paris and was on my way back to the city when I crossed paths with a man who told me: 'What are you doing here, you with your Arab curly hairs?' What surprised me at that time was the 'normal look' of this guy. I would rather have expected it from a skinhead or somebody of that type. Clearly, since 9/11, if you show that you belong to Islam it triggers negative comments."

By showing her concern for unfortunate people without having been a victim of such acts herself, Lila reoriented her whole life. She quit her job as a lawyer, which may represent some sacrifice in terms of earnings. (She is now paid by the legal aid association that works together with the Collectif Contre l'Islamophobie en France.) Whereas Yasmina was a spectator of the suffering of others, Lila frames the suffering of an individual person into a legal argument, making it a "case." Lila, as a spectator, nevertheless "can point towards action by putting herself in the position of having to report" on what the victims tells her (Boltanski 1999, 19). The metaphor of the theater for public space is extended with the figure of the spectator, with the position of those who observe and act (e.g., Yasmina and Lila), on the one hand, and, on the other, with those who observe without being willing to be seen as Muslims (e.g., Kenza), who act as a representative for the CFCM (e.g., Larbi), or who choose to play a "clandestine" role, pretending to be a representative of an association of which he is not a member (Morad).

They all related to me individually that they had suffered from the spectacle made of Islam and Muslims in France, on television talk shows, in books, in politicians' discourses, in their daily interactions with actors in the public sphere. Kenza's phone conversation with the director of her daughter's school is a good example of situations in which the meaning attributed to being Muslim reaches a level that comprehends "community concerns." Kenza's daughter goes to a public school in the center of Paris. Once, while working at home, Kenza received a phone call from the director of the school, precisely at the moment of the parliamentary discussion preceding the vote in March 2004 on the law on *laïcité*.

"'Why is your daughter excused from gym course, and why is she not going to the swimming pool with the rest of her classmates?' When I heard this question, I immediately thought, 'This woman has never seen me, she cannot imagine that my daughter is not going to these lessons because of medical problems, and she certainly has the image of me wearing a burnous! Or a headscarf.' ... That was con-

---

26 For more details on the association, see the Web site http://islamophobie.net.

firmed when, after having explained the reason why my daughter had the medical certificates for exempting her from sports training at school, the head of the school started to speak about her last trip to Morocco. Through this discussion, I just realized how unnatural it is for my daughter to be good at school."

Kenza's choice about how she directs her discourse on being a Muslim in France differs from those made by Lila and Yasmina. While she was studying sociology and working in public offices dealing with migrant populations, she tried as much as she could to draw publicity to issues and to act against certain forms of racism or in support of policy aimed at helping Muslim populations. She felt close to socialist party proposals. Her itinerary is now one of a frustrated activist, focusing exclusively on protecting her privacy (and her daughter's life) from external aggressions. In these three cases, decisions about and motivations for discourse are anchored in the individuals' emotions. What makes people act or react to injustice, racism, or unfair treatment is based on their position as spectators of this injustice and racism. But even as simple spectators, people cannot avoid being emotionally invested, even by proxy, in the suffering of others. They are not strategic options in a rational-choice perspective.

Performances or Ascriptions?

A scientific silence still seems to surround the so-called invisible majority of Muslims. Indeed, a common feature of the five individuals discussed in this chapter is the contingency of their commitment to accomplish something good and therefore help others (both Muslims and non-Muslims). Circumstances affect individuals' trajectories of commitment: a particular event may change its course, be it an event of a strictly private nature or one by proxy (e.g., 9/11, racism). Moreover, when it comes to the public expression of one's private religious convictions, the French context is especially difficult. This difficulty is not so much embedded in the principle of laïcité as it is anchored in the perceptions that individuals have of its meanings. One positive aspect of the discussions preceding the vote on the law banning conspicuous religious symbols from public schools, which was passed on March 15, 2004, lies in the improved knowledge of its content among French citizens at large (Baubérot 2004; Gresh 2004).

When it comes to religious belief, the dominant representation of laïcité is articulated in the notion that nobody knows who you are or who you believe in (or whether you believe at all). As one young interviewee told me as I was holding a collective round of discussions at an occupational high school: "That's laïcité, Madam. You shouldn't know what people believe in. You don't know it. And you don't even see it."[27] So how can we identify Muslims

---

27 "C'est ça la laïcité m'dame, c'est q'tu dois pas savoir c'que les gens y croient. Tu peux pas l'savoir, en plus tu l'vois même pas" (Muslim girl born in France,

if they are not visible? Does being visible necessarily make one a public actor?

A common development has emerged over the last two decades: Islam and Muslims are said to have become more visible. They certainly have received rather negative publicity; but although this process has been accelerated since 9/11, it was not instigated by it.[28] Morad kept telling me that his main motivation for abandoning his position as a teacher in a public school was that he wished to help his own community find jobs and training opportunities. He therefore switched to working with computers and opened his own company. How do Muslims living in non-Muslim contexts experience such movement? What does visibility refer to in their case? What is public in all that?

Visibility and publicity have become fashionable words. But where do they become visible, and what makes them visible? Beards and veils are perhaps the most easy markers for recognizing Muslims walking in the street—just as membership in an Islamic association or one's presence in a mosque makes one a Muslim in the eyes of French sociologists. Yet this does not mean they are the only Muslims we should consider. Can belief be traced in behavior? If one fasts, is one then a Muslim?[29] What about money and religion, economy and religious belief?[30] If one does not eat pork, is one then a Muslim?[31] The practices linked with religious beliefs are social acts that give a sociological dimension to belief. This connects practices not only with rituals, but with making decisions, raising the children, being part of a work environment, socializing, voting, and so forth; that is, religious beliefs should be traced in situations other than exclusively denominational ones, even if as motives they are always inferred rather than observed (Lenclud 1990). No one believes in the same way as another, even within the same realm of significations and symbols. Moreover, as in the case of the five persons at the core of this research, practice and convictions vary from one individual to another, even though such variations are not always well accepted. So investigating beliefs as part of the social positioning of individuals also means looking at the degree of pluralism accepted within a given community of belief.

---

18 years old, Malian parents, during a focus group in a classroom, professional high school, Mantes la ville, April 5, 2005).

28 Some events appear to be more central than others in sustaining the emergence of specific representations in European public opinion. The Iranian revolution was one of these central episodes, launching in particular a specific iconography of how Muslims look. This process of "publicization" continued through other events, wars, terrorist attacks, and suicide bombings; 9/11 was just one of them.

29 In certain neighborhoods, non-Muslims fast during Ramadan (see Ville 2004).

30 For an ethnographic and more anthropological point of view on the halal business, see the study by Laurence Bergeaud-Blackler, 2004.

31 In a study I am conducting in public schools and public services providing the people with catering services, the emergence of the category of *sans porc* or *pas de porc* kids.

The reference to the notion of "visibility" has some methodological consequences. The identification and localization of Muslims remain almost exclusively associated with the existence of organized (institutionalized) visible structures, mostly based on authoritative relationships. When visiting these places, individuals perform as Muslims, for insiders and outsiders. Of my five discussion partners, three have been or are still members or such structures. Larbi is a leading imam in a mosque and the head of a cultural-religious center. Morad was for six years the president of a local association of Muslims that he helped to create. Lila is a founding member of the association against Islamophobia. Yet, neither Yasmina neither Kenza go to mosque in Paris. Both prefer to visit churches. One's profession to be a Muslim and one's performance do not correspond to similar identifications. Indeed, identifying Muslims on the basis of their membership in a Muslim association does not give much information about the nature of their commitment. It rather ascribes people an identification to a religious group. On the one hand, it gives priority to organized forms of belonging that of course trace the existence of the belief in the real world. On the other hand, it focuses only on the margins of European Muslims' performances as Muslims. Thus, one important issue is the relation between performing as a believer (showing one's belonging to a religious community) and declaring one's faith (believing). Second, is it possible for religion to exist outside its institutional definition? In other words, is a Muslim in France allowed to follow other paths to exist as a citizen than the one performed by the visible institutional sites linked to his or her religion?

Moreover, visibility is an interactive phenomenon. A person becomes visible to others in a context in which the codes of behavior and patterns of attitudes are quite precisely determined. Wearing a headscarf makes one visible to people who do not share its meaning, in a society where it does not refer to common cultural and religious values. By wearing a headscarf, Muslims girls perform as Muslims.[32] But wearing a Muslim headscarf in public schools makes one visible in France in a different way than it does in the United Kingdom.[33] It also makes one visible in a Muslim society in which

---

32 Here I should add that most of the veiled Muslims interviewed about their experience of wearing the headscarf in non-Muslim contexts expressed a wish for an "invisible headscarf," meaning one not noticed by others and not producing a distinction. I thank Anne-Sophie Lamine for having reminded me of this paradox.

33 For instance, since April 2001 the Metropolitan Police in London have accepted hijab as a uniform option for Muslim women serving in the police force as part of a broader message that Muslim values are valued within the force. This may be different since the terrorist bombings in July 2005, but it also depends on local appreciation. In Nottingham, for instance, a police chief asked his four thousand officers to wear green ribbons ("good fair ribbons") to express solidarity with Muslims fearing persecution after the July bombings in London (see *Times*, August 12, 2005).

the public status of religion has come under the control of the political world and in which, therefore, symbols that deviate from state-defined orthodoxy in terms of religious behavior are publicly stigmatized. This is the case in Turkey, for instance. In the post-9/11 (and post-3/1 and post-7/7) context, most Muslims living in Europe insist on discretion and respect for their belief in the private sphere: they do not want to be visible. The gap between those who are effectively visible and those who are not is growing. The majority of Muslims living outside Muslim societies prefer invisibility and silence, whereas a minority engages on the path to visible, somewhat spectacular (in a horrific sense), and noisy actions.[34] In itself, this does not reveal any specificity of Islam and Muslims: generally speaking, the activists engaged in defense of a cause or the promotion of interests are always a minority. The fact that a majority of Muslims do not wish to make of their religious identification anything special beyond privacy informs about the discrepancy with the public media and political discourse overemphasizing religious determination for explaining actions and discourses of "Muslim populations."

The emphasis on institutions to understand religion is certainly related to two factors: the specificity of the French context of secularization and the way the theoretical discussion on public space was shaped. Public space cannot only be conceived of as a pure site for deliberation on abstract issues. Its theatrical dimension, the dramatic dimensions of some scenes that occur on public stage is something that should be taken into consideration when thinking about the division between intimacy, private life, and the public positioning of Muslims. The fact that in some situations, one may be invited to play a role that is not related to one's convictions and political stance may well happen. For instance, in November 2002 my discussion partner Morad decided to accept the proposal made by one Islamic Tabligh association to take part as their representative in the group sessions preparing the implementation of the CFCM. In private, Morad describes himself as a "normal Muslim": "I have values, I believe in certain principles, I want to raise my kids as Muslims. But I would find it difficult if my wife would say she wished to wear the veil. I just feel that things need to be done by persons who have skills, not by the usual illiterates" (interview in Saint Denis, December 2002). Morad is not a follower of the Tabligh, nor did he join them in order to sit as their representative. He just considered it an opportunity to be present and active within the negotiation process. A charismatic speaker, a good specialist of the juridical aspects related to the discussion on Islam in France, he also felt "the moral obligation not to leave people who would not have been able to make their voice heard because they don't have the knowledge or just because they don't speak French well enough."

---

34 In generational terms, both categories include young men and women, better educated than their parents, using new languages, having developed skills in different domains of knowledge and technology, and having access to the media and the political realm (see the chapter by Annalisa Frisina in this volume).

Morad played his part, following both his own personal agenda (getting to know the minister of the interior, becoming an insider) and defending the position of the association. This idea of putting oneself on a stage to perform a role and play a scene was the reason why Kenza decided to withdraw from politics. Her decision intervened in a very tense context emerging after the election of the first CFCM in 2003. Many choruses started to sing in the name of the "unrepresented Muslims" in public space, the most active ones being the *musulmans laïcs*.[35] These new voices demand a clear distinction between politics and religion, but one that does not require sacrificing one's private religious convictions. These profiles of activist are not radically new in the French context.[36] What is new is their wish to come back as central actors, including "Muslim" in their label. To them, religion is not an obligation, but rather a free option that any individual, male or female, can choose to adopt or to abandon in the course of his or her life. My five discussion partners share this sentiment. From the outside, this secular/religious distinction resembles the private/public one. It appeals to the idea that going public imposes constraints and rules to be respected (e.g., conventions, laws, codes, and symbols specific to the French context), while at the same time not canceling all cultural peculiarities of the individuals nor reducing believers to the ritual dimensions of their faith.

Kenza's recent choice (2003) to retreat from any form of political commitment is the result of a multifaceted decision. She had experiences in different political forums, right and left, with similar outcomes in both cases:

"I agree to be an activist if I am entitled to talk. The problem people of my generation are facing is that we are not accepted in the competition, whether it be political

---

35 Many initiatives were launched under this label: the Conseil Français des Musulmans Laïcs (the French Council for Laïc Muslims), led by Amo Ferhati and Tokia Saïfi (the latter used to be a minister in a previous Chirac government, both are members of the Union pour un Mouvement Populaire [UMP] party); the Convention laïque pour l'égalité des droits et la participation des musulmans de France (Laïc Convention for Equality of Rights and Participation of Muslims from France), under the presidency of Yazid Sabeg, another prominent figure of the UMP and a businessman who in 2004 authored a report on affirmative action and discrimination in employment (directly inspired by the Jewish Representative Council for Jewish Institutions in France [i.e., the Conseil représentatif israélite de France]); the Mouvement des *musulmans laïcs* de France (Movement of Laïc Muslims from France), founded by Rachid Kaci and Djida Tazaït. Kaci belongs to the ultra-liberal side of the UMP party. Tazaït was an activist for the Green Party and for a time was elected to a European deputy position for the same party. She created a local association for young Arabs based in Lyon, the Independent Laïc Movement, and the Coordination for Democrat Muslims. See Frégosi 2004, 2005.

36 Earlier in the 1970s and 1980s, similar profiles could be found in civic movements, human rights and antiracist associations, leftist organizations. What is more surprising is their rightist orientation while they would have been rather committed in left parties in the 1980s (see Geisser 1997).

or social. So long as we stayed in our cellars and our neighborhoods, we were tolerated as citizens. Now that we want to speak up, now that we have skills and competencies, and equality finally amounts to something, we are labeled as Muslims to make us feel that we are not yet there. In particular when it comes to public agencies: they see Muslims everywhere! One should stop that. People need to be looked at differently." (Kenza, discussion in May 2004)

The articulation between religious self-definition (regardless of how regularly one practices) and politics can take various forms. In some cases, it serves the interests of an individual willing to be elected or chosen as a representative within political parties. It also can be purely strategic and opportunistic. Morad explains his decision to take on a Tabligh disguise also as his desire to promote his personal interests in getting access to prominent figures of the ruling party (e.g., Nicolas Sarkozy and the members of his cabinet). His main motivation remains his local political career ("I will end up as a mayor"). Morad plays the gambler's game. He went up to the office of the minister, negotiating with him a position at the Union pour un Mouvement Populaire (UMP), "frightening him. In his department [a neighborhood of Paris], I told him: 'Mister Minister, you'd better not treat us badly. We can make a difference with the ethnic electorate! You have to deal with us now'" (discussion in Le Bourget, April 2003).

But it can also reflect general discomfort related to the public stigmatization of Muslims, to the greater tendency to see an Islamist behind every Muslim, or even to the difference of treatment between Jews and Muslims. The omnipresence of an unhappy public discourse on Islam and Muslims interferes with positioning oneself as a Muslim in a network of activism, among Muslims as well as in other types of civic and political activities. In that sense, expressing oneself as a Muslim on public occasions depends also upon the existence of positive or negative perceptions in the immediate surroundings.

The desire to act as a laic Muslim in the French public sphere is common to the generation that is around forty to fifty years old, and can be summarily described as the former "beur generations" (the ones that went to the streets in the 1980s to defend equality for the children of immigrants and mostly kept away from mobilization in religious terms).[37] They have strong anti-Islamist positions and denounce all associations and initiatives that can be suspected of having links with Muslim Brotherhood or radical movements. In that sense, they can be compared to the secular/Muslim line that divides the Turkish communities living in Germany (see the chapter by Gökçe Yurdakul in this volume). To them, religion should not be made a visible sign for recognition and distinction. It should be kept a private choice. They position themselves as representative of an elite that wish to get recognition for its competence, speaking out their religious feelings more in cultural terms. They consider

---

37 Some other movements emerged that define themselves as movements of nonbelievers.

themselves as the voices of the silent majority of Muslims in France, those who do not feel attached to the newly created CFCM. On the French scene, they demand an increase in the number of antidiscriminatory practices and policies, but also improved protection of the public image of Muslims and an active fight against all forms of Islamism and radicalism (most of them were in favor of the March 2004 law on religious symbols). They also claim to represent the common and anonymous Muslim, the one who is never shown on television because his or her life does not correspond to the dominant stereotypes. The emergence of this new category of Muslims has attracted attention: they indeed represent the alliance of supposedly antithetic identities (i.e., Muslim and republican), and claim the right to live this identity publicly, making no secret of it (Morad), but also without using it systematically as an entry ticket to politics (Kenza).

This positioning, defended in particular by Morad and Kenza, questions the coexistence of plural forms of believing and belonging to a religious family. Grace Davie's famous distinction, elaborated on the basis of her study of British society, perfectly conveys the tensions that each of my five speakers experienced at certain stages: You may believe, but not belong. This is illustrated by Kenza's life history. She defines herself first as an Arab and a Muslim, and has an unusual family history. Her family has lived in France since the end of the nineteenth century. She was born in Marseille. Her mother died when she was six years old, and she was raised by the second wife of her father ("my second mother," as she calls her). She has three brothers and was educated in a private Catholic school.

"My father kept telling me not to go to the Arab part of Marseille. He said Arab men make no distinction between streetlamps and women. We lived in a part of Marseille where we were alone in our situation. The women of my family have always been extremely committed politically. My mother joined the resistance against the French military in Algeria. All of the women in her family went to school and university, married whomever they wanted to. So when I started my studies in sociology, I was not perceived as an eccentric but as a very normal girl."

Living in Paris, raising her child alone—"You know how men are. My daughter's father got tired all of a sudden when she was born. So I told him: 'I don't need you.'"—she defines her belonging to Islam not in terms of practice.

"I never enter a mosque. I hate those places. I'd rather go to churches. And I take my daughter with me. That's where I pray. They are to me normal places for praying. After all, I spent my entire education in Catholic institutions, so I could not betray those who have contributed to my education! So I tell my daughter that we are visiting these places out of courtesy." (Paris, June 2004)

Assuming a clear distance from the institutions of the religious Muslim community in France, Yasmina, coming from a very different background, shares a similar relationship to other denominations, in particular to parochial

Catholic communities. During Christmas of 2004, while she was earning money wrapping up gifts in a luxury shop in Paris, she had her lunch everyday beside the chapel of the closest church. Talking about how she came to be interested in getting to know her religion better, she spoke of the various encounters she had with people from other faiths (including Buddhists and Jews) who helped her to move towards more spirituality in her daily life. Working in the center of Paris, she goes to the closest church during Ramadan to sit, pray, and meditate during her lunch break. She wears a medallion representing Maria, which she always hides when visiting her family.

"They would ask me too many questions and would not be able to understand me. They are not that spiritual, even as Muslims. They would all think I'm weird. But I bring my nephew [age four] to church, and I explain to him the meanings of the architecture, of the paintings."

In France, at a strictly institutional level, there can be no doubt about the primacy of the polity and the marginal character of the public role of religion. As an individual, one's choice of worldview becomes optional, with religion being pushed out of the political center. But at a personal level, it is also anchored in emotions and affects that may connect an individual to other traditions and cultures (Yasmina and Kenza), without pushing them out of their community of belief. Kenza constantly repeats to her daughter that she is not like her classmates. When dealing with religious beliefs, institutions appear to be the way to domesticate a system of symbols, practices, and messages that otherwise would escape (Favret-Saada 1994). It is true that the institutionalization of Islam in France through the creation of the CFCM makes it socially viable and politically acceptable. But at the same time, the public visibility of Islam becomes a problem in French society not so much in terms of its institutional existence, as when it is "carried by corporeal performances and self-presentations rather than by textualized forms of subjectivities and discursive practices" (Göle 2002, 183).

Going Public as an Everyday Citizen

Is there a path that enables one to consider Muslims as participating, as being excluded, as elaborating strategies in order to gain access to the public sphere, independent of institutional structures? International frameworks of course interfere with national and local representations of Muslims. Since 9/11, for instance, the dichotomy between good and bad Muslims as competing categories has emerged more strongly as a central archetypal construction dominating the political international arena (Bonnefoy 2003) and determining policymakers' decision-making.[38] Nationally, non-Muslims' perceptions of Muslims

---

38 The categorization of "good and bad Muslims" may remind one of "good and bad nationalism." "At the core of each instance, as it is generally understood, is

are very much influenced by the way specific controversies unfold. In France, since 1989 the headscarf controversies have constituted the epicenter for the pattern of conflicts involving Muslims. The notion of a "public" therefore has to be considered in its complexity and as encompassing at least three levels of meaning. First, it refers to the idea of a concrete audience. In our case, a legitimate question could be to inquire about the existence of a "Muslim public." This is the audience Yasmina met during her job at La Villette, the persons whom Lila is trying to defend and protect. Second, the notion of a public entails a reference to a social totality (e.g., France as a nation). This is the political space in which Morad projects his future career as mayor of a city north of Paris, where he lives. Third, it refers to a public coming into being in relation with the circulation of discourses (written or not). For instance, public space is also a space where different discourses of identity circulate, compete, and sometimes clash with each other (Bayart 1996; Calhoun 1991). It is a space where some collective identities are accepted and tolerated more easily than others. Some are never accepted. In this respect, Kenza explains that

"one day, my daughter returned home, saying somebody at school told her she was a 'dirty Arab' (*sale arabe*). Some weeks before, a boy at school told another one that he was a 'dirty Jew' (*sale juif*). In the latter case, the school administration and the parents demanded that the boy be punished; he was sent to the discipline committee. In the former, they just asked me not to say anything."

In their perspective, being a Muslim and expressing it in public has a cost, sometimes with social and economic consequences, and even physical ones. Larbi was arrested in August 1994 on the order of the then minister of the interior, Charles Pasqua. He was charged with threatening the republic and supporting Groupe Islamique Armé and Front Islamique du Salut activists in France. He was sent to jail, where he stayed one month. Soon, an important campaign of support was organized by scholars, academics, and journalists who were familiar with his activities in the mosque. Once he regained his freedom, he was asked not to leave the neighborhood for five months. In that context, he launched his social and cultural activities, adding to the ritual religious activities an array of conferences to take place once a month on Saturdays. Over the last ten years the Saturday afternoon conferences of the Rue de Tanger mosques have become an institutional gathering where Muslims and non-Muslims, religious authorities, academics, and opinion-makers make presentations and hold discussions in front of an audience of men and women, younger and older persons, whether French-speaking or not. The

---

an ethnic solidarity that triumphs over civility and liberal values and ultimately turns to horrific violence." Nationalism could be replaced by Islamism. Calhoun (2002, 150) continues: "To treat nationalism as a relic of an earlier order, a sort of irrational expression, or a kind of moral mistake is to fail to see both the continuing power of nationalism as a discursive formation and the work— 'sometimes positive'—that nationalist solidarities continue to do in the world."

topics covered are as varied as the protection of youngsters from drugs, equality and justice in democratic societies, what can be done against AIDS, the reform of Islam, and solidarity in a global world. Larbi usually acts as the host and stays out of the discussion, which lasts most of the afternoon; he reintegrates his role of imam in the very last minutes in order to make concluding remarks. Larbi has created his own, sometimes extremely controversial, public forum of discussion, in which he appears at the beginning and the end of the meeting to perform a sermon.

"What my time in jail changed for me was my relation to politics. Not to culture or French civilization. I have asked myself, 'Why did France do that to me?' I think the answer is pretty much linked with reciprocal ignorance. I often say to my fellows that France and Islam coexist only geographically. The challenge to all of us, Muslims and non-Muslims, is to transform this geographical proximity into a historical proximity. That is to say, building up something together. To produce history. Giving a true meaning to history. And that can only happen with meetings, opportunities to come together and discuss. Otherwise, you stay in your tiny little corner, and I'll never know you. And if you don't know me, you'll end up having wrong ideas and projections of who you think I am."

There are, of course, different ways of showing one's identity as a Muslim. It may be done in the framework of recognition of a faith-oriented perspective: "We Muslims demand our rights as believers." The discourse is in this case a plea for the equality of all citizens. This is pretty much the position assumed by Larbi within his mosque, which was first accommodated in the 1970s in a small Paris church (Ménilmontant). Another type of discourse among Muslims in France insists on the right to be treated free of stigmatization: "You don't need to address my Muslim identity." Morad, for instance, defends his right to be treated as a citizen with no marker. Laughing, he mentioned once on the phone a comment by his son (five years old at that time), refusing to go to Arabic courses and arguing, "Papa, I am not an Arab!" This position is grounded in the interaction with a secular and republican laic tradition. A third position is the one held by individuals who are sometimes also members of associations and who defend the standpoint of "We are not the same as you." They articulate a will to have their rights as believers recognized, but argue in favor of recognition by state authorities and non-Muslim French citizens of the specificity of their history and moral values. In the more radical version, it may even end up with a minority community discourse. None of my discussion partners is defending that position, even if Lila's activism can be related to it. The commitment behind the banner of "fight against Islamophobia" belongs to a strategy of denunciation, accusation, claims-making, naming of adversaries, and a definition of the self that gives meaning to the actions of the Collectif Contre l'Islamophobie en France. In parallel, the decision to act as a collective should be conceived of as part of the institution of a specific public order. In this perspective, going public means that one accepts to perform on a stage, a theater where dramas are shown and where actors accept to perform according to certain rules. In the fight against Islamophobia and religious discrimination, the case is easy as it is mostly a discourse based on a strong dichotomy between victims and criminals articulated along a line of acts that goes from injuries to murder. The fact that discrimination is mostly defined in legal terms seems at first to be a facilitator. But as Lila says, "We cannot limit our activities to the legal arena. It is also a political fight" (interview, November 2004).

The ability to share grievances with other communities, other groups of victims remains in fact open and for now unsolved. The "fight against Islamophobia" discourse remains quite isolated, in the field of the broader antiracism discourse (Lila keeps saying that SOS Racisme, a key nongovernmental organization in the fight against racism, demonstrated hostility towards the Collectif Contre l'Islamophobie en France on many public occasions, accusing them of being fascists), but also more largely in the television and press arena. For instance, no alliance or even comparative perspectives have for the moment been elaborated with anti-Semitism and the situation of Jews in France. On the contrary, Lila but also Kenza and Larbi pointed out, albeit differently, their frustration about seeing Muslims and Jews considered differently when the issues of racism and exclusion for religious reasons come to the fore.[39]

Going public is also made possible by the opportunities offered by the context and the institutional landscape. Therefore, the notion of public space needs to be explored by keeping in mind at least two dimensions. It is first a public space for visibility where social actors play their public role, represent themselves in front of the others. In a way, it is the sensitive dimension of public space, the one that gives opportunity to all participants to consider otherness. The experience of pluralism is indeed central in debating Muslim identity in non-Muslim societies where social control on religion-related practices is relatively smooth. Pluralism among Muslims is something hardly discussed among Muslims themselves. Yasmina, for instance, had the following experience when she was organizing a visit to the Grande Mosquée de Paris with a guided tour provided by the Algerian mosque administration:

"The man who was guiding the group of persons I had brought to the mosque was not very well prepared. Among the visitors, I had brought some particularly difficult students almost excluded from school, and they gave him a hard time during the visit by being noisy and making stupid comments. But I felt offended when he told me in front of them that I was not a good Muslim because I had just said to one of the students—who then repeated it to him—that eating halal food was not an obligation."

---

39 This is a central postcolonial issue in the current French context. On the "victims competition," see Chaumont, 1997. On the postcolonial context, see Liauzu, 2005.

The debate over being a good or a bad Muslim is seen by my discussion partners less in terms of theological good and bad behavior than in relation to a broader assessment of what effects on others good practices can produce. It therefore appears to be extremely difficult to precisely assess the deep significance of the decision to work as a lawyer in a Muslim association: Is the motivation based on the sense of community and can it be at the same time related to a commitment to social justice, therefore carrying a political meaning? Here the reader should not be confused between what my discussion partners say about their own commitment (whether it is Muslim, whether it is public) and what the sociologist qualifies as such. In most of the interviews, they make no distinction between what seems to be conceived of as irreconcilable proposals in the French republican context. The same question remains open while trying to identify the motives of Larbi's preaching, the reason why Morad prefers to employ Muslims and the children of migrants, or when Yasmina helps to organize interreligious dialogue conferences. Acting backstage, my five discussion partners avoid politics and even proclaim their inability to affect others' life courses. Even when they express their awareness of the broader public debate on Islam in France, their remain at a distance from it or at least minimize their potential effect on it. Nina Eliasoph's work on parents volunteering in anti-drugs groups is enlightening here, as she evokes similar attitudes of "silencing public-spirited political conversation" that she considers to be a paradoxical

"way of looking out for the common good. [...] Volunteers work embodied, above all, an effort aimed at convincing themselves and others that the world makes sense, and that regular people can really make a difference. [...] Community-spirited citizens judged that by avoiding 'big' problems, they could better buoy their optimism. But by excluding politics from their group concerns, they kept their enormous, overflowing reservoir of concern and empathy, compassion and altruism, out of circulation, limiting its contribution to the common good." (Eliasoph 1998, 63)

In the French context, some Muslim associations try to organize their own arena for discussing the articulation between being a Muslim and being a citizen of a non-Muslim society. The Union des Organisations Islamiques de France is one of these; Tariq Ramadan's networks also act in a similar manner. But in the eyes of my discussion partners, these initiatives are excessively based on the interested motivations of leaders. In a way, they do not take it for genuine.

In considering individual, everyday citizens, I share Calhoun's perspective on "the people" in his critique of Habermas's constitutional patriotism: "It is crucial to understand not simply which constitutional arrangements are in some abstract sense good, but what makes them have force for specific people" (Calhoun 2002, 153). It is also a question of individual identity, which produces passions that escape conventional categories of the political. The situations in which individuals experience injustice (Lila and Kenza by proxy, Larbi more directly) evoke anguish and hardship, which possibly will lead them to commit to somebody or some cause (Morad for the "community," Yasmina for improved understanding of Islam and Muslims). Situated arrangements poses as a starting point the claims made by individuals (Boltanski and Thévenot 2000). For the Muslims quoted in this chapter, public space or the public sphere is essentially about discourse and interaction. Members of a society may join together in the public sphere, performing through debates and conversations (Calhoun 2002). Participation is therefore not exclusively based on personal connections, and remains open to everybody. It is supposed to include everyone within the field at stake (Warner 2002). Public space is thus a scene of performance, a stage where individuals perform a role that may be composed of several profiles. This refers to situated practices: working on the coming to public of Muslims takes as point of departure the observation of situated practices. Public space is an arena where one fights for the defense of one's identity and its related positions, but it is also a place where one performs in front of a public (Cefaï 2003)—as Yasmina did during the exhibition at La Villette and Larbi does during the Saturday conferences he organizes in his mosque. Leaving the floor open to people whose views he may not share, Larbi nevertheless keeps for himself the concluding remark and plays his authoritative role of preacher and moral guide for the Muslims sitting in the conference room, encouraging them to be "active citizens and active, enlightened Muslims" (personal observation during a conference in June 2003). This towering position does not systematically result in communication between divergent voices or opinions expressed in different registers (e.g., religion, faith, and theology facing political and secular questions). The absence of communication among Muslims themselves is absolutely dominating the public dimension of the debate, not only in Larbi's mosque. "People may live side by side and have no sense of closeness fostered through privileged knowledge of everyday details [...]. Rather they may feel trapped together as strangers who know nothing of each other's inner worlds" (Jamieson 1998, 8).

Connecting these remarks with the dominant narratives mentioned earlier, I would argue that the borders delimitating what is private and what can be publicized seem to have been displaced. Dominique Mehl (2003) evokes a process through which social deliberation is defined by the private space of personal conversation. Society speaks to itself in this articulation between private and public. This is facilitated by the increasing number of discussions touching upon personal stories, upon affective and emotional episodes. Everybody knows the other exists. However, the direct confrontation of minds and divergent opinions never takes place. Comparison is made possible between different lifestyles (Bouzar and Kada 2003) and modes of behavior, thereby rejecting or establishing norms. These singular narratives speak and echo each other. Public space appears as a space for experiencing and testing difference in the way one lives as a Muslim.[40] Public presence brings value to singular voices, illustrating various paths of authentic ways of living. This "extreme individualization of examples" (Mehl 2003, 492) takes place in a moment of unprecedented exposure to public stories through the mass media (Jamieson 1998). The idea behind this narrative form is, "I am not the only one in this case. My life is the same as hundreds and thousands of others." The content is thus considered to be representative. But on the question of knowing whether the discussion encourages reflection among Muslims in France, the answer is rather that it facilitates the superimposition of opinions. "In these public spaces, identities and lifestyles are performed, contested and implemented" (Yavuz 2004, 223).[41]

Conclusion: Invisible but Publicly Active Muslims

Based on the life experiences and challenges that Larbi, Morad, Kenza, Lila, and Yasmina related to me, this chapter focused on individual voices. Haphazard as such a choice must remain, it helps to describe the many forms taken in a process of commitment as Muslims in France. Insisting on particularities, on snapshots, rather than relying on the feeling of security that comes from working on association, is of course a slippery option for an author. Highlighting the silent Muslim majority occurred to me a necessity, even if it remains difficult to grasp. I thus do not want to generalize my findings. Rather, I make a claim for singular experiences, for the need to describe individual itineraries.

In public space that remains fundamentally secular, four aspects are central in the five itineraries. The first one is that the classic division of social worlds into private and public is insufficient to gain an understanding of the multiple and fragmented aspects of individuals' everyday lives, even though reading public space as a theater and emphasizing the notion of stage and performance remain of relevance in case studies. The second one stems from the observation that public engagement cannot be limited and restricted to an associative membership. From one moment to the next, through changing one's place or situation, the meanings given by individuals to their self-definition as Muslims vary. Each of them is able to articulate different means to become engaged. They may have as an objective for discourse and action the "Muslim public" (e.g., Larbi when he is preaching, Yasmina when she is

---

40 Pluralism does not exist unless it is concretely experienced, such as on the day of Eid ul-Adha, when different communities of Muslims meet for the first time in front of the slaughtering house, and do not bring all the same animals to slaughter.

41 This point recalls Mehl's observation (2003) about the nature of discussion in television programs dealing with intimate issues. Rather than a proper discussion including divergent views on different ways of life, the shows explicitly rely on a superimposition of different opinions and lifestyles.

explaining what Islam is to youngsters visiting the exhibition, Lila fighting against Islamophobia), non-Muslims (Kenza arguing with her daughter's teachers, Yasmina organizing interreligious conferences), or a local community (Morad employing Arab Muslims from the area in which he lives when he launched his firm) as a framework for justifying their commitment. The ways each of them define the representation of his or her commitment do not end in a unique imaginary, even if in linguistic terms Islam may appear to the external observer to be a similar link to a common social and cultural imaginary.[42] In these diverse situations, being a Muslim and acting and speaking as such do not mean the same thing from one person to the next, from one place to the next, from one moment to the next. The third aspect regards the need to take a broader view of the activist's individual trajectory, seeing it not so much as a linear career, but rather as an experience primarily developed on the basis of interactions that may create breaks, generate affects (in all directions), or provoke a shift from one type of discourse to another, from commitment to silence (Kenza), or the other way around (Yasmina and Lila). The fourth aspect concerns biographical dimensions and the need for careful description in order to map the complexity of the repertoires and discourses that an individual can draw from to tell his or her story.

This chapter reflects an ambiguous configuration in which Muslims in France currently find themselves. On the one hand, they have made their coming out in the sense of demonstrating their ability to make their voices heard in a context of political interest in their involvement.[43] This development is not restricted to the French context, but can be seen in the so-called growing international visibility of Islam on the international and national scenes: "Islamic social movements represent the 'coming out' of private Muslim identity in public spaces" (Yavuz 2004, 223). On the other hand, hostility towards Islam is growing; the public discourse relayed by the media is ill-informed and contributes to the diffusion of stereotypes and reductionist views of the religion and its believers. In this context, a focus on individuals is the only level that enables a description of situations where one can pose the question "What does it mean to be a Muslim?"

The silent majority, the invisible Muslims, those who "do adapt without problems" (Roy 2005, 166), should not be too quickly reduced to "absentees of public space" just because they have no words and no organization to represent them (Mehl 2003, 495). In this chapter, I illustrated how some individuals have chosen different forms of commitment that do not follow the expected associative structures. They represent other ways of having a voice. By the end of this chapter, some echoes of the silent majority of Muslims

---

42 The idea of Islam playing the role of a link for an imaginary bond is advanced by Nilüfer Göle, for instance, when she speaks about the tie between "sozial entwurtzelten Muslimen," or "socially uprooted Muslims" (2004, 17).

43 I used the wording "coming out" once in an interview for the newspaper *Libération* and received a phone call from Larbi the next day, congratulating me on the adapted wording.

living in France have reached us. How do individuals autonomous from the sphere of institutionalized religion have their intimate and private convictions go public? The sample at the core of this text was supposed to open up readings about Muslims in France which escape organized, institutional, and visible frameworks, illustrating how one comes to terms with plurality within one's community of belief.

References

Abd al Malik. 2004. Qu'Allah bénisse la France. Paris: Albin Michel.

Abdelkrim, F. 2002. Na'al bou la France? (Maudite soit la France). Bobigny, France: Gédis.

Althabe, G. 1990. Ethnologie du contemporain et enquête de terrain. Terrain 14:126–131.

Amara, F. 2003. Ni Putes Ni Soumises. Paris: La Découverte.

Amghar, S. 2005. Les salafistes français: Une nouvelle aristocratie religieuse. Maghreb-Machrek 183 (spring): 13–31.

Amiraux, V. 2004. Expertises, savoir et politique: La constitution de l'islam comme problème public en France et en Allemagne. In Les sciences sociales à l'épreuve de l'action, ed. B. Zimmermann, 209–245. Paris: EHESS.

———. 2005. Representing difference. Open Democracy Web site (published November 15): http://www.opendemocracy.net/democracy-resolution_1325/difference_3026.jsp.

Amiraux, V., and O. Roy, eds. 2004. Musulmanes, Musulmans au Caire, à Téhéran, Istanbul, Paris, Dakar ... Marseille: Indigène.

Babès, L. 1997. L'islam positif: La religion des jeunes musulmans en France. Paris: Editions de l'Atelier.

———. 2005. Le voile démystifié. Paris: Bayard.

Basdevant-Gaudemet, B. 1996. Le statut de l'islam en France. Revue du droit public et de la science politique en France et à l'étranger 2 (March–April): 355–384.

Baubérot, J. 2004. Laïcité 1905–2005: Entre passion et raison. Paris: Seuil.

Baubérot, J., J. Costa-Lascoux, and D. Bouzar. 2004. Le voile: Que cache-t-il? Paris: Editions de l'Atelier.

Bayart, J.-F. 1996. La greffe de l'Etat. Paris: Karthala.

Bellil, S. 2002. Dans l'enfer des tournantes. Paris: Denoël.

Bergeaud-Blackler, L. 2004. Social definitions of halal quality: The case of Maghrebi Muslims in France. In The qualities of food: Alternative theories and empirical approaches, ed. M. Harvey, A. McMeekin, and A. Warde, 94–107. Manchester: Manchester University Press.

Berger, P., and T. Luckmann. 1967. The social construction of reality: A treatise in the sociology of knowledge. Harmondsworth, UK: Penguin Books.

Boltanski, L. 1999. Distant suffering: Morality, media and politics. Cambridge, UK: Cambridge University Press.

Boltanski, L., and L. Thévenot. 2000. The reality of moral expectations: A sociology of situated judgement. Philosophical Explorations 3 (3): 208–231.

Bonnefoy, L. 2003. Public institutions and Islam: A new stigmatization? ISIM Newsletter, 13 December: 22.

Bouzar, D., and S. Kada. 2003. L'une voilée, l'autre pas. Paris: Albin Michel.

Calhoun, C. 1991. Imagined communities and indirect relationships: Large scale social integration and the transformation of everyday life. In Social theory for a changing society, ed. P. Bourdieu and J. S. Coleman, 95–120. Boulder, CO: Westview.

———. 2002. Imagining solidarity: Cosmopolitanism, constitutional patriotism, and the public sphere. Public Culture 14 (1): 147–171.

Cardon, D. 1995. "Chère Ménie ..." Emotions et engagements de l'auditeur de Ménie Grégoire. Réseaux 70:41–79.

Cefaï, D. 2003. Qu'est ce qu'une arène publique? In L'héritage du pragmatisme, ed. D. Cefaï and I. Joseph, 51–81. Paris: Editions de l'Aube.

Cesari, J. 1994. L'islam dans l'immigration: Un bilan de la recherche. Pensée 299 (July–September): 59–68.

Chaumont, J. M. 1997. La concurrence des victimes: Génocide, identité, reconnaissance. Paris: La Découverte.

Eickelman, D. F. 2000. Islam and the languages of modernity. Daedalus 129 (1): 119–135.

Eliasoph, N. 1998. Avoiding politics. Cambridge, UK: Cambridge University Press.

Favret-Saada, J. 1994. Weber, les émotions et la religion. Terrain 22:93–108.

Frégosi, F. 1998. Les problèmes d'organisation de la religion musulmane en France. Esprit 239:109–136.

———. 2004. Vous avez dit "musulmans laïcs"? Les Cahiers de l'Orient 76 (winter): 59–72.

———. 2005. Les musulmans laïques en France: Une mouvance plurielle et paradoxale. Maghreb-Machrek 183 (spring): 33–44.

Galembert, C. de, and M. Belbah. 2005. Le Conseil Français du Culte Musulman à l'épreuve des territoires. French Politics, Culture and Society 23 (1): 76–86.

Gamson, J. 1998. Freaks talk back: Tabloid talk shows and sexual nonconformity. Chicago: University of Chicago Press.

Gaspard, F., and F. Khosrokhavar. 1995. Le foulard et la République. Paris: La Découverte.

Geisser, V. 1997. Ethnicité républicaine: Les élites d'origine maghrébine dans le système politique français. Paris: Presses de Sciences Po.

———. 2003. La nouvelle islamophobie. Paris: La Découverte.

Geisser, V., and K. Mohsen-Finan. 2001. L'islam à l'école. Paris: IHESI.

Goffman, E. 1981. Footing. In Forms of talk, 124–159. Philadelphia: University of Pennsylvania Press.

Göle, N. 2002. Islam in public: New visibilities and new imaginaries. Public Culture 14 (1): 173–190.

———. 2004. Die Sichtbare Präsenz des Islam und die Grenzen der Öffentlichkeit. In Islam in Sicht: Der Auftritt von Muslimen in öffentlichen Raum, ed. L. Amman and N. Göle, 11–44. Bielefeld, Germany: Transcript.

Gresh, A. 2004. L'Islam, la République et le monde. Paris: Fayard.

Guénif, N., and E. Macé. 2004. Les féministes et le garçon arabe. La Tour d'Aigues, France: L'Aube.

Jamieson, L. 1998. Intimacy: Personal relationships in modern societies. Cambridge, UK: Polity Press.

Khedimellah, M. 2001. Jeunes prédicateurs du mouvement Tabligh: La dignité identitaire retrouvée par le puritanisme religieux? Socio-Anthropologie 10:5–18.

Khosrokhavar, F. 1997. L'Islam des jeunes. Paris: Hachette.

———. 2004. L'islam en prison. Paris: Balland.

Laermans, R., B. Wilson, and J. Billiet, eds. 1998. Secularization and social integration: Papers in honor of Karel Dobbelaere. Sociology Today 4. Leuven, Belgium: Leuven University Press.

Lenclud, G. 1990. Vues de l'esprit, art de l'autre. Terrain 14 (March): 5–19.

Levy, L., and A. Levy. 2004. Des filles comme les autres: Au-delà du foulard. Entretien avec Véronique Giraud et Yves Sintomer. Paris: La Découverte.

Liauzu, C. 2005. Empire du mal contre Grand Satan. Paris: Armand Colin.

Lorcerie, F., ed. 2005. La politisation de l'affaire du foulard. Paris: L'Harmattan.

Mehl, D. 2003. Le témoin, figure emblématique de l'espace privé/public. In Les sens du public: Publics politiques, publics médiatiques, ed. D. Cefaï and D. Pasquier, 489–502. Paris: PUF.

Meliane, L. 2003. Vivre libre: Itinéraire d'une marcheuse des Ni Putes Ni Soumises. Paris: Oh éditions.

Mucchielli, L. 2005. Le scandale des "tournantes." Dérives médiatiques, contre-enquête sociologique. Paris: La Découverte.

Nordmann, C., ed. 2004. Le foulard islamique en questions. Paris: Èditions Amsterdam.

Pew Research Center. 2005. Support for terror wanes among Muslim publics. Islamic extremism: Common concern for Muslim and Western publics (Pew Global Attitudes Project, released July 14). Washington, D.C.: Pew Research Center.

Roy, O. 2005. La laïcité face à l'islam. Paris: Seuil.

Stokes, B. 2005. Easing Muslim alienation in Europe. National Journal 16 (July): 2304.

Tarraud, C., ed. 2005. Les féminismes en question. Paris: Éditions Amsterdam.

Taylor, C. 2002. Modern social imaginaries. Public Culture 14 (1): 91–124.

Tietze, N. 2002. Jeunes musulmans de France et d'Allemagne. Paris: L'Harmattan.

Venel, N. 2004. Musulmans et citoyens. Paris: PUF.

Ville, M. 2004. L'héritage recomposé: Étude des pratiques du Ramadan en France. Paris: EHESS (DEA, unpublished thesis).

Warner, M. 2002. Publics and counterpublics. Public Culture 14 (1): 49–90.

Yavuz, H. 2004. Is there a Turkish Islam? The emergence of convergence and consensus. Journal of Muslim Minority Affairs 24 (2): 213–232.

Zitouni, R. 2005. Comment je suis devenue une Beurgeoise. Paris: Hachette.

Nadia Fadil

"WE SHOULD BE WALKING QURANS":
THE MAKING OF AN ISLAMIC POLITICAL SUBJECT

Introduction

Recent events and developments such as the attacks in New York and Madrid, the murder of Theo Van Gogh in the Netherlands, the Islamic terrorist threat, and the emergence of Islam in the Western European public sphere have led to an increased interest in Islam in the Western world, which is seeking explanations for what is going on. While many have turned to polarizing, Huntingtonian visions in which Islam and Muslims are framed as the new enemy, others, in the hope of avoiding such polarization, have hoped to find "new" Islamic leaders who are able to offer "new" discourses and approaches to Islam and citizenship. Questions of representation and leadership are important not only for a broader Western European public; they are crucial for Muslims themselves.

In this chapter I focus on a group of young Muslim professionals who are actively engaged in issues of representation and citizenship. Three years ago, some younger members of the Union of Mosque and Islamic Organisations of Antwerp (UMIVA) decided to organize a conference in response to the negative representation of Islam in the aftermath of 9/11. Faced with an increasing level of Islamophobia and stereotypical representations of Islam, they came up with the idea of organizing "Treasures of Islam," a conference on the scientific contributions of medieval Islam. In the process of preparation for the conference, new members—both men and women—were attracted, resulting in the establishment of a stable group of young professionals within the existing umbrella organization.

This chapter focuses on how some of the members frame their political and religious involvement in this working group. The working group is characterized by its explicit references to Islam, which plays a prominent role in both a normative framework and a framework for defining identity. I attempt to describe and analyze how the engagement of the members of the working group is an expression of the creation and performance of an Islamic political subject. By questioning the existing and dominant representations of Muslims on the one hand, and by articulating an alternative, politicized discourse on the self on the other, the members of the working group process and construct a particular vision of their identity. Identity politics refers to collective actions that aim not only at accessing equal rights but also at

53

questioning and refusing imposed or prescribed identities (Calhoun 1994, 21). After briefly situating and presenting the working group, I discuss how the challenging of dominant essentialist discourses on Muslims involves the articulation of and reliance on alternative, but equally essentialist, accounts. In the third section I focus in more detail on the group's discourse of active citizenship and how it relates to dominant accounts of this issue.

The UMIVA Working Group

In 1974 Islam was recognized as the third official religion in Belgium. This year also ushered in both the end of the large-scale Belgian labor immigration policy, which attracted workers from North Africa, Turkey, and the southern Mediterranean, and the worldwide oil crisis. It is estimated that around 400,000 Muslims now live in Belgium, and that this group is mainly composed of Moroccan and Turkish nationals (Landman 2002, 100). Initially, most Muslim immigrants were located in the coal-mining regions of Le Borinage, Liege, and Limburg. Bigger cities like Brussels and Antwerp also attracted a large number of Muslims in the early 1970s, when alternative industries such as metallurgy and car assembly were developed in these regions. The working group upon which this chapter focuses is situated in the city of Antwerp, the second-largest city of Belgium, with 457,739 inhabitants.[1]

Institutional and Political Setting

The city of Antwerp has a history of migration and international contacts due to its international port and diamond trade (Bousetta 2001, 144). Moroccans make up the highest share of non-nationals among the overall average of 13.3 % for non-nationals (4.6 % for Moroccans; 1.5 % for Turks). Due to the increasing number of naturalizations, however, it is difficult to estimate the number of Moroccan Muslims actually residing in the city (Peleman 2002, 115).[2] Antwerp is home to a variety of contradictory political and sociological trends, making the city an interesting setting for observing multicultural developments.

One striking characteristic of the city is the presence of an extreme right-wing political party, previously called Vlaams Blok and recently renamed Vlaams Belang. With its 33 % of the votes in the last municipal elections

---

1   DIA-Antwerp, November 2004, http://www.antwerpen.be/feitenencijfers/diversiteit//.
2   Estimates vary between 20 % and 25 %. According to the city of Antwerp, "new Belgians" (naturalized Belgians) and non-nationals represented 22.1 % of the city's population in 2005 (http://www.antwerpen.be/feitenencijfers/demografie/diversiteit.htm).

(2000), it is the largest party in Antwerp.[3] After its major electoral break-through in 1994, a *cordon sanitaire* was formed around Vlaams Blok, obliging all other elected political parties to form a "monster coalition" and thereby obtain the majority of seats needed to govern.[4] Although kept out of the local administration, Vlaams Belang clearly has a great impact on this political constellation. To begin with, the composition of divergent political parties in city government hampers smooth operation of the coalition, result-ing in regular crises between the coalition partners, which Vlaams Belang, as the only opposition party, eagerly exploits. In addition, the strong presence of Vlaams Belang since its political breakthrough in the late 1980s has influ-enced the political positions and measures proposed and taken up by estab-lished parties and institutions. Hassan Bousetta has pointed, for instance, to the difficulties of building new mosques and the propositions of the Antwerp mayor in 1990 to create immigrant-exclusive neighborhoods (2001: 154). More recently, knowledge of Dutch has become a criterion in the allocation of social housing in Antwerp.[5]

As mentioned, the presence of a strong extreme-right party goes hand in hand with the broad spectrum of ethnic and economic diversity in the city, which has a major port and is one of the leading capitals in the global dia-mond trade. Among the city's diverse mix of ethnic and cultural minorities, the presence of a strong and visible Chassidic Jewish community is particu-larly noteworthy.

As noted, there is also a sizable Islamic community, with Moroccans rep-resenting the largest ethnic minority from outside the European Union. This group is characterized by a weak socioeconomic position and a strong concentration in neighborhoods like Borgerhout, where 25 % to 30 % of Moroccan nationals live (Peleman 2002, 120).[6] This concentration coincides with a high level of unemployment, low levels of education, and poor hous-ing. The highest Flemish unemployment rate is in the city of Antwerp, with 32 % of the unemployed 18- to 29-year-olds of Moroccan origin.[7] A majority of pupils of Moroccan origin do not finish their secondary schooling, and

---

3   The last regional elections of June 13, 2004, only confirmed its leading position, with 34 % of the votes in the city of Antwerp.

4   This coalition included the SP, VLD, Agalev, CVP, and VU. Only the small party Waardig Oud Worden (WOW), with its one seat on the council, was not included (Bousetta 2001, 153).

5   The newspaper *De Standaard* reported on December 30, 2004, on agreements made between several social-housing companies to refuse social housing to peo-ple who do not speak Dutch.

6   Borgerhout is often cynically called "Borgerokko," in reference to the consider-able Moroccan community in this neighborhood.

7   Data from the following Web site (in Dutch): http://www.wvc.vlaanderen. be/minderheden/minderhedenbeleid/icem/publicaties/jaarrapport1998/04werk~1. htm#P7_8.

persons of Moroccan origin are only marginally present in higher education.[8] Moreover, only 1.6 % of the Moroccans in Belgium live in houses of good quality (Bousetta 2001, 102).

Snapshots of Moroccan Civil Society

These weak social conditions are combined with relatively active and diverse social and political activities. Four types of organizations within Moroccan civil society in Antwerp can be differentiated.[9] The first is small-scale and locally based ethnic organizations, often established for concrete needs and purposes: Arabic/Dutch language courses, homework tutoring, sewing lessons, and so forth. These organizations are often gender-segregated and are mainly composed of first-generation Moroccans (with the exception of homework tutoring). They have no explicit "political agenda,"[10] and tend to be integrated in the neighborhood.[11]

A second type consists of Islamic organizations whose clear aim is *da'wa*, the religious duty of each Muslim to spread the message of Islam.[12] They tend to organize Arabic language courses, lessons in Islamic history or *fiqh*, and

---

8   Data from research carried out at the University of Brussels and the University of Antwerp. Further information is available at the following Web site (in Dutch): http://www.studentfocus.be/UA%20onderzoek%202004.pdf.

9   These descriptions are based on observations from my fieldwork for a doctoral research project with the working title Secularisation and Individualisation Processes in the Religiosity of Organised and Non-Organised Moroccan Muslims in Antwerp and Brussels (2002–2006). This rough typology does not include mosques, but instead is oriented to organizations whose primary function is not the organization of Islamic rituals such as prayer. Furthermore, this typology focuses only on what Bousetta calls "ethnic organisations," that is, organizations established and run mainly by and for members of the Moroccan community (2001, 352). Other ethnic groups or "mixed organizations" are not included.

10 I use the term "political agenda" to refer to organizations that, among other things, act as pressure groups through their interactions and/or their interventions in the public sphere and that negotiate with political officials. I am aware of the restrictiveness of this definition and concept of what is political (see Mahmood 2005).

11 Examples of the first type in the neighborhood of Borgerhout are Nibras (Islamic organizations for religious and leisure activities, primarily for women and children), El Moustaqbal (a first-generation women's organization offering sporting activities, Dutch classes, and the like), Safina (a first-generation, mainly men's organization, arranging Arabic courses for children and lectures and debates on different social topics), and Al Kitaab (a homework tutoring organization, mainly run by highly educated second-generation Moroccan Muslims).

12 This is not to say that the first type of organization is not Islamic. The difference lies in their explicit purpose of spreading knowledge about Islam and orienting all their activities to this purpose.

lectures on various religious themes. They reach a large number of people—mainly young persons and sometimes people from outside Antwerp—and are not involved in the political scene.[13]

Third, there are the federations and umbrella organizations with a clear political agenda embedded in an institutional logic.[14] Established in reaction to the paternalistic approach of Belgian integration policies and the political interference of Moroccan authorities, these organizations seek more autonomy in community affairs. They not only act as unofficial representatives of the community in dealing with city officials, but also are called upon during times of conflict (Bousetta 2001). In the Ramadan period of November 2002, when riots broke out after the racist murder of a locally well-known Islamic teacher by his Flemish neighbor, the different federations and umbrella organizations were called together to act as intermediaries with the city officials and to prepare the teacher's funeral.

The last type of organization is an outsider in the Belgian political scene because of its outspoken political positions and radical discourse on multiculturalism: the Arab European League (AEL). Its noninstitutional logic and grassroots approach also differentiate it from the other organization types: through its emphasis on popular mobilization and its strategy of pursuing its own network of organizations (e.g., in media, scouting, and schooling) within the pillared structure of Belgian society, the AEL challenges the established institutions as well as the strategies of other Moroccan ethnic organizations.[15] The visibility of the organization reached a national level with the organization of civil patrols to check and document the alleged racist behavior of the Antwerp police force, as well as with its political positions on Belgian integration policy. It gained international attention in November 2002, when the leader of the movement, Dyab Abou Jahjah, was held responsible and imprisoned for the outburst of riots following the murder of the Islamic teacher, only to be released soon afterwards because the case against him was weak.[16] After a tumultuous year characterized by extensive media coverage,

---

13 The most prominent example of this type for Antwerp is the Islamic organization Jongeren Voor Islam (Youth for Islam).

14 Three umbrella organizations representing mainly Moroccan ethnic organizations are based in the city of Antwerp: Federatie van Marokkaanse Vereniging, Vereniging voor Ontwikkeling en Emancipatie van de Moslims, and Unie van de Moskeeën en Islamitische Verenigingen van Antwerpen (UMIVA).

15 Here I am borrowing from McAdam's definition of social movements, which limits it to "those organized efforts, on the part of the excluded groups, to promote or resist changes in the structure of society that involve resource to noninstitutional forms of political participation" (1999, 25).

16 Abou Jahjah's imprisonment was highly contested not only because the evidence against him was weak, but also because of a suspicious entanglement of political and judiciary powers: Abou Jahjah's arrest was preceded by a heated parliamentary debate in which the minister of the interior and the prime minister insisted on the need to immediately stop the activities of the AEL.

offensive political attacks on the movement, and poor election results,[17] the AEL was weakened and marginalized in the public arena (see Abou Jahjah 2003; Jacobs 2003; Fadil 2003; De Witte 2004).

I stress the importance of this movement because of the impact that its discourse, activities, and actions in November 2002 had on the local Antwerp setting and on ethnic associations. The rise of the AEL and the climactic events in the fall of 2002 led to a number of proposals, formulated by local and regional officials, on the different social problems that the Moroccan community was facing. Some political parties even spoke of a "Marshall Plan" for Borgerhout.[18] Moreover, the presence of the AEL had a direct and indirect impact on other ethnic organizations and the larger Moroccan community. Organizations and Muslims were asked to take a position on (and preferably against) the AEL. The organization's rise led to a stronger political and social consciousness among the Moroccan community, which was evident both in the increasing number of public debates on socioeconomic issues related to the community and in the support and creation of new organizations.[19]

The UMIVA Working Group: Description and Presentation

Established in 1995, UMIVA brings together mainly Arab-language mosques and strives for an active partnership with local and regional officials by acting as a representative and mediator for the Moroccan Islamic community.[20] The members work on themes ranging from issues related to Islamic worship to youth issues and social problems. UMIVA also joins other regional mosque

---

17 The AEL ran in two elections: in the federal elections of May 2003 under the open list "RESIST!", which was an alliance primarily between the AEL and the far-left party Partij Van De Arbeid, and in the regional elections of June 2004, for which it established the Muslim Democratic Party. The results of both elections were weak, with 2.32 % in 2003 and only 0.62 % in 2004 for the city of Antwerp.

18 G. Timmerman "Agalev wil een Marshallplan voor Borgerhout," *De Morgen*, December 2, 2002.

19 The presence and positions of the AEL also influenced the activities of the UMIVA working group. An example is the intervention of UMIVA members in the Carim Bouziane affair, a politician of the Green Party. Bouziane announced in September 2003, in a documentary on homosexuality in the Islamic community, his intention to distribute posters depicting covered Muslim girls kissing each other; he planned to distribute these posters in neighborhoods where many Muslims live. After the AEL's sharp reaction and condemnation, which led to a small public riot, the group of young UMIVA professionals contacted Bouziane in order to convince him to abandon the plan. In the end, however, it was internal problems in the Green Party which prevented the plan from going through.

20 The union brings together thirty-five mosques; most of these are Moroccan, with the exception of a Chechnyan, a Bosnian, an Afghan, and a Roma mosque.

unions in a larger structure that interacts with Flemish and federal officials.[21] The working group presented in this chapter acts within this larger structure, but has a quasi-autonomous status. Meetings take place in UMIVA's meeting room and are often attended by the union's secretary. There is, however, no explicit interference of the UMIVA board in the activities and decision-making of the working group.

Most male members were already active within UMIVA before the working group came into being. Informally called "the group of young people" (*groupes de jeunes* in French, or *jongerengroep* in Dutch), the working group began in 2003 as an organizational committee for the conference Treasures of Islam. Female members and new external members were attracted to support preparations for the conference. What started as an ad hoc working group soon became a stable group of professional volunteers meeting on a regular basis, discussing societal developments, and organizing activities and projects. The group is composed mainly of higher educated people and includes both sexes. Whereas the women are all second-generation Moroccans born in Belgium, the male members comprise second-generation Moroccans as well as recently arrived first-generation Moroccans and one converted Muslim. There is no official structure within the group, which does not mean that there are no key figures.

The material presented in this chapter was gathered during the months of October, November, and December of 2003. At that time, the group had existed for almost a year and was busy preparing a large Islamic fair and making public interventions on different social and political matters. The ethnographic material includes notes taken during three group meetings (on October 16, 2003; October 19, 2003; and December 14, 2003), one group interview (on November 13, 2003), and individual interviews with five members of the group.[22] The following description of the group is based mainly on the accounts of Fouad, Amina, and Nora. Fouad could be described as the "informal" president of the working group. Ever since his migration from Morocco to France, and later to Belgium, in order to pursue his studies, Fouad has been involved in different Islamic organizations. He was one of the main sources of inspiration for the organization of the conference as well as for the enlargement of the working group to include female members and external members. The second member presented is Amina; born in Belgium, she holds a university degree and is currently working as a civil servant. Her professional and educational career was always accompanied with civic engagement, first in student affairs and later in women's issues. For several years she headed a Muslim women's organization aimed at deconstructing the media's stereotypical representation of Muslim women and at promoting

---

21 Umivel (for the province of Limburg) and Umivow (for the province of Eastern and Western Flanders).

22 Although the "strict" gathering of information took place in October, November, and December of 2003, some relevant events that occurred after this period also will be discussed.

equal rights within an Islamic framework. Two other members mentioned are Nora, an Islam teacher, and Ahmed, an engineer; both are second-generation Moroccans.

My interviews with the working-group members attempted to trace the motivations and reasons for their engagement. The Treasures of Islam conference and the plan to organize an Islamic fair reflect the two main lines of their engagement: to work against negative and stereotypical representations of Muslims and to empower Muslims who too often find themselves in weak socioeconomic conditions and without a strong sense of identity. The common thread for all members of the working group is an active reference to an Islamic framework. In what follows, I shall show how this active use of and reference to Islam is a means to resist and challenge existing stereotypes about Muslims and Islam, and how their active discourse on Islamic identity constructs and reflects a certain vision of the Islamic subject and its relation to the political sphere.

Recognition through New Representation

One of the main features of identity movements, as Craig Calhoun explains, is resistance to imposed identities and the search for recognition and legitimacy (1994, 21). Dominant discourses about and representations of particular groups are not abstract, but affect and influence the identity formation of the concerned subjects and the relationship to outsiders. Hence, questioning and challenging dominant representations is of fundamental importance (Jordan and Weedon 2000, 170). In this section I show how the conference Treasures of Islam, which featured scientific discoveries and advancements made by Muslims in the Middle Ages,[23] served to deconstruct dominant and stereotypical representations of Islam and Muslims.

In Search of a New Essence

Nora described the problem of negative representation as follows:

"After 9/11 everything was observed from a negative perspective ... Most people, whether they have a PhD or a university degree, know Islam only through books or the media. And generally it's only from one specific perspective that things are reported. So it's not real Islam, but more extreme variations of Islam, like the attacks that were committed in Bali and America ... So they only know that Islam." (Nora, Islam teacher)

---

23 More information on the conference can be found at the conference Web site: http://users.pandora.be/abdelhay/favorite.htm.

The problem, according to Nora, is that Islam is systematically considered from a negative point of view. To illustrate the reach and dominance of this negative representation, she uses two references: "most people" and "people with PhDs." "Most people" stands for broader public opinion, presumably non-Islamic, whereas "people with PhDs" counters the idea that this negative representation is a matter of ignorance, hence emphasizing that it is a vision widely shared by groups with quite different educational backgrounds.

In order to deconstruct this general idea, she describes existing stereotypes as "extreme variations," which contrast with what she calls "real Islam." In this juxtaposition of real versus extreme, Nora's account is situated on the side of the "real," whereas "other" accounts of Islam, notably media representations, are dismissed as being marginal and extreme versions of Islam to which only a small group of people adhere.

Fouad also pursues this line of describing dominant accounts of Islam as nonrepresentative and false. The following quotation illustrates how this deconstruction of dominant discourse goes together with the establishment of an alternative essence and narrative for contemporary Islam, namely, science.

"We thought the best answer was through science. This science was the essence, the soul of Islamic civilization. By showing Islam through this perspective ... we could show people that Islam is not the WTC [World Trade Center], but it's algorithms, it's Avicenna, it's people who weaved a whole Islamic civilization lasting for centuries and centuries, at the source of a European civilization. Therefore, in a way we have our roots in Europe, and we have something in common ... On the other hand, this scientific approach could also describe our contribution to European civilization, which is marginalized in all the educational programs. There are fifteen hundred years within the history of humanity which are called the Dark Ages, but for us they were enlightened years." (Fouad, scientist)

For Fouad, the main aim of the conference was to present Islam through a new narrative, and in particular a scientific one. Algorithms and philosophy provide Islam with an essence, not 9/11. A major advantage of using science as a "new" account for the presentation of the self is that it allows the integration of Islam into one of the main narratives of modernity. This becomes explicit when Fouad contrasts the history of the Middle Ages, also called the Dark Ages, with the simultaneous developments in Islamic civilization in science, culture, and philosophy. By arguing "for us they were enlightened years," Fouad not only points at a Western-biased and ethnocentric vision of history; his use of the term "enlightenment" also insists on the compatibility—or even causality—between Islam and (Western) modernity.

Consequently, the use of science as an alternative narrative allows Fouad to deconstruct the opposition between the West and the Orient and to insist on the connection between Europe and Islam. This strategy is also evident in sentences like "We have our roots in Europe," which allows Fouad to counter the Orientalizing discourse of Islam as the ultimate other, as the alien outsider (see Said 1995).

In Search of Legitimacy

The deconstruction of dominant representations of collective identities is not only about challenging stereotypical representations; it also involves a quest for legitimacy. Calhoun links identity politics to the question of *recognition*: identity is constructed not only through *self-recognition* but also through *recognition by the other*. Hence, the relationship with this "constitutive other" remains central in the process of acquiring an autonomous and legitimate self (Hall 1996). This need for recognition emerged again and again in the accounts of several members of the group as a reason to organize the conference and, more generally, as a reason to present alternative accounts of their identity.

"They say that a silent person is someone who consents. We wanted to break that vicious circle [of polarization] by letting ourselves be heard, and we have done so by organizing a conference to make clear to the outside world, to policymakers, politicians, youth workers, and all organizations in civil society, to show them that there is no clash of civilizations and that Islam is not at all a foreign religion." (Amina, civil servant)

When Amina speaks of the outside world, she speaks of politicians and actors in civil society. The target audience of the conference were people active in the field and involved in political topics. The political purpose of the conference was thus explicit: the conference was intended to inform and—more important—to establish an alternative form of recognition, and thus an alternative societal discourse on Islam and Muslims.

The need for an alternative form of recognition of Muslims and Islam is also linked to daily interactions with the mainstream—in this case, non-Muslims—and the wish to be recognized, as Amina puts it, as a "normal citizen":

"My main motivation is to prove by doing it, through my engagement in the union, that Muslims are normal people ... The main aim is to stop the abnormalization so that Muslims, like any other citizen, can participate and be seen as a normal citizen." (Amina, civil servant)

Amina frames the negative and stereotypical discourses on Muslims as a process of "abnormalization," a process through which the category of Muslim gradually becomes deviant. Being a Muslim thus becomes a stigma, which limits Muslims' ability to participate in broader society. Nilüfer Göle (2003) describes the process of celebrating and actively referring to Islamic discourses and using embodied practices (like the Islamic headscarf) in the public sphere as the voluntary adoption of stigma symbols in order to achieve a reversal of their meanings. The domestication of such stigmatic practices and symbols and their inclusion in the secular public sphere are, according to Göle, not only acts of self-empowerment and self-definition (2003, 820).

They are also a form of cultural resistance to dominant and hegemonic (Western) cultural models of modernity that oppose the idea of modernity and Islam (or religion in general): they become both Muslim and modern (2003, 818, 824).

"It [working on representation] is a priority. Why? At school, I teach in four schools, I always get the same questions. They come from what they see on TV. So if the representation was positive, they won't ask that number of questions ... I mean, of course there will be questions, but not the questions about an inexistent Islam ... It is also a duty of a Muslim to ... Religion is, Islam is not like a job or something you only do at home. You live according to it: at work and everything. So it's normal that as a Muslim you talk about your religion to non-Muslims ... Da'wa, preaching the religion, is a duty of any Muslim. Every Muslim knows it's a duty to do something about it." (Nora, Islam teacher)

In this last quotation Nora illustrates how she, as a Muslim, is always confronted with the same questions related to negative media representations, questions, she emphasizes, about "an inexistent Islam." She also repeats the distinction between the *false* Islam, that is, the one conveyed through the media, and *her* Islam, which she considers the real one. In the second part of the quotation she also introduces a new motivation to work towards a more positive representation of Islam. She frames this task of offering new, more positive accounts as "da'wa," or the religious duty that each Muslim has in terms of spreading the message of Islam. Hence, to work towards a more positive representation is not only about deconstructing stereotypes and being recognized; it is also simply a religious practice and part of being a devout Muslim. In the next section I show how this discourse on religious duty is linked to the larger question of citizenship.

Empowering the Islamic Community

So far I have observed how Treasures of Islam aimed at challenging mainstream representations while offering alternative accounts of Islam and Muslims. In this section I continue to explore this formation of a political Islamic subject and show both how questions of identity and citizenship are interrelated and how a particular discourse and vision of the Islamic subject are performed. I explore this question on the basis of the motivations of the working-group members to plan the second major project, namely, an Islamic fair organized by and for the Muslim community of Flanders, inspired by Le Bourget, the major annual fair in France.

Becoming an Active, but Anonymous, Citizen

Each spring about three hundred French Islamic organizations and over seventy-five thousand participants gather in the exposition halls of Le Bourget, a few kilometers outside Paris, in order to present their associations, to network, to buy or sell literature, and to discuss contemporary issues. Started in 1983 with nearly two hundred participants under the banner of the Union des Organisations Islamiques de France, the yearly gatherings in Le Bourget have become one of the largest and most important mass events of and for Muslims in France (see Amghar 2003). The gatherings in Le Bourget attracted publicity throughout France in 2003, when Minister of the Interior Nikolas Sarkozy was booed at during a speech in which he positioned himself against the possibility of wearing the headscarf in pictures for official documents.[24]

Inspired by the success and importance of Le Bourget, the members of UMIVA wished to organize similar gatherings for Belgian and Flemish Muslims.

"The idea is to answer, to start from zero in order to build a dynamic of associations. When you go to the Bourget, there is a life, an Islamic model: there are people who sleep, people who cry, it's a society. We would like to create that climate here, to export it at the level of the community here. To tell others that we exist: there is an Islamic presence. And that's what is lacking here in Flanders, in a very basic way." (Fouad, scientist)

Fouad describes the main motivation for organizing such a gathering: he speaks of the importance of networking, but also of creating and affirming an "Islamic model." Le Bourget shows that Muslims are present, that they can and do organize themselves, and that they are more than only passive subjects. This idea of making the Islamic presence visible—almost of proving that Muslims are organized and alive—is one of the main themes in dealing with the question of citizenship.

As I have shown in the previous section, the quest for visibility is closely linked to the question of recognition. Invisibility in the public sphere is tantamount to inexistence, which explains the importance of a quest for active citizenship, for visibility, for recognition. Becoming visible, however, is not the end; it is a *means* to this process of normalization. The final aim is to remain unnoticed but visible. The political claim is thus paradoxical: the ultimate ambition of identity movements in their struggle for recognition and visibility is to be unnoticed while being part of the picture.

---

24 This was the first time that a French official was invited and present at this gathering. Moreover, it was one of the major events that relaunched the headscarf debate on a national level in France, which eventually led to the creation of the Stasi commission and the law prohibiting religious symbols in public schools.

This section illustrates how this question of visibility in the public sphere also entails a certain vision and articulation of the collective identity. The point of departure for most members of the group is an existential question about who they are. Making the Islamic presence visible therefore is not only about a certain vision of citizenship, it is also about fostering and shaping an Islamic subject.

Forging a Muslim Identity

"It is precisely due to our concern about the negative representations, and the identity crisis of Muslims, that we want to dedicate our second conference entirely to Muslims, to the community, in order to make clear to Muslims that Islam is present here in a manifest way, and that we can proudly tell Muslims in a constructive and playful way that Muslims are starting to organize themselves in a very good way." (Amina, civil servant)

For Amina, the first function of visibility is to empower people by showing their positive presence. Moreover, she presents an Islamic framework as a way out of the identity crisis that she identifies. By referring to the negative representations, Amina acknowledges that the image of the self is highly influenced by dominant negative discourses. Consequently, making "the Islamic presence" visible is not only about countering stereotypical images of Muslims but also about offering new, alternative, and positive messages about and images of their identity. This becomes clear when Amina refers to the question of pride and emphasizes the need to show in a "constructive" and "playful" way what Muslims are doing: they not only are there; their presence is also a positive and constructive contribution to society at large.

The lack of an assumed and positive identity among Muslim youth appeared to be one of the main problems identified by the group.

"I have always said that the young people here are the result of street culture, television, and education at school and at home. At home things are seen in a certain way; on the street another image of life is offered; television offers a different image; school offers an ideal of another way of life. Young people are the result of all this, and there is no compatibility … When you ask a kid, 'Are you Moroccan or Belgian?', he answers, 'Neither.' This is the problem: Who is he?" (Fouad, scientist)

To Fouad, the root of the problem lies in the scattered identity that most youngsters of the second generation have to cope with. He enumerates different frames of reference that young people encounter, each with its own expectations, visions of the world, and normative values. The incompatibility of these frames leads to incomplete identifications. Hence, for Fouad one of the main challenges is to find an answer to these existential questions about a cultural identity that is neither Moroccan nor Belgian.

The members of the working group find in Islam a way to deal with the question of identification. This observation corresponds with much of the literature, which describes Islam as a new, alternative identity that transcends ethnic and cultural dilemmas, thereby allowing youngsters to fully find their place in the European context (Khosrokhavar 1997; Cesari 1994; Vertovec and Rogers 1998; Roy 2002; Amiraux 2001; Kanmaz 2003). Terms such as the "ethnicisation of Islam" (Modood and Werbner 1997) refer to this process of differentiation between a cultural and a religious identity, with the latter developing into a new ethnic identity: "European Muslim" is the new and preferred self-appellation. This religious framework, however, is more than merely a cultural resource for identity claims; it is also a normative framework that deals with questions of meaning and life orientation (Beyer 2000, 67). Yet within the literature on the Islamic revival and Islam as an identity, this second dimension—the normative framework—is often overlooked.[25]

In my conversations with members of the working group, the normative implications linked to an Islamic identity were clearly evident. As Amina explained, when asked why it is important to emphasize the presence of Islam:

"To Muslims, religion is an important part of life, in the sense that the Islamic value system is a component of a Muslim's daily life. You already see it, for instance, during the year; Ramadan—clearly visible—shows for instance how Muslims fast for a month, and are busy with Islam for at least one month each year. Also, the fact remains that people go actively to the mosques. Muslims don't really have a process of de-churchification. Quite the contrary: Islam remains an important part of life." (Amina, civil servant)

For Amina, Islam is more than just a cultural resource: when she states that "to Muslims, religion is an important part of life," she first associates Islam with religion, and describes Islam as a normative framework and "value system" with a dominant place in and influence on daily life. When speaking about Islam, the members of the working group speak not only about the cultural resources but also—and more important—about the normative framework behind it. Fouad not only confirms this observation; his words also reveal an important implication of the normative dimension of Islamic identity.

"For a Muslim, it is that: if he doesn't have an ideal, a clear vision, if he doesn't have a goal, whether it is an intermediary goal, or a final goal, he is always disoriented … Where are we going? Even the philosophy of the Quran always speaks about a clear set of goals. What is this goal? Judgment Day. And if you lose this reference, you lose all references. The molding of your life changes in such a way that you are destabilized. Why? Because you don't have a clear set of goals. And, by the way, this is human nature. If I tell you, 'In a week you have an exam,' you will make a

---

25 When the "normative" dimension of Islamic identity is assessed in the literature, its compatibility with the citizenship issue tends to be explored (see, for instance, Roy 2002 and Cesari 1994), whereas other dimensions remain relatively unexplored or receive little recognition (see also Asad 2003; Mahmood 2005).

plan, you will change your life to achieve that goal, which in this case is passing the exam. This means that you will take two hours to study, two hours to eat ... You will organize yourself in order to achieve that goal and pass the exam. So it's about that. Even Ramadan is about that. What is Ramadan? It's about having well-defined behavior for thirty days, and about being in a specific psychological state of mind in order to achieve that goal, which is the end of Ramadan. There is even a hadith that says that life is like Ramadan. Ramadan is life, and during this life we have to abstain from things, we have to do other things, we have to behave in a specific way. It's in fact the Muslim's ideal. And the end of Ramadan is the triumph, it's the gift, it's *al-Jahana* [paradise], it's that ... Hence, life for a Muslim is about reaching an ideal, achieving a goal, which is: to satisfy Allah. *Soebhana-wa-Ta'ala* [Praise Allah the great/all-knowing]. And if this goal is disrupted, everything is disrupted ... I always say: The *shari'a Islamiya* [Islamic path] is a positive means of integration into society." (Fouad, scientist)

In this quotation, Fouad tells us that Islam is about having a clear set of goals and orienting one's life towards these goals. The ultimate goal he identifies is Judgment Day: the moment when all actions of earthly life will be assessed and the ultimate verdict will follow. The view that civic (or other) activities are a means to achieving a larger religious purpose—Judgment Day and/or satisfying Allah—was frequently expressed by other members of the group as well. It was also observable when Nora presented the need to work on the representation of Muslims as a form of da'wa, the religious duty of each Muslim to spread the message of Islam. By using concepts such as da'wa or, in this case, Judgment Day, Fouad and Nora frame their actions within the realm of religious duties and obligations. Furthermore, Fouad's reference to the "final goal," or Judgment Day, is not merely allegorical; rather, it is consistent with a strong insistence on disciplinary actions. God's blessing is not something that one acquires by longing for it; it is something that one must work for by "molding" one's personality and actions in that direction.

These insights converge with Saba Mahmood's observations and analysis of women active in pious movements in Cairo (2001, 2005). She argues that the literature on pious and Islamist movements tends to overlook and under-value existing discourses on the moral subject and the way in which this moral subject is actively constructed and transformed. When religious practice is included in the analysis, it is often framed as something functional to nationalistic claims and/or claims about identity.[26] The respondents' accounts, which situate these practices within a "religious logic," are rarely included in the broader analytical framework or are only viewed as "phantom imaginings of the hegemonized" (Mahmood 2001, 209).

Mahmood has analyzed the religious discourse of women active in "nonliberal" women's movements in order to understand their relation to

---

26 Mahmood gives the example of the veil, which is often described as a nationalistic symbol or a means of resistance, but rarely as a religious practice.

religious practices and the notion of subject implicitly involved.[27] She discovered a seeming "paradox": a discourse of submission to prescriptions, combined with active agency in performing this submission. For many of the women with whom she worked, the attainment of religious virtues (e.g., patience, shyness, modesty) was not considered something "natural," but rather something one had to work on. Mahmood has recounted the efforts of these women to acquire these virtues, and how this process went together with a conscious and active drilling and molding of their subjectivities and bodies. The activities of these women are not aimed at resisting certain norms or prescriptions but rather at actively disciplining subjectivity in order to make it compatible with a discursive tradition, that is, the Islamic moral and ethical subject.[28]

My emphasis on Mahmood's writings is prompted by similar observations about what Fouad tells us in the last quotation, which is crucial in this respect, as well as about other conversations with members of the working group. The members' introduction of the Islamic subject as a means to frame their identity was not only about having a cultural resource; it also fits with a larger discourse on the moral subject and its compliance with an ethical and discursive tradition, namely, Islam.[29] The reference to an Islamic identity and religious practice not only points to the larger goal—Judgment Day—but also to the necessity of forging and molding a certain subjectivity, one in which religious practice is not only a means to reach an ultimate goal but also a means to perform and shape a specific kind of subjectivity. Religious practice therefore becomes "the means to both *being* and *becoming* a certain kind of person" (Mahmood 2001, 215; italics in original).

Fouad not only describes this Islamic identity as a "mold" for forging one's subjectivity in a certain way; he also strengthens this claim by describing this process in secular terms. He does so by arguing, first, that it is a normal thing, proper to the way that society is organized, and, second, that it is present in all aspects of religious life, even in its most elementary forms. This normalization takes place in three steps: making the process seem

---

27 Mahmood uses the word "nonliberal" to refer to movements with a conception of selfhood and subjectivity which contrast with the liberal tradition.

28 Mahmood asserts that, from a poststructural perspective, this insight is compatible with descriptions and observations of *any* subject formation. She refers to Judith Butler's *paradox of subjectivation*: the active subject acquires its agency (and its potential to resist) by paradoxically inscribing itself in and submitting itself to a discursive tradition. Thus, the subject is *always* formed through the obedience to certain norms, and it is precisely this obedience to (and acquiring of) these norms which makes resistance possible. This leads Mahmood to argue for a conception of agency not solely as a "synonym for resistance to a relation of domination, but as a capacity for action that historically *specific* relations of subordination enable and create" (2001, 203).

29 Or, to be more precise, compliance with a specific ethical and discursive tradition within Islam.

natural, referring to the example of taking exams, and relating the process to Ramadan. The first step in normalizing the process is to describe it as part of "human nature." Second, the reference to taking exams serves as a "secular" example that illustrates the broadness and validity of his claims and dissociates it from the religious sphere. Fouad concludes by arguing that this method of disciplining the subject is also present in the most elementary forms of religious practice, such as Ramadan. Thus, this disciplining of the subject is not something exceptional, nor something limited to extremely pious Muslims; it is something natural, general, and present in all aspects of society, in both religious and secular life.

To conclude, and in line with Mahmood (2001, 2005), I argue that this quest for and/or reference to a framework for an Islamic identity coincides with the construction and disciplining of an Islamic ethical and moral subject. When people like Fouad refer to Islam as an alternative framework, they also refer to and perform a certain moral and ethical subject. Hence, identity movements—in this case Islamic ones—are not only about seeking and establishing an alternative narrative about the self, but also about constructing and disciplining the self in order to make it compatible with a specific Islamic tradition. In the following subsection I illustrate how the working-group members view a relationship with the political sphere as a vital aspect of this moral and ethical subject.

Active Citizenship as Part of Religious Practice

Active citizenship is viewed by all members in the working group as a worthy objective. They all support the idea that political involvement in society at large is a sign not only of good citizenship but also of being a good Muslim. Furthermore, active citizenship includes reaching out to non-Muslims and striving together for shared political aims. It is therefore not surprising that members of the group appreciate an intellectual like Tariq Ramadan. His vision and ideas were often mentioned, and one of the ambitions of the working group was to organize discussion seminars on citizenship issues with Tariq Ramadan.

"And that's where we come to the new discourse of Tariq Ramadan; it is about active involvement in society. The idea of the social contract, the idea of testimony: the *shahada*. He is revolutionizing, he is leading a silent revolution of the second generation. And that's what youngsters like; they recognize themselves in a way in Tariq Ramadan. And *al-hamdu-lilah*, it works, even in different communities, even if he is French-speaking, because it is an Islamic discourse." (Fouad, scientist)

According to Fouad, many Muslims, regardless of their origin, recognize themselves in Tariq Ramadan's discourse through the universal weight of the Islamic message. This discourse calls upon Muslims to fulfill their prime responsibility, the first pillar, the shahada: to testify that God exists and that

Muhammad is his prophet. By equating the idea of the social contract with the first pillar, Fouad inscribes the political sphere within the Islamic engagement and prime duties of Muslims, thus clearly challenging and rearticulating secular-liberal notions of citizenship and its relation to religion. In the discourse of Fouad, both become interlinked: active citizenship stands for being a good Muslim, and being a good Muslim becomes synonymous with active involvement in society.

"Even the act of taking a stone from the street is part of our religion, is part of *laïcité* [being an active citizen in a secular environment]. And this should be understood ... Our duty, the effort we have to make, is to present a positive image of Islam ... Efforts should be made from both sides. We always talk about the internal effort we have to make to go to the others. I forgot to say something: Even if we spend one thousand or twenty-four hundred hours telling people about Muslims and Islam, if each one of us is not a walking Quran, we will always have problems explaining things to others. They see Islam, but don't see the Muslims." (Fouad, scientist)

Fouad expresses a vision of political and religious engagement in which both are interlinked, if not equated. In the first sentence of the quotation, he not only links civic involvement with religious duty but also insists on their compatibility: it "is part of *laïcité*." These last words indicate that he is aware that his approach—linking religious duty to civic duty—could be considered deviant when compared to the "common" secular-liberal separation of religious duty from civic duty. But Fouad seeks a way out of what might appear to be an inconsistency by arguing that his vision is perfectly compatible with the concept of *laïcité*. He thus dissociates the definition of *laïcité* from a secular-liberal tradition and makes it compatible with a vision in which religion and politics are interlinked.

"If the existing rules are in contradiction with your rules, then you have to adapt your rules to those of the community, to the rules of the country ... and it is possible to do so. Our religion is a very flexible one. The goal of each religion is to guarantee the internal stability of human beings; it's to live in harmony with others. Certainly for the Islamic religion. Seventy percent of the Quranic verses are about social relations; at least thirty percent are about the spiritual aspects of faith. And all the *'ibadaat,* they are about good behavior towards others: *ahlaq*. Why do we pray? To be good with others. We fast to feel the hunger of others. We do the *hadj* [the pilgrimage to Mecca] in order to meet people from all over the world. *Zakat* is about helping others, to have a sense of social responsibility. Hence, our religion is made to live in society." (Fouad, scientist)

This quotation illustrates once more how Fouad links religious and civic engagement. Hence, his discourse on active citizenship is related not only to the question of identity but also to his religious practice. On several occasions, and with reference to various examples, Fouad emphasized the intrinsically social and civic dimensions of Islam. In his conciliation of Islamic and civic engagement, however, he tries to remain within the boundaries of a "mainstream" understanding of citizenship. He does not fundamentally question the way in which larger society conceives of political citizenship; a telling indication of this is his emphasis on the flexibility and adaptability of religious rules to society's expectations.

This observation has already been made by other authors analyzing active citizenship, especially those focusing on Tariq Ramadan's discourse (Frégosi 2000; Mohsen-Finan 2002). Khadija Mohsen-Finan, for instance, describes Ramadan's discourse as the development of a faith-based citizenship that questions the strict French separation of state and religion and calls for a middle way between the British communitarian model and the French model of assimilation (2002, 139). Franck Frégosi (2000), on the other hand, maintains that the success of the "Ramadanian verbs" derives from the combination of presenting active citizenship as part of religious practice—as a message of Islam—while fully embracing the dominant discourse on citizenship, and simultaneously opening up possibilities for changes to and adaptation of some Islamic rulings.[30] A call for flexibility and openness is also evident in Fouad's discourse.

One could, however, also construe Fouad's emphasis on the flexibility of his religion as a defensive stance, almost as if to avoid accusations of being "fundamentalist" or a "threat to society." The hegemonic discourse on secularism and citizenship, certainly when dealing with Islam, is such that any public appearance of religion is quickly viewed as an illegitimate interference, as "'inflecting' the secular domain or as replicating within it the structure of theological concepts" (Asad 2003, 191). This becomes explicit in Fouad's answer to my question about how far this flexibility can go and whether it also would have implications for prescriptions such as the headscarf.

"But concerning the headscarf issue, the secular context in which we live allows it since it respects the religion and faith of everyone among us. Hence, by wearing the headscarf we have to—and this is also our responsibility, of our community—we need to say that for us, that we do not practice Islam but we live Islam. And this we have to make clear to people. But how can you explain that in a context that always stigmatizes Islam, in a context that always says, 'What's this covered woman, this guru coming to invade us?' There is a fear fed by the media, which remains unexplained." (Fouad, scientist)

Clearly, flexibility to Fouad does not mean the alienation or far-reaching adaptation of religious prescriptions; his position on the Islamic headscarf illustrates this. In order to resist the suggestion of simply adapting or abandoning religious prescriptions, he frames prescriptions such as the Islamic headscarf within the liberal principle of freedom of religion, which, according to him, is characteristic of the secular organization of society. Furthermore, he

---

30 The most well-known adaptation, popularized by Tariq Ramadan, is without a doubt the abolition of the theological categories *dar-al-harb/dar-al-islam* (house of war/house of Islam), thus enabling theologically the full participation of Muslims in a non-Islamic setting (Ramadan 1999, 202–204).

argues that it is the responsibility of Muslims to make clear that to them religion is not practiced but lived. This sentence supports my earlier observation about a strong articulation of both the political subject and the religious subject. Hence, and certainly when reading the sentences in which Fouad describes the "stigmatization" that persists towards Muslims, I argue that the need to legitimize Islamic discourse within the "mainstream" liberal framework is also motivated by a defensive approach, and does not strictly deviate from a vision in which religious practice is framed within liberal and secular political accounts.

Frégosi observed a similar mechanism in Tariq Ramadan's discourse, which he described as a "paradox": although Ramadan states that he does not claim a "special status" for Muslims and that he embraces the existing concept of citizenship, he nevertheless describes religion as a way of life, as a civilization and culture (2000, 211). My position differs from Frégosi in that I do not observe this "ambivalence" as a paradox, but rather as an illustration of the difficulties inherent in an approach to religion as a political subject which differs from those prescribed by dominant secular-liberal frameworks. The reason these claims appear to be "ambiguous" is mainly linked with the need and urge of people like Fouad to remain within the boundaries of accepted consensus and not be marginalized because of their approach and vision. Fouad's reference in this quotation to suspicions towards Muslims illustrates this claim. Hence, I argue that what appears to be an "ambivalence" is rather the articulation of the difficulty of reconciling an "imposed" secular-modernist vision of the religious and political subject with an alternative vision in which the political and religious subject are more interlinked. What appears to be a "paradox" thus not only reveals the tension between the two visions; more important, it unveils the particularity of the dominant framework, its implicit definition of and approach to religion, and its effect on other approaches to religion.

Hence, I argue that the interpretation of this ambivalence as a "paradox" is linked to the use of analytical frameworks that rely on a secular opposition between "the religious" and "the political." Consequently, when one departs from analytical concepts that reproduce a sharp differentiation between the "religious" and the "secular" spheres, interactions between the two tend to appear paradoxical or at least inconsistent. I argue that it is not enough to observe the interaction between "the secular" and "the religious"; rather, one also needs to be reflexive about the assumptions and a priori conclusions on which both concepts rest. Not doing this will hinder social scientists from tracing the complexity of existing dynamics and will lead them to reproduce too quickly the normative differentiation between "the religious" and "the secular," which is implicitly present when one speaks of the "paradoxical" combination of a religious and a civic discourse.

On this point I rely heavily on Talal Asad's *Formations of the Secular* (2003), in which he urges scholars to scrutinize and question the traditional concept of secularization, which opposes a "religious sphere" with a "secular sphere." The latter is described as the space in which human freedom and individual rights prevail; in contrast, the religious sphere is where authoritarian obedience to rules is said to dominate. Asad questions this equation: "I am arguing that 'the secular' should not be thought of as the space in which real human life gradually emancipates itself from the controlling power of 'religion' and thus achieves the latter's relocation" (191). Hence, when one questions the way in which secularity is traditionally defined, one's analytical conception of the world also needs to be revised. This also entails examining how "politics" and "religion" have come to be defined and how the two "turn out to implicate each other more profoundly than we thought" (200). The concept of religion is not only *opposed* to the secular, it is also *produced* by it (193; see also Smith 1968).

Discourses like those of Fouad enable one to see how this process of constructing "the religious" through "the secular" takes place. Fouad's active, though "subversive" (with respect to religion), engagement with the notion of citizenship shows how a dominant definition of citizenship relies on a particular relationship between religion and politics, one which only allows religion as a discourse and not as a practice, one which defines religion in a specific way and recognizes it as long as it does not transgress prescribed limits (Asad 2003, 199). In Fouad's description of his civic and religious engagement, one can see how a specific "secular" articulation of religion (i.e., religion as a discourse and a private practice) conflicts with his vision of religion (i.e., religion as a way of life and a total practice), and how an equilibrium is sought to conciliate both visions.[31] It is too early to know what the end result of such negotiation will be, but one thing can be said: discourses like those of Fouad reveal the dynamics behind societal narratives and challenge "us" (i.e., social scientists) to unpack the normative, a priori conclusions of these narratives (see also Bracke 2004).

The Process of Internal Negotiations

The internal difficulties encountered in promoting a vision of citizenship were another recurrent element in the way members of the working group framed their engagement.

---

31 This point constitutes the main difference between Islamic movements that reproduce discourses on "active citizenship" and "pious movements" that do not actively intervene in the political sphere, like those described by Saba Mahmood (2005). Although both are "political" in the sense that they actively reshape the way society is organized through an Islamic ethical framework, discourses like Fouad's actively seek to negotiate an approach to citizenship with the dominant secular framework, whereas pious movements consciously withdraw from this kind of negotiation and do not seek compromise.

"We first need an internal debate; we should harmonize the different opinions. Within the Islamic community there are too many differences … There are those who say that the environment is haram [illicit], that we are in *dar-al-harb*.[32] There is the Shi'i fraction; there is the *hizb-a-tahrir*. They have different views on Islam, and this makes the task more difficult on the intracommunitarian and intercommunitarian levels … That's why we need time. We first have to agree among ourselves, before being able to bring things to the outside world. It is a major challenge, and I think we can do it. The means are there for it, we just need the will to live together." (Fouad, scientist)

According to Fouad, divergent opinions must be harmonized before Muslims can act within society at large. In this quotation Fouad refers to the existing ideological and sectarian divisions within the Islamic community not only to illustrate its diversity, but also to show the difficulty of reaching a consensus over citizenship issues. To strengthen his argument, he refers to the disagreements over the use of concepts such as dar-al-harb when referring to Western Europe. Fouad views this diversity as problematic because it hampers his political aim of constructing a strong and internally coherent political subject in order to achieve certain political goals.[33] Thus, what is needed is the creation of a stable ground, a consensus, in order to be able to engage at the political level. Internal debate is a way to achieve this vision of citizenship and to harmonize opinions on this matter.

Not all Muslims, however, were included in these discussions about harmonizing existing differences. One of the most recurrent divisions referred to by members of the working group was that of generational difference. Most members saw a clear difference in approach to the citizenship issue between the second and the first generations. As a group operating within a union of mosques, it also specifically targeted the mosques, with the aim of opening them up to larger segments of society.

"I always say that the first generation was a generation of mosque builders … It then falls to the second generation to get involved in mosques, to make the mosque come to the outside. That is, I think, the challenge for the coming five to ten years. The second generation has to enter into mosques in order to make them come outside through open-house days, cultural activities … to show that mosques are not only a place to pray, but also a place to meet, a place of interaction between Muslims and non-Muslims. This is in a way our challenge for the coming five to ten years." (Fouad, scientist)

---

32 Some traditional scholars divide the world into *dar-al-harb* (the house of war) and *dar-al-islam* (the house of Islam) in order to differentiate an Islamic from a non-Islamic region. Muslims in a non-Islamic region are considered a minority and have special rules and prescriptions. Lately, however, this traditional dichotomy has increasingly been called into question. Several scholars, including Tariq Ramadan, have called for abandoning this outdated differentiation.

33 The need for and dangers of essentialism in the construction of a political identity have been extensively debated in poststructuralist feminist theory (Calhoun 1994; Fuss 1989).

Fouad's notion of the role of mosques reflects his conception of citizenship. Mosques should be not only a place to pray, but also a space for interaction, a *new public sphere* for Muslims and non-Muslims. Hence, two shifts are made in his conception of the mosque: first, by adding to it alternative functions such as meetings and cultural activities and, second, by opening it up to non-Muslims. In addition, Fouad clearly frames this new approach as something befitting the second generation. This generational dynamic has been observed by several researchers (Kanmaz and Mokhless 2002; Sunier 1996).

Generation thus becomes the ultimate factor for explaining differences in orientation. Without disputing this claim or observation, I would argue that this insistence on the generational factor can also be viewed in terms of its functional capacities of constructing a stable and coherent Islamic political subject. By locating the existing disagreements mainly within a generational framework, rather than a framework of ideological or sectarian difference, one presumably has better control over the identified internal differences, as there is an underlying conviction that these differences will be "solved" in the long term. An emphasis on sectarian or ideological differences, on the other hand, would hamper the smooth construction of a stable political subject.

As for the observed generational differences, it was striking to note how the working-group members avoided a confrontational approach with the first generation. They instead called for patience and acceptance of this difference.

"Most of them are stubborn. If you try to explain something like that to a first generation, they don't always understand you ... There are people of the first generation who understand us and can follow us, but the majority doesn't want any contact with the outside world. They just want to stay separated in their mosques. It's up to us, the second generations, and converted Muslims, to have contact with the outside world." (Ahmed, engineer)

Ahmed describes a generational rift, without arguing for change. By using the word "stubborn," he characterizes the disagreements in terms of personal traits and features of the first generation, rather than differences in point of view. Consequently, Ahmed argues that both the second generation and converted Muslims should lead the way to active citizenship.

Conclusion: Which Space for Political Interactions and Negotiations of Religious Subjects?

One of the most frequent topics in the literature and in mainstream media is the recent upheaval of Islamic identity among second-generation youths in Western Europe. Labels such as European Muslims and the "ethnicisation of Islam" indicate a shift: Islam is becoming a new identity for participation in the European public opinion. This reference to and use of the Islamic label is often analyzed as a dual process. On the one hand, there is a differentiation and distancing from ethnic identity, which enables young Muslims to position themselves in Western Europe; on the other hand, this practice can be read as a defensive identification with Islam in reaction to the negative stereotypes about Muslims and Islam (Roy 2002; Göle 2003). In this chapter I have observed and analyzed how a group of young professionals frames and uses Islamic identity in their political engagement.

The two main threads running through their involvement are representation and empowerment. Challenging stereotypical discourses on Islam and offering alternative representations not only are ways to frame their identity in a different—and to them, more accurate—light; they also are ways to achieve recognition. The ability to influence public opinion about Muslims is felt to be crucial, as public opinion affects their daily interactions and contributes to their societal marginalization. A second thread in their involvement focuses on the empowerment of Muslims in the light of their weak socioeconomic integration. In this case, Islam is presented as a solution for these weak conditions, which are linked to a lack of an assumed and positive identity.

This chapter has examined how an active reference to and use of an Islamic framework also entails and performs an Islamic ethical, moral, and political subject. Referring to positive representation as da'wa, building a strong Islamic identity through religious discipline, considering citizenship a religious duty—such perspectives and strategies imply that Islam is not only an identity but also a religious and normative framework. In addition to a "new" identity, Islam is, above all, a religion with prescriptions for and expectations of the moral and ethical subject (Asad 2003; Mahmood 2001, 2005).

This is also evident in the relationship between citizenship and religion: religious identity is not only inscribed within a discourse on citizenship; civic involvement is also framed as a religious duty. The difference between the two formulations is important, for the latter stresses that Islamic citizenship not only *adapts* to the secular expectations and norms of modern life, it also *interacts* with it and *questions* it. The "subject" implicitly assumed in secular modernity is a subject for whom religious and political life are clearly differentiated, for whom there is no problem adapting to the expectations of secular social life. People like Fouad, for whom religious, political, and other elements are largely interwoven, do not simply try to conform to the implicit expectations of modern life; they also try to find a compromise with the explicit and implicit expectations of society as a whole. Hence, to seek a compromise is something other than "adapting" to the expectations of modern life, and the limits of "flexibility" are not endless. The balancing act remains difficult and fragile, with people like Fouad in a weak position for negotiation, particularly in the current political climate, in which every public manifestation of Islam (or other religions) is suspiciously observed or even hysterically and repressively attacked.

References

Abou Jahjah, D. 2003. Tussen twee werelden. De roots van een vrijheidsstrijd. Antwerp, Belgium: Meulenhoff.

Amghar, S. 2003. Le congrès du Bourget: une 'fête de l'Humanité' islamique. Confluences Méditerranées 46 (summer).

Amiraux, V. 2001. Acteurs de l'Islam entre Allemagne et Turquie. Parcours militants et expériences religieuses. Paris: L'Harmattan.

Asad, T. 2003. Formations of the secular: Christianity, Islam, Modernity. Palo Alto, CA: Stanford University Press.

Beyer, P. 2000 [1994]. Religion and globalization. London: Sage.

Bousetta, H. 2001. Immigration, post-immigration politics and the political mobilisation of ethnic minorities: A comparative case-study of Moroccans in four European cities. Brussels: KUB.

Bracke, S. 2004. Women resisting secularisation in an age of globalisation: Four case studies in a European perspective. Ph.D. dissertation, Utrecht University, the Netherlands.

Calhoun, C. 1994. Social theory and the politics of identity. In Social theory and the politics of identity, ed. C. Calhoun, 9–36. London: Blackwell.

Cesari, J. 1994. Être Musulman En France. Paris: Karthala/Iremam.

De Witte, L. 2004. Wie is bang voor moslims? Aantekeningen over Abou Jahjah, etnocentrisme en islamofobie. Leuven, Belgium: Van Halewyck.

Fadil, N. 2003. Débat sur l'intégration de l'Autre, débat sur la définition de Soi. Nouvelle-Tribune: Quand la Belgique intègre 31/32 (March/May): 123–127.

Frégosi, F. 2000. Les contours discursifs d'une religiosité citoyenne: laïcité et identité islamique chez Tariq Ramadan. In Paroles d'islam. Individus, sociétés et discours dans l'islam européen contemporain, ed. F. Dassetto, 205–221. Paris: Maisonneuve & Larose.

Fuss, D. 1989. Essentially speaking: Feminism, nature and difference. London: Routledge.

Göle, N. 2003. The voluntary adoption of Islamic stigma symbols. Social Research 70 (3): 809–828.

Hall, S. 1996. Introduction: Who needs 'identity'? In Questions of cultural identity, ed. S. Hall and P. Du Gay, 1–17. London: Sage.

Jacobs, D. 2003. The Arab European League: The rapid growth of a radical immigrant movement. Paper prepared for the European Consortium for Political Research Conference, Marburg, Germany.

Jordan, G., and C. Weedon. 2000. When the subaltern speak, what do they say? Radical cultural politics in Cardiff Docklands. In Without guarantees: In honour of Stuart Hall, ed. P. Gilroy, L. Grossberg, and A. McRobbie, 165–180. London: Verso.

Kanmaz, M. 2003. Onze nationaliteit is onze godsdienst. Islam als identity marker bij jonge Marokkaanse moslims in Gent. In Migratie, zijn wij uw kinderen? Identiteitsbeleving bij allochtone jongeren, ed. E. Cornelis and M. C. Foblets, 115–133. Leuven, Belgium: Acco.

Kanmaz, M., and F. Mokhless. 2002. Sociaal-cultureel werk in de Moskee? Vorming, Vaktijdschrift voor volwasseneneducatie en sociaal-cultureel werk 17 (October): 425–442. Also available at the following Web site: http://www.flwi.ugent.be/cie/CIE/kanmaz_mokhless1.htm.

Khosrokhavar, F. 1997. L'Islam des jeunes. Paris: Flammarion.

Landman, N. 2002. Islam in the Benelux Countries. In Islam, Europe's second religion, ed. S. T. Hunter, 97–120. Westport, CT: Praeger.

Mahmood, S. 2001. Feminist theory, embodiment, and the docile agent: Some reflections on the Egyptian Islamic revival. Cultural Anthropology 16 (2): 202–236.

———. 2005. Politics of piety: The Islamic revival and the feminist subject. Princeton, NJ: Princeton University Press.

McAdam, D. 1999 [1982]. Political process and the development of Black insurgency, 1930–1970. Chicago: University of Chicago Press.

Modood, T., and P. Werbner. 1997. The politics of multiculturalism in the new Europe: Racism, identity and community. London: Zed Books.

Mohsen-Finan, K. 2002. Promoting a faith-based citizenship: The case of Tariq Ramadan. In New European identity and citizenship, ed. R. Leveau, K. Mohsen-Finan, and C. Wihtol de Wenden, 133–139. London: Ashgate.

Peleman, K. 2002. De rol van de buurt: de maatschappelijke participatie van Marokkaanse vrouwen in een ruimtelijk perspectief. Ph.D. dissertation, Department of Geography and Geology, Catholic University of Leuven, Belgium.

Ramadan, T. 1999. Être un musulman européen. Lyon, France: Tawhid.

Roy, O. 2002. Vers un Islam européen. Paris: Editions Esprit.

Said, E. W. 1995 [1978]. Orientalism: Western conceptions of the Orient. London: Penguin.

Smith, W. C. 1968. The meaning and end of religion. London: SPCK.

Sunier, T. 1996. Islam in Beweging. Amsterdam: Het Spinhuis.

Vertovec, S., and A. Rogers. 1998. Muslim European youth: Reproducing ethnicity, religion, culture. Aldershot, UK: Ashgate.

Annalisa Frisina

THE INVENTION OF CITIZENSHIP
AMONG YOUNG MUSLIMS IN ITALY[1]

"Islamophobia" precedes the tragic events of 9/11, but, as in many other countries, it was above all after this date that some opinion-makers and politicians began to depict Muslims who live in Italy as potentially dangerous (Sciortino 2002; Rivera 2002; Schmidt di Friedberg 2001).[2] Faced with this difficult situation, the Association of Young Italian Muslims (GMI), an active group of youths born in and/or raised from infancy in Italy, entered the public sphere, participating in various activities involving interreligious and intercultural dialogue at the local and national levels. Through this work the group gained extraordinary visibility among the media in a relatively short amount of time.

The main innovation of these youths' approach was that they did not limit themselves to "reversing the stigma" (Sayad 2002), that is to say, they did not simply deny the association of Islam to violence, declaring themselves to be Muslim pacifists. Their ambitious objective has been to change the framework and shift the discussion about Muslims in Italy from one concerned with safety issues to one focusing on citizenship. But what is the meaning of citizenship in their speeches and in their practices? What are the outcomes of their demands within the public sphere? How have Islamic associations for adults reacted to their activism?

In this chapter I attempt to answer these questions. I first introduce the Italian context in which Muslims seem to serve as a screen against which some Italians project themselves as a unity, and then show how the Association of Young Italian Muslims has opposed a representation of Italian identity based on a common Catholic matrix by declaring themselves Italian citizens of Islamic faith. Moreover, I analyze their various forms of belonging and

---

1   This chapter is based on my doctoral thesis in sociology entitled "Difference as Opportunity? Young Italian Muslims and Demands for Citizenship" (supervisor: Chantal Saint-Blancat). Heartfelt thanks to Stefano Allievi for having introduced me to the stimulating research group composed by the authors of this book.

2   See, for example, the long article "La Rabbia e l'orgoglio" (Rage and Pride) by O. Fallaci, which appeared on September 29, 2001, in Corriere della Sera (one of the main national newspapers) and later became a best-selling book. With respect to political forces, Lega Nord is the main agent of anti-Islamic xenophobia (Guolo 2003, 58–80). For the historical origin of the perception of Muslims as "enemies," see Allievi, 2003,143–144, and Khader, 1992.

participation, showing that they are Muslim democrats practicing "ordinary citizenship" in their everyday life (especially at the local level) and that their main feature is their commitment to the legitimation of a public representation of Italy as a multicultural and multireligious country. Finally, I illustrate how the visibility of this youth association is challenging the "defensive logic" of the previous generation.

Italy: A Catholic and Secular Country?

According to prevailing theories, Italy discovered cultural diversity with the arrival of immigrants.[3] What had been a nation of emigrants until the 1970s became a country of immigration. And according to the collective representations circulating in the mass media, what was, from a religious point of view, a homogeneous country found itself confronted with a problematic alternative: Islam. And so with the settlement of immigrant families came multicultural policies: for example, there was experimentation with intercultural projects in schools, and linguistic and cultural mediators were introduced in hospitals and other public institutions.

Anthropologists Ralph Grillo and Jeff Pratt (2002) tell us a different story, maintaining that, basically, the Italian nation was born through a "policy of identity." To quote Massimo d'Azeglio (1861), "We have created Italy, now let us create Italians." In actuality, the country continued to remain plural, marked by profound regional differences and above all by differences between the North and the South, the famous "southern issue." Jeff Pratt (2002) adds that this "hierarchised cultural diversity" in which the North stigmatized the South is the principal leitmotif of Italian history.[4]

This internal plurality also affects the sphere of religious belief (Garelli, Guizzardi, and Pace 2003, 299): for instance, 45.1 % of the Italian population believe that religious celibacy should be abolished, and more than half of the Italian population maintain that there is something true in all religions and,

---

3 Since the last regularization campaign launched by the center-right government, immigrants in Italy now total about 2,400,000; it is estimated that among them about 800,000 are Muslims (Pace 2004b). The original nationalities are extremely varied, though the most consistent group is that of Moroccans. As regards youths, the Agnelli Foundation gave an early estimate of young Muslims in 2004: they are thought to amount to around 300,000, of which 140,000 to 160,000 were born in or grew up in Italy. For a report on the statistics on Muslims and on the process of identity allocation, see Amiraux, 2004.

4 In Italian history there are other, even more stigmatized differences, such as the "racial" differences under the fascist regime. According to historian A. Del Boca (1998), up to the present day in Italy there has never been serious public reflection on Italian colonialism, and the myth of the "good Italian people" survives along with racist stereotypes.

therefore, that Catholicism cannot be the only true religion.[5] Despite all of this, Italy continues to represent itself as a homogeneous society from a cultural and religious viewpoint. There are those who believe that Italian Catholicism might at its base be "a romantic idea" to be shared for the sake of unity (Pace 1998, 75–101).

Nowadays Islam is often socially constructed as the "unassimilable difference" and as the "internal enemy" against whom "Western values" must be defended (Rivera 2003). However, if Islam causes such apprehension in Italians, it is perhaps in part because it reopens issues that are controversial independent of the presence of Muslim immigrants. Once again, the outsider becomes a mirror (Hervieu-Léger 2000; Amiraux 2004) and reveals tensions already existent in Italian society, such as secularism versus the Catholic Church's monopoly of cultural values (Saint-Blancat and Schmidt di Friedberg 2005).[6] As evidenced during the recent referendum on assisted insemination (Law 40), when the Church aggressively intervened in the public sphere by inviting Catholics to stay away from the polls in order to prevent voter turnout from reaching the necessary minimum, the relationship between religion and politics is not a specifically Muslim problem but rather a general challenge for all Italians (Rusconi 2000, 2005).

Hence, starting from the hypothesis that Muslims serve as a screen against which some Italians project themselves as a unity (i.e., as a "Catholic country"), and imagining Italy to be modern and secular (as opposed to Muslim immigrants, with their "traditionalism" and "incapacity to separate religion and politics"[7]), let us see if and in which manner the Association of Young Italian Muslims has managed to question these collective representations, which have the effect of excluding them.

Why the Association of Young Italian Muslims?

The Association of Young Italian Muslims (hereafter the "GMI") is composed of about four hundred children of immigrants. The majority were born in Italy or were raised there since primary school. They are between 15 and

---

5   This internal pluralism within Italian Catholicism is rarely acknowledged. However, according to Garelli, Guizzardi, and Pace (2003, 297–298), cultural and political differences among Catholics have been present since the foundation of Italy: for example, there were papal extremists, but also modernists. These variances crossed over class divisions: think of peasant religiosity and of the social solidarity inspired by Catholics during the first workers' movement, or of the liberal Catholicism of the enlightened bourgeoisie or of conservative Catholicism among farmers.

6   According to Sciolla (2005, 316), we are witnessing an increasingly pervasive interference of the Italian Church in issues of public or directly political interest along with the Church's growing visibility in Italian mass media.

7   For the historical roots of these representations, see Said, 1991.

17 years of age; the association's leaders are somewhat older, between 18 and 24. Girls are both more numerous and more active in the association. The majority of GMI members are high-school students; the leaders (both male and female) attend university and are majoring in science or the social sciences.[8]

Most of the parents are Moroccan, but there is also a significant Syrian component among parents of the more active members. Other nationalities represented in the association are Egyptian, Palestinian, Jordanian, Tunisian, and Algerian. The members' fathers are for the most part factory workers, but there is also a significant number of doctors and entrepreneurs.[9] Their mothers usually are housewives, but there are also maidservants and cleaners, intercultural mediators, social workers, and entrepreneurs.

The largest local sections of the GMI are those in Lombardy, where it has its headquarters in Milan; Emilia Romagna; Piedmont; Trentino Alto-Adige; Tuscany; and Umbria. The best organized regions are in northern Italy; in many regions of southern Italy there are no local sections of the GMI.

The social composition of the association mirrors in certain respects the population of the children of immigration in Italy: GMI's members are concentrated in northern and central Italy, and the most common nationality of origin is Moroccan.[10] On the other hand, the association is interesting not because of its representativeness,[11] but because it is currently the only Islamic youth association active in Italy, because it came into being just ten days after 9/11,[12] and because it was able to give a voice to all the youths who are continually "called into question" as Muslims.

---

8 This case study is informed by my doctoral thesis work, for which I conducted qualitative research for over three years in the form of participant observation of the GMI, fifty in-depth interviews with children of immigrants born or raised in Italy (who now live in Milan), and four focus groups with young Muslims (militant and nonmilitant). My entry in the GMI was facilitated by a friend who became the first secretary general of the association (she answered for my seriousness). I met the other young people who were not GMI members in Milan, first in high schools and universities and second through "snowball sampling."

9 Whereas Syrian parents are doctors, parents of Moroccan origin usually are factory workers.

10 Because the stabilization of immigration in Italy is relatively recent, most "foreigners born in Italy" are much younger than GMI members and still attend nursery and primary schools.

11 The reality of young Muslims in Italy is surely much more diversified—one need only think of the many different nationalities of origin which are not represented in the association.

12 It was created from the ashes of previously existing Islamic youth associations (first, the group Islamic Youth; in 1999, AGESMI; and in 2000, The Mediator); with the exception of the latter all were dependent on the Union of Islamic Communities and Organizations in Italy (UCOII), the main Islamic immigrant association and one of the organizations that requested a formal accord (*intesa*)

"Nowadays Islam is being bombarded in every sense and thus it is important to be practical and to be visible and make yourself understood with your words and behaviors ... We young Muslims feel extremely responsible because with every move we make and every time we speak we feel as if we are being observed. Even at school I have to watch every word I say because I feel like I am being watched ... I do not feel like all the others ... You are the only one with a veil at school ... you are like a reference point ... They look at us and say, 'This is Islam.'" (Z. K., 17 years old, Syrian Italian, GMI member)

Some youths have in fact managed to make the best of a bad situation and to change this social pressure into an opportunity. Whereas adult Islamic associations still adopted defensive logics (by opposing "us Muslims" to "them Italians"), the GMI entered the public sphere and introduced a new, more inclusive category: "Italian citizens of Islamic faith." Participating in various public debates and organizing activities for the children of Muslim immigrants, they have attempted to reach two main objectives:

1. An "external" objective: they aim to become involved on the local, national, and European levels "for the cause of justice, peace, and defense of human rights" (from the statute of the association, Article 3).
2. An "internal" objective: the GMI work to promote the identity construction of young "Italian and European" Muslims through educational activities aimed at promoting and deepening their faith.

What Kind of Citizenship?

In the course of three years of empirical research (2001–2004), the issue of citizenship has progressively assumed greater relevance, on the one hand because the GMI has had a central role in the discussions about belonging and the practices of participation,[13] and on the other because the concept of "citizenship" has been invoked often enough by members of the association, to the point of becoming one of the slogans of the GMI.[14] For instance, the fifth convention of the group (in Marina di Massa, December 25–27, 2003) was significantly entitled "New Citizens, Good Muslims," and in the workshop in which they discussed what it means to be a Muslim Italian citizen it clearly emerged that it was not a "passport issue" but depended on "being part of a territory or not." Also on that occasion diverse stories of discrimination and racism were shared, in such great numbers that participants proposed the

---

with the Italian government (Allievi 1994; Guolo 1999; Pace and Perocco 2000; Elsheikh 2001).

13 According to Delanty, 2000, belonging and participation are two key dimensions in a democratic conception of citizenship, which is based not upon ownership of rights, as in the traditional liberal model, but upon the fact of residing in a certain territory, feeling that one is part of it, and actively participating in social life.

14 Another "slogan" of the GMI is that of participation in public life motivated by faith, that is to say, to be "protagonists, with the help of God!"

creation of a "database on the state of Islamophobia in Italy" through the gathering of daily experiences of young Muslims. At the end of the discussion different proposals for "becoming citizens" emerged: knowing how to compare yourself to others at school and in the workplace, being present in the social realm, doing volunteer work,[15] and participating in public events and organizing meetings and seminars for discussing the challenges facing society as a whole.

For these young people, as for young Muslims in other European countries such as France (Cesari 1998, 2003; Tietze 2002; Venel 2004), Islam is lived as one reference of identification, but not as the only one. Its importance is in bringing it to a level equal with other ones. As opposed to what their parents did and do, it is no longer simply a matter of claiming "the right to be different" (e.g., asking for mosques, Islamic cemeteries) but entails real and actual issues of citizenship.

The GMI's calls for inclusion come on different levels: local, because these youths actively participate in the life of the area in which they live;[16] national, because they feel Italian and want "formal citizenship" in order to be officially in possession of rights and duties. Moreover, there are symptoms of much larger claims, such as in the first steps that the association has been taking on a European level: the GMI is part of the European Federation of Young Islamic Associations and of the Youth Forum (which comprises lay and religious youth organizations from various European countries).

The GMI have faced the theme of "formal citizenship" many times, discussing it both inside and outside the association. For example, in one of the constitutive meetings of the National Youth Forum (in Rome on May 30, 2003), the GMI came up with the idea of starting a "campaign for direct access to citizenship for all children of immigrants,"[17] in de facto support of a "citizenship of residency" (*ius soli* rather than *ius sanguinis*) of the sort in which civil, social, and political rights await those who are born in or live in a particular region or territory. This took a particularly innovative form in that the National Youth Forum concerned itself with opening a discussion on a European level as well, namely, within the European Youth Forum.

---

15 Some GMI members related their experience of volunteer work inspired by Christian associations. Furthermore, the GMI recently reached an agreement with lay environmentalist associations to organize communal activities.

16 The first GMI candidate (in Reggio Emilia, in the center-left Margherita Party) ran for office in the most recent town government elections, and the first public appearance of the new mayor of Reggio was organized with the GMI in order to strengthen a "pact of citizenship with Muslim youth."

17 According to the law on Italian nationality, reformed in 1992, children born in Italy to foreign parents acquire the citizenship of their parents. They can request Italian citizenship within one year from their eighteenth birthday only if they have been continually residing in Italy from their birth up to the date of their application. On children of immigrants and citizenship, see Andall, 2003, 289–294.

However, in almost all interviews with GMI members, there is a growing conviction that formal acknowledgement is a lengthy procedure and that it can instead be constructed "from below," thanks to the visibility of youths who become an active part of society. For instance, Latifa is active in various associations, among them the GMI, and works as an intercultural mediator.[18] She participates in the public life of her region, expanding her social network as much as possible, in the conviction that this will help her to obtain formal recognition of Italian citizenship.

"I'm 22 years old, born in Morocco, and now a student of sociology in Trento. I'd like to be a researcher ... I try to meet a lot of people and to make myself known ... I am not an Italian citizen, even if I feel Italian ... You need to have a full-time job, years of contributions; it takes a long time ... I've been here for twelve years. I grew up here like other young people from Trento, but I have an unstable life ... I must find a job immediately, before graduation. If I don't, I can't study; my parents are unable to help me. I have permission to stay for educational reasons, and I don't have a full-time job to make the request ... which they can then refuse to grant. Without knowing why ... It's a problem that many of us feel; with the GMI we try to speak about it, to do something [...]."

National identification among GMI members, their "feeling Italian" despite their passport, does not exclude other bonds of belonging. As is common among many Italians, local identification—above all with the commune in which one lives—is very strong (Sciolla 2004, 57–66). There are certain GMI members who find motivation for their social commitment in "the love for the town in which they live."

For example, Badra is 19 years old, of Syrian origin, and lives in Carrara, Tuscany. She is known locally because she wears a veil: since she has gone to school she has had to answer questions about Islam and international terrorism (e.g., "Do you know Bin Laden?"). Growing up she learned how to entertain contacts with Christian friends and, with the support of the GMI, to participate in local activities on interfaith dialogue and at demonstrations of the global peace movement. Badra says, however, that this is not enough for her. She wishes "to help society, beginning with her town," in a very concrete way: for example, by achieving the repainting of the station wall. As an "active citizen," she believes that the community can become involved in the decisions that affect them and appears to hope that the "participatory budget"[19] of the town of Porto Alegre, in Brazil, will be implemented in her beloved Carrara, too. In the meantime, thanks to the support of her family, she is occupied with her studies at the university, because she thinks that without that she would end up "accepting things just as they are." Badra hopes instead

---

18 "Latifa" is a pseudonym, as are all other names of interviewees and participants quoted in this chapter.
19 See the book by the Chilean sociologist Marta Harnecker, Delegating Power to the People, free for download at http://www.verademocrazia.it.

to be able to change them, beginning with herself and the region in which she lives.

"I think Carrara is very beautiful: the sea, the mountains ... I'd like to help society beginning with my city, you know? I don't want to do things on a big scale ... That's why demonstrations aren't enough for me; I want to do something concrete. Because the little things can be changed, you can see it. Like with the station: I kept talking about it, and, I swear, they finally painted it! Honestly! They painted the whole thing and now you can arrive at the station of Carrara and see that it's decent ... These things are very important to me. I'd love to know where all this money goes to ... What in the world is the city government doing? What is it doing for our city? What projects are there for improving the city? Because we are going downhill ... and this makes me sad. I'm interested in the experiences where citizens are aware of the expenditures and are given a voice ... These are things that affect us. I'd like to be informed, to participate ... I think they already do that in some other parts of the world [...]."

Although acting locally, some of the interviewed youths "think globally" and express transnational belonging as well, recognizing themselves in the composite social universe that has been called "movement of the movements" because of its many facets: it is a global movement for peace (Kaldor 2004), it is critical of the neoliberal model of development, and it aspires to an "other-worldliness" (Ramonet et al. 2004), practicing a sort of "globalization from below" (Pianta 2001).

So-called nonconventional participation (i.e., not related to political parties or politics) is in fact their "normal politics," that is to say, the most common form of participation among these youths, as it is for Italians in the same age group (Albano 2005). It can take the following forms: participating in a procession or demonstration, collecting signatures for petitions, sending press releases or letters to newspapers, writing to public authorities, and participating in events related to local problems.

It is a "politics of everyday life" (De Certeau 2001; Ginsborg 2004), in which social actors express their power by means of small acts of autonomy: for example, by keeping themselves informed about events of public interest or by making responsible choices as consumers. Although these forms of participation are more common among urban youth (such as those inter-viewed in Milan), in the course of my empirical research I also found this kind of activism among GMI members living in small towns of central Italy. Such is the case of Farida, of Sirian origin, who lives in Macerata, a small town in central Italy. She is a cyber-activist who finds on the Internet the sociality that she misses in her provincial town.

"I'm 24 and I'm about to graduate, God willing ... I'd like to leave Macerata and run away from the South! I'd like to go to Rome or Milan: there are more people there, more things happening ... Because I'm an active person, I try to keep myself busy, but here it's pretty hard! ... I was at the big demonstration on February 15th ... We were all there asking for peace, mostly young people ... Millions of people, young

86

people from all around the world who were asking for peace and justice! ... At home, I ask myself, 'What can be done?' ... So I surf the Internet and try to get a better understanding ... See, if I say 'No global,' you think about people who go around destroying ATMs ... I try it in a different way ... For example, the counterinformation I find on the Net, I take it to the university ... I really pester everyone to boycott products that finance Bush. It isn't easy ... Some of my classmates think that they'll die if they can't eat Kit-Kat! I've never heard of anyone dying from a lack of Nutella! But I've got some friends who help me make photocopies and hang up flyers ... On the Net I find advice about how to be active without leaving home ... There are mailing lists where you can find exchanges of updates about which products to boycott. You can even do it from Macerata!"

As we have seen, there can be different levels of belonging (national, local, and global) binding these youths to the rest of society. Their commitment is above all of a civic nature, and the prevailing form of citizenship emerging from what they say and do is democratic citizenship, based on active participation in the region in which they reside. However, when one observes the public initiatives in which GMI members participate as an Islamic youth association it becomes clear that the distinctive involvement of this organization has been in the domain of intercultural and interreligious dialogue in public space.

GMI activism in this realm has included participation in the following events: the annual interfaith meetings organized in Modena by the Associations of Italian Catholic Workers (ACLI); the "ecumenical days of Christian-Islamic dialogue," promoted over the last three years by some Catholic and Protestant magazines (*Il Dialogo, Confronti, Tempi di Fraternità, Mosaico di Pace*); the yearly summits of the Secretariat for Ecumenical Activities;[20] the various interfaith dialogue activities organized on a local level together with various Catholic groups (e.g., the Focolarini in Turin, the Giovani Impegno Missionario linked to the Combonians in Trento, the Comunità di Sant'Egidio in Rome); the "Un calcio alle differenze" project ("A kick in the face of differences" project); the "meeting of civilizations in a soccer game" at the Tre Fontane Stadium in Rome;[21] the day for "positive interdependence in memory of 9/11," proposed by political expert Benjamin Barber and organized by the city council of Rome; the drafting of a common document with the Union of Young Italian Jews (UGEI) and ACLI youths entitled "Different Identities, Equal Rights" (2002); and the meeting called "Creators of a Plural

---

20 See AA.VV, Abitare insieme la terra. Comunità ecumenica e giustizia (Milan: Ancora, 2003), in which speeches from the 2002 meeting are collected (among them those of GMI's former president).

21 Organized to coincide with President Bush's visit in Rome by the Triciclisti (an informal association that sprung up on the Internet) and by GMI members, it had the following objectives: "promoting dialogue and constructive cultural exchange between peoples of different cultures; proposing new ways to solve international controversies." Among participating associations: the national association of sports champions, the national actors soccer team and the Italian association of referees.

Community: Young Italian Muslims, the Union of Young Italian Jews, FUCI and ACLI Youths in an Experience of Communal Life on the Themes of Politics, Religion, and Brotherhood" (in a Camaldolite cloister in Albano Laziale, March 19–21, 2004).

This last event gained even further significance because it was preceded just a week prior by the tragic terror attack in Madrid. The opening press release for the meeting stated: "In an age in which any religion risks becoming instrumental and seen as a cause of wars and conflicts, we want to reaffirm that communal living, sharing of the same spaces, mutual acceptance, and dialogue on an equal level are still possible. Religions are a resource for any society: they are society's possibility for hope." This experience was an important step in the strategy of social inclusion promoted by the association. In comparison with the dynamics of other meetings, in this meeting power was more equally distributed, and all of the interlocutors met and compared their experience and their ideas about the same issues, starting from the accepted point that they were unsolved matters for all three faiths. In other words, in Albano Laziale GMI members experienced what Baumann (2003) calls a process of "convergence," in which social actors are able to cross borders (in this case religious borders), constructed by others and/or themselves, in order to reach common objectives: in this case, a transformation of the way in which "religions" are present in public space.

These youths have challenged together the monolithic representation of Italy as a Catholic and secular country, discussing thorny issues such as the relationship between religion and politics and the meaning of being believers and citizens at the same time. To convey the innovative nature of these meetings, it is useful to present contributions to a focus group (on March 19, 2004) involving around twenty young men and women active in Catholic, Jewish, and Islamic associations.[22]

Young man from UGEI: "Where is the secularism of the Italian state? In public schools, in religion classes? In public television, where the pope is omnipresent in the news? In Parliament, where they are voting for the law on assisted insemination?"

Young woman from FUCI: "They are different things ... and there is independence from power structures: you can see it from the position the pope took against the war, a position differing from that of the Italian government ... which did not seem to be much influenced by it […]."

Young man from GMI: "Let us think one step ahead. With the ongoing unification of the European Union we will have to consider issues on another level ... What will

---

22 The discussion group comprised two boys and three girls from the ACLI, one boy and one girl from the FUCI (University Federation of Italian Catholics), five boys and two girls from the UGEI, and three boys and four girls from the GMI. I had been sent by the GMI to serve as an observer of the discussion group, which was entirely self-managed.

secularism be like on a European level? Consider France. They forbid Muslims to wear the veil, but they celebrate holidays for everybody. Isn't it contradictory?"

Young man from UGEI: "We do not want crucifixes in classrooms because institutions have to be secular, but citizens should be allowed to wear the kippah, the veil [...]."

Young woman from GMI: "Think about Germany. If the teacher wears the veil, what should you do? Expel her? It is discriminating because she is not proselytizing!"

Young man from ACLI: "And think also of the issue of the Christian roots of Europe ... Either we mention everybody, or it is better not to mention any religion."

Young man from GMI: "I would like a plural society where there is room for all points of view, religious or not."

Young man from UGEI: "Yes, but crucifixes are historically a part of proselytism by the Catholic Church. If you want to see a crucifix you should go to church, not to schools or public offices. It is OK to respect Italian and European Christian traditions, but nowadays the Church has to get out of the way of institutions."

Young man from ACLI: "The European Union is born out of the endeavor to leave World War II behind us [...]."

Young man from UGEI: "[...] and maybe the Crusades too!"

Young man from GMI: "OK, religions have messed things up a bit ... But they can help dialogue and change. We at GMI do not want separation; we do not want different, separate schools, but common spaces where dialogue is possible."

The youths participating in this discussion engaged in "social criticism" through their religious difference (Colombo 2003): they questioned secularism and the level of democracy of the Italian state, and expressed their wish for a society that guarantees to a greater degree the right to religious freedom.[23] Together they demanded the introduction of a "pluralist teaching of religion" in public schools, because "nowadays Italian society no longer is only Christian" and because "only public schools can teach believers to also be citizens."[24]

But what does it mean for these young believers to be citizens? During the same interfaith meeting, the GMI introduced the question to Catholic and Jewish participants who were discussing the ties between "religion and citizenship," not knowing that the young Muslims present did not possess Italian citizenship. A very interesting discussion developed and was then

---

23 On the limits of the 1984 agreement between the Catholic Church and the Italian state, see Pace 2004a.

24 This approach is currently being tested in Alsace Lorraine, in northeastern France, where different religious teachings are set in a broader framework of "education to values and citizenship" (Willaime 2000).

more deeply examined thanks to the participation of a young Jewish woman in a doctoral program in history at the University of Rome.

Young woman from GMI: "As regards religion and politics, young Muslims are working inside democratic states ... Yes, well what you hear about us wanting theocratic states makes no sense for young European Muslims ... We are pluralists ... It is written in the Koran that God created different tribes and peoples in order for them to get to know each other ... What is important are the relationships between those who are different ... That is the policy for a European Muslim and it is influenced by religious values, but in the sense that it is important to do good ... together with others. We are influenced by the way in which we are perceived; it's necessary to move forward, to stop thinking about Islam and about immigration. Let us speak as citizens ... We must participate more ... citizenship is very important because it gives the sense of belonging to a country, the desire for its well-being. There needs to be a different policy ... They rejected my citizenship request three times, there is too much discretion involved ... It's hard psychologically. Where would they send me? This is my home."

Young man from FUCI: "Yes, there needs to be a different policy. I didn't realize that you had these problems [...]."

Young man from GMI: "It's not only her ... Listen, it's terrible to be forced to stand in that queue en masse for a piece of paper ... It makes you feel ... inferior. It's most upsetting for those of us who were born here."

Young man from UGEI: "Well, there is a need for security ... With terrorism there is a need for ... checks ... but these are bureaucratic things that will be resolved with time."

Young man from GMI: "Pardon me? I'd like to hear you explain more on this topic ... Because giving citizenship to young people like us is ... is ... arbitrary. It depends on the city you're in. There is no general rule [...]."

Young man from UGEI: Yes ... well I come from Turin, San Salvario ... And there the Muslims are closed, they're not like you ... There are illegal immigrants; there is petty crime [...]

Young woman from GMI: "The danger exists ... On the other hand, correct policies will make the youths more responsible."

Young man from UGEI: "It's not like there are only young people in San Salvario [...]."

Young woman from GMI: "We began talking about the young people in Turin and then it reverberates to the adults ... It takes time ... These are peripheral problems [...]."

Young man from UGEI: "Yes, actually. Also in France there are problems with young Muslims, I think. They are closed ... there are problems with anti-Semitism [...]."

90

Young woman from GMI: "We have contacts with other young Muslims in other European countries ... We compare ourselves ... and it is true that there can be closure. For instance, the English have a lot of complexes, they keep more to themselves ... and until just a short time ago they held different meetings for young men and young women! ... But here the earth is fertile, it can be worked ... We're the first generation of young Italian Muslims ... We must use the time wisely ... being here isn't enough. It takes ... an act of conscience ... To know our objectives."

Young man from GMI: "It must be understood that there are Italian Catholics, Italian Jews, and Italian Muslims."

Young man from FUCI: "Like the title of the meeting, "a plural community," right?"

Young woman from UGEI: "I'll give you a bit of Italian history that may help this discussion. Historically, in Italy religious minorities, the Jews and also the Waldensians, were not citizens like the rest (and they helped each other). Because the Waldensians were considered heretics they were persecuted by the Holy Inquisition ... The Jews were seen by the Church as the murderers of Christ and were discriminated against ... It can be said, however, that they were considered citizens, but with a few limitations ... There's no need to complicate the issue though: the Church sought conversions, but it was only the racism of the twentieth century that attempted extermination ... The Jews came out of the ghetto during the Renaissance ... With the Risorgimento they thought they had participated in the unification of Italy ... so much so that until the Shoah they felt more Italian than Jewish ... The Jews were patriots, they couldn't believe what was happening, with race laws—there were even Jewish Fascists! Now ... that blind faith in the state doesn't exist ... It is important to understand history in order to be citizens."

Young woman from GMI: "That is also our point: to have the same rights, to be Italian Muslims."

Young woman from UGEI: "But you've been here for less time. Not since the birth of Rome! Many young Jews ignore history ... But they can't afford to. Because to each one of us is asked, 'Where were you born, in Israel?'"

As opposed to other interfaith meetings in which the emphasis was on agreement, on mutual reassurance in the face of wars and other dramatic events, these young people were able to go beyond "a pleasant intercultural exchange" (Demorgon and Lipiansky 1999) and confront complex issues, succeeding in developing and comparing conflicting points of view. What is the relationship between Islam and politics? The response that many experts give reveals an essentialist vision of Islam, for which any political undertaking by Muslims—because they cannot "distinguish between public and private" and they have a "totalizing religious identity"—must be suspect and have as its secret agenda the "Islamization of the state." The young woman from the GMI instead talks about democratic participation and a pluralism of values which guarantees the collaboration of all citizens for the "common good." For her it is important that young Muslims be more active in the public sphere so that they can emancipate themselves from "how they are viewed," which is to say, as "foreigners." Although she was born in Italy, she has been refused Italian national status, and her case is not isolated. Another member of the GMI adds that this is a status shared by "those who have been raised in Italy" (but born elsewhere). To not possess documents means, for example, having to undergo what seems like a ritual degradation: waiting for hours and hours in a queue outside Italian police stations (where residence permits are issued), amidst bureaucratic red tape and discretionary margins that have been denounced many times, even by Catholic associations.

Faced with this demand for citizenship, a young Jewish Italian showed his concern by saying that not all of the Muslims are like those present at the discussion: in his opinion, the checks are necessary in times marked by international terrorism and criminality by illegal immigrants. Speaking of his experience in a part of Turin where many immigrants live (Semi 2004), the young man asserted that the recent political choices that have been made in the name of "security" are legitimate. The point of view of the young woman from the GMI was that these problems might be better solved through more adequate social policies, especially those aimed at young people. The young man from the UGEI then proceeded to develop another conflictual point, reporting episodes of "anti-Semitism" perpetrated by young Muslims: Can what has happened in other countries also happen in Italy? According to a young member of the GMI, it is still possible to anticipate those types of slips: young Italian Muslims are the first generation in Italy, and the experiences of other countries can be useful. Again taking up the "strength" of the associa-tion ("we are Italian citizens"), a young woman from the GMI stated that the main challenge is cultural: it is necessary to understand that nowadays Italians no longer are only Catholics, but that there are also Italian citizens of Islamic faith. The final discussion with the young woman from the UGEI refers to the slower times of development in history: in Italy the Jews and Waldensians were not considered to be "citizens like others" for a long time. In order to obtain the same rights, they had to follow a path beset by obstacles. Not even someone like the young Jewish woman who considers herself autochthonous since "the beginnings of Rome" is protected from discussions that can exclude her and treat her as "foreign."

As we have seen, there is a part of Italian society which continues to imagine Italy as a "monoreligious" country, but from below there are those who are trying to change this representation and demand citizenship in a secular, multicultural, and multireligious country. GMI members are Muslim democrats, and together with young Catholic and Jewish leaders they are challenging the strong resistance to change, not only from the outside but from the inside too. All of the youths from religious organizations who participated in the Albano Laziale meeting in fact declared that in their experience "intracommunity" dialogue is often more difficult than dialogue between "peers of different faiths" (that is to say, among youths from the ACLI, GMI, and UGEI). Moreover, they expected difficulties in "reporting to headquarters" the discussions that they had amongst each other. Let us therefore consider the difficulties that GMI members are facing, above all with the previous generation and with adult Islamic associations.

Breaking Defensive Logics

Relations with institutions and the media have elicited lively debate both within the association and with other institutions representing Islam in Italy, particularly with the Union of Islamic Communities and Organizations in Italy (UCOII). Young Muslims have, in fact, often met with opposition in the "control mechanisms which operate as guardians of the access to public space," intended both as a space of representation and as a site of normative and institutional regulation (Amiraux 2004, 125). But what can be done when faced with this censorship, with the "framework shifts" and the imposition of the "security framework"? GMI's approach is to continue to act as active citizens, though one consequence of this approach is to face phases of deep crisis on the "home front."

In January 2003 Interior Minister Giuseppe Pisanu publicly appealed to Muslims to make "a covenant with Muslim moderates," declaring that "Italian Islam cannot be left to the mercy of its different souls" (*La Repubblica*, January 21, 2003). At first, GMI members tried to reframe Pisanu's proposal in an interpretive framework in which Muslims are first of all "citizens."

"We believe that the only way to accomplish a real "Italian Islam" is through the new concept of Islam and Italian Muslims as actual and complete citizens, although with a different faith ... We will be able to really say that Islam is well established when mosques are considered by all to be a part of the cultural legacy of towns and cities, as has already happened in other European countries. When Muslim citizens are subjects and not only objects of debate." (La Repubblica, February 9, 2003).

In the same interview, the journalist obtained the following answer to the question of "who represents Italian Muslims": "Parliament, beyond a doubt. For us 'new citizens,' the state and its institutions are the guarantors of our rights, of the rights of the community." In a press release of May 24, 2003, in response to a new appeal by Pisanu, GMI members not only condemned violence but also declared that it is necessary to create "a society in which all can feel like citizens," "based on equal rights and duties for all, in observance of individual freedoms and under the supreme guardianship of the Italian constitution." In other words, GMI statements abandon the "security framework" and the "reactive" and "defensive" position of "Muslim moderates," and instead take up a democratic perspective, demanding, along with an end to violence, an acknowledgment by the state of equality of rights and duties. But with what results?

Almost one year later, Pisanu once again talked about the representation of Italian Islam and, as always, he did so by using an interpretive framework of "safety" and "war against terrorism." Members of the "Council of Moderates," said the minister, would not be elected, but would be chosen for their "reputation as moderates" (Corriere della Sera, February 13, 2004). GMI members were among the "chosen ones." Some months later, as a consequence of the Beslan slaughter, GMI members signed a "manifesto for life and against terrorism" together with other "Muslim moderates" (Corriere della Sera, September 2, 2004).[25] His signing of this document is one of the reasons that led former GMI president Anouar to turn in his resignation on December 11, 2004.[26]

To understand what was at stake, it is useful to refer to the national convention "Young Muslims and the New Europe" (in Chianciano Terme; December 27–29, 2004) by means of a brief ethnographic account. After three years of participant observation, during which I had followed the development of national conventions and the gradual acquisition of autonomy by the youth association, I noticed that there was a strong tendency towards lack of leadership in adult associations. The resignation of their president certainly brought confusion in the higher ranks of the GMI—so much so that up to the last moment the program for the three days had been suspended. For example, the program was supposed to include the participation of "professors external to the Islamic community" and the organization of workshops in order to provide the youths with more room for discussion. In the end there was no time for group work, and it was always the same persons who spoke from the stage (and from the audience): the vice president of the Association for Islamic Culture and Education (ACEI) and the president and vice president of the UCOII—that is to say, three fathers of sons and daughters who also were participating.

Conflict was "tamed" through continual official declarations of "fraternity": not only between generations, but also among the youths themselves. Even when new elections were called, the candidates felt the need to make a communal public statement: "We are not competitors, we are brothers." Afterwards they had pictures taken of them embracing each other. In the face of an event that the media had presented in dire tones (e.g., the daily newspaper Libero interpreted the resignation of GMI's president as the result of "Islamist threats"), the young leaders chose an approach that seemed to me to be aimed at "playing down the tones" and reassuring the very young participants (as at the other conventions, the majority of participants were in the 15- to 16-year-old age group).

I consider the following to be the most salient moments of the convention: (a) the speech by the ex-president on the reasons for his resignation and the

---

25 The text of the manifesto can be found at http://www.stranieriinitalia.it.

26 Here, too, a pseudonym is used, even though it is easy to identify him because of his popularity (e.g., through frequent appearances on television, especially on a popular evening talk-show). He is 21 years old, comes from Casablanca, and grew up in Reggio Emilia. He recently moved to Naples, where he is pursuing a degree in Arabic Studies at the university. He writes articles for local newspapers and is very active in volunteer work (and has been since high school).

new elections; (b) the showing of the film *East is East* and the ensuing debate on "Muslim families"; (c) the round table between various leaders of Italian Islamic associations and the difficult "intracommunity" dialogue.

GMI: One of the Many Paths for Young Muslims?

Anouar resigned after one year as president, retracing the steps taken by the youth association ("We began within the UCOII, and then we sought more autonomy and founded the GMI"). According to Anouar, crucial points were "the process of taking responsibility and reaching self-awareness" among youths who want to "feel like protagonists" and the ability to "give a voice to those who did not have one." Anouar was embittered because he felt that he had undergone a "campaign of pure defamation" and that he had received little support from within the association. Moreover, he wanted to stress that being a citizen means engaging in criticism and participating actively in social life. This is exactly what he tried to do.

"We can never be full citizens if we are not aware of the fact that we are. Dialogue is not a strategy or a tactic for interaction. Believing in the values of pluralism, freedom, and democracy means living by them. It means we are within society and we participate. We communicate with the media not to be in the spotlight, but because we really believe that we are citizens."

The implicit reference is to the "fathers" who still adopt defensive logics towards Italian society and who blame the youth of having gone "too far" for personal ambition. Anouar invited all participating youths to feel free to "see it differently," reminding them that in Islam there are four different juridical schools and that internal divergence runs deep. Only then, he argued, is it possible to discuss the problems they are facing without fear of betraying someone. "If there can be no confrontation and comparison, only defamation is left ... Islamic Brotherhood? Yeah, right!" Anouar did not spare his peers from criticism either:

"I thought that our vision was to become a launching pad to become full citizens ... Our internal debate is fundamental. Otherwise, we will not have the strength to be autonomous and drive our decisions home ... I will continue my commitment, I will try to be a critical mind and to support the GMI in another manner ... as one of the many possible paths for young Muslims ... May Allah accept and bless our journey. I hope that the brothers I am referring to will not feel offended but will instead take my words as a starting point to reflect together."

Anouar believes that one can be a "good Muslim" outside Islamic associations as well, and he views his participation in and contribution to the GMI in this new light: he will try to contribute to the good of his brothers by means of cultural criticism.[27]

Although Anouar's speech definitely was disturbing, nobody took up the issues he had presented in order to challenge him. Some members of the leadership were evidently moved, though it seemed the interpretation circulating among them was that it was a matter of Anouar's "personal problems." By calling new elections, the leadership did not explicitly face the issues that had been raised, but it did express generic gratitude for what the former president had done. The central issue of autonomy from adult associations returned in the speeches of the three candidates, but in effect the conflict was passed over in silence. All were just concerned to declare themselves "autonomous"—though in full respect of their parents.

But how is autonomy *practiced*? For example, one of the candidates (the son of the UCOII vice president) said that he wanted to invest more in religious training—which in recent years was quite limited, as the association was more occupied with external issues. He suggested that they ... follow ACEI directives. Another candidate raised the issue of funding the association and he sought help ... from the associations of the fathers. In other words, the presence of the previous generation made clear that independence has not yet been fully attained. The speeches of the youths also revealed a reluctance to pursue actual autonomy by creating the necessary conditions to practice it.

The election was won by a 21-year-old man of Tunisian origin who studies political science at Padova University. His slogan ("Strong with our principles, positive in our society") seems to have pleased many of the participating youths: it made a twofold claim (as Muslims and Italians) in continuity with the history of the association. Perhaps what helped the new president the most was the emphasis he placed on the participation of youths at the local and regional levels to re-establish from the ground up the priorities and activities of the GMI.

GMI: A Nonhostile Space to Express Oneself and Discuss Freely?

East is East is an ironic cinematic tale (Ferro 2005) about the intergenerational conflicts within a British Muslim family (the father originates from Pakistan). The showing was accompanied by strong opposition and criticism by those who saw the film as a provocation. According to them it was a "dirty film" containing obscenity and vulgarity. Others were instead interested in the story and tried to follow its thread despite the noise and chatter. With some difficulties, the showing was followed by an intense debate introduced in this way by the daughter of the UCOII's president: "Who among you feels that he is represented in this film?" Silence followed. "Nobody, so this film does not represent us. In the film there is a bad Muslim father and a good English

---

27 See his first book, Salaam, Italia (Reggio Emilia, Italy: Aliberti editore, 2005).

mother." The UCOII's vice president then added, "The Islamic family depicted in this film is the exception confirming the rule. Islamic pedagogy is the best. Next time you will choose a different film."

Obviously, this "literal" reading of the film created an underlying misunderstanding (i.e., film = reality) and did not entertain them or make them laugh. This reaction was not, however, universal. A young man from a Moroccan family living in Perugia said that "these things happen every day" and that there was no reason to be shocked if it did not depict reality, because a movie inevitably conveys one point of view, that of the director. A young girl of Tunisian origin from Novara also spoke up for the film, explaining that "comedy always exaggerates things" but that it still can be useful to think about issues like mixed marriages, or the fact that the children in the film are de facto English but the father can hardly understand it—something that many young Italian Muslims can identify with. The opposing faction then stated that the film was "anti-Islamic" and that it was time to fight to change the image of Muslim families, telling stories in which "the best image of Islam" could emerge. Once again confounding film and reality, a woman from the Association of Muslim Women in Italy, who had some of her children in the room, added that "if the mother had been a Muslim there would not have been all those problems." She later warned against "mixed marriages" and ended with a panegyric on "Muslim women." A member of the leadership at this point tried to calm the situation by saying that the issues dealt with in the film were not "typically Islamic" but could just as easily apply to "a family of immigrants from Apulia in Germany." He invited the audience to consider the GMI a "nonhostile space to express oneself and discuss freely."

Clearly, showing and then discussing the film was an experiment in pluralism and democratic participation: a demanding exercise to try to break free from the apologetic "cages" of Islam which paralyze the thoughts of many Muslims, an attempt at (self-)criticism. It was possible to observe in action the issues raised by the resigning president. Of course, these challenges concern not only the GMI, as nowadays it seems particularly difficult for any Muslims to find a "nonhostile space to express oneself and discuss freely." The considerable socioeconomic problems that many immigrant families face daily (Frisina 2005) and the prevailing interpretive frameworks of "security" and "culture" with respect to Islam surely do not help. As anthropologist Lila Abu-Lughod (2002) has pointed out, in order to engage in self-criticism one needs time and tranquility. As long as the rhetoric on the "clash of the civilizations" and on "Muslim women in need of rescue" prevails, intracommunity debates and "transverse alliances" will be that much more difficult.[28]

---

28 Discussions about the veil issue also suffer from this kind of approach, so much so that during the convention there were those who defined the veil as "the flag of Islam." In this case it is not easy to discuss what it means, for instance, to be modest, because everything is interpreted through a framework of bearing witness against a society that stigmatizes Muslims. This is another example of how a

Towards a "Critical Brotherhood"

Of the association leaders invited by the GMI leadership, only Nour Dachan from the UCOII, Abu Soumaya from the ACEI, and Omar Camilletti from the great mosque in Rome (Islamic League) showed up. The latter supports the controversial "manifesto against terrorism" and was the first to speak up: "Let us not allow that only Islamophobics criticize us; let us do it ourselves, too. For example, let us not cover for the brothers who err, be it a matter of a violent father or a political issue." He then invited the youths to study in order to "make of knowledge the distinguishing feature of Muslims" and to commit themselves to interreligious dialogue with Jews "because one must learn to distinguish between the Jews and the policies of Israel." Dachan's contribution was rather declamatory: "They thought we were done for, and instead here we are! Let us not compete amongst ourselves; we must cooperate together with the government ... Beware of journalists who sow discord! Long live the GMI, long live the UCOII!" The ACEI's vice president also followed this defensive approach, taking a stance against the outside world and for a new alliance of Italian Muslims: "Those who do not hold Islam dear try to exhaust us ... We do not want youths who work only to make a show of themselves; we want youth who work for the good of all Muslims."

The resigning president was in the room and, perhaps feeling that such speeches were in reference to him, intervened in the debate:

"The clash is not personal ... We are not within a family; we are talking about the activity of an association that is public and political! We all share respect for our parents and the value of a fraternal relationship, but we are members of civil society! We youths want the good of our society. Confrontation must not be private, for we must learn to answer for what we do in the society in which we live ... The media must not be demonized! We do not live in an Arab regime; we are citizens in a democratic state! ... And real pluralism requires rules and above all mutual acknowledgement [...]."

The young man was visibly tense and straining to measure the weight of every single word he spoke, but in exchange he got only a chilling response from the speakers on stage. The UCOII's president refused to answer him, and Camilletti declared that he felt embarrassed and that he censored himself "out of respect for his senior brother from the UCOII," thereby preferring to leave criticism for another time. What about his own encouragement to engage in criticism of and among Muslims just a few minutes earlier?

Observing the actions of the only "external" figure at the convention, Camilletti, the young participants perhaps have come to understand that "brotherhood" can lead to even a grown-up man being reluctant to openly express his dissent. "Intracommunity" dialogue was therefore merely hinted at. It was, however, the youths who felt a need for it, and the new GMI

---

defensive approach eventually paralyzes internal discussions and ends up legitimating a normative version of Islam.

president seems determined to follow this route towards a "critical brotherhood" in which there can be room for dissent and change.

References

Abu-Lughod, L. 2002. Do Muslim women really need saving? American Anthropologist 104 (3): 783–790.

Albano, R. 2005. I giovani e le nuove forme di partecipazione. Il Mulino 54 (2): 320–330.

Allievi, S. 1994. Organizzazione e potere nel mondo musulmano: Il caso della comunità di Milano. In I musulmani nella società europea, ed. Fondazione Giovanni Agnelli, 155–176. Turin, Italy: Edizioni della Fondazione Agnelli.

———. 2003. Sociology of a newcomer: Muslim migration to Italy— Religious visibility, cultural and political reactions. Immigrants and Minorities 22 (2–3): 141–154.

Amiraux, V. 2004. Les musulmans dans l'espace politique européen: La délicate expérience du pluralisme confessionnel. Vingtième Siècle. Revue d'histoire 82 (April–June): 119–130.

Andall, J. 2003. Italiani o stranieri? La seconda generazione in Italia. In Un'immigrazione normale, ed. G. Sciortino and A. Colombo, 281–307. Bologna, Italy: Il Mulino.

Baumann, G. 2003. L'enigma multiculturale: Stati, etnie, religioni. Bologna, Italy: Il Mulino.

Cesari, J. 1998. Musulmans et Républicains. Paris: Editions Complexe.

———. 2003. Muslim minorities in Europe: The silent revolution. In Modernizing Islam: Religion in the public sphere in Europe and the Middle East, ed. J. Esposito and F. Burgat, 251–269. Newark, NJ: Rutgers University Press.

Colombo, E. 2003. Quando il vicino è straniero: Il multiculturalismo quotidiano come spazio di costruzione della differenza e di analisi sociologica. Working Paper 8/2003, Dipartimento Studi Sociali e Politici, University of Milan. Also available at the following Web site: http://www.sociol. unimi.it/papers/2003-5-7_Enzo%20Colombo.pdf.

De Certeau, M. 2001. L'invenzione del quotidiano. Rome: Edizioni Lavoro.

Delanty, G. 2000. Citizenship in a global age: Society, culture, politics. Buckingham, UK: Open University Press.

Del Boca, A. 1998. Il colonialismo italiano tra miti, rimozioni, negazioni e inadempienze. Italia Contemporanea 212:589–603.

Demorgon, J., and M. Lipiansky, eds. 1999. Guide de l'interculturel en formation. Paris: Retz.

Elsheikh, M. S. 2001. L'Islam come nuovo soggetto religioso in Italia. In La religione nella società dell'incertezza: Per una convivenza solidale in una società multireligiosa, ed. R. De Vita and F. Berti, 173–193. Milan: Franco Angeli.

Ferro, L. 2005. La sfera pubblica cinematografica: L'analisi della comunicazione interculturale nella rappresentazione del matrimonio di diaspora. Ph.D. dissertation, Università di Padova, Italy.

Frisina, A. 2005. Potersi sentire a casa anche qui. In Voci di famiglie immigrate, ed. A. Marazzi, 81–117. Milan: Franco Angeli-ISMU.

Garelli, F., G. Guizzardi, and E. Pace. 2003. Un singolare pluralismo: Indagine sul pluralismo morale e religioso degli italiani. Bologna, Italy: Il Mulino.

Ginsborg, P. 2004. Il tempo di cambiare: Politica e potere nella vita quotidiana. Turin, Italy: Einaudi.

Grillo, R., and J. Pratt. 2002. The politics of recognizing difference: Multiculturalism Italian-style. Aldershot, UK: Ashgate.

Guolo, R. 1999. Attori sociali e processi di rappresentanza nell'Islam italiano. In L'islam in Italia: Una presenza plurale, ed. C. Saint-Blancat, 67–90. Rome: Edizioni Lavoro.

———. 2003. Xenofobi e xenofili: Gli italiani e l'islam. Rome: Laterza.

Hervieu-Léger, D. 2000. Miroir de l'islam. Vingtième Siècle. Revue d'histoire 66 (April–June): 79–89.

Kaldor, M. 2004. L'altra potenza. La società civile globale: la risposta al terrore. Milan: Università Bocconi Editore.

Khader, B. 1992. L'Europe et le monde arabe: Cousins, voisins. Paris: Publisud-Quorum.

Pace, E. 1998. La nation italienne en crise: Perspectives européennes. Paris: Bayard Editions.

———. 2004a. Un Concordato con la modernità. Quaderni di diritto e politica ecclesiastica 12 (April): 17–21.

———. 2004b. L'islam in Europa: Modelli di integrazione. Rome: Carocci.

Pace, E., and F. Perocco. 2000. L'Islam plurale degli immigrati in Italia. Studi Emigrazione 37 (March): 2–20.

Pianta, M. 2001. Globalizzazione dal basso: Economia mondiale e movimenti sociali. Rome: Manifestolibri.

Pratt, J. 2002. Italy: Political unity and cultural diversity. In The politics of recognizing difference: Multiculturalism Italian-style, ed. R. Grillo and J. Pratt, 25–39. Aldershot, UK: Ashgate.

Ramonet, I., et al. 2004. Altermondialistes de tous les pays ... Manière de voir 75 (June–July). Paris: Le Monde diplomatique.

Rivera, A., ed. 2002. L'inquietudine dell'islam. Bari, Italy: Dedalo.

———. 2003. Estranei e nemici. Rome: DeriveApprodi.

Rusconi, G. 2000. Come se Dio non ci fosse: I laici, i cattolici e la democrazia. Turin, Italy: Einaudi.

———. 2005. La legge sulla fecondazione: Un'occasione mancata di democrazia laica. Il Mulino 54 (2): 221–228.

Said, E. 1991. Orientalismo. Turin, Italy: Bollati Boringhieri.

Saint-Blancat, C., and O. Schmidt di Friedberg. 2005. Why are mosques a problem? Local politics and fear of Islam in northern Italy. Journal of Ethnic and Migration Studies 31 (6): 1083–1104.

Sayad, A. 2002. La doppia assenza: Dalle illusioni dell'emigrato alle sofferenze dell'immigrato. Milan: Raffaello Cortina Editore.

Schmidt di Friedberg, O. 2001. Sentimenti anti-islamici in Italia e in Europa. Europa-Europe 10 (5): 26–36.

Sciolla, L. 2004. La sfida dei valori: Rispetto delle regole e rispetto dei diritti in Italia. Bologna, Italy: Il Mulino.

———. 2005. Italiani che cambiano. Il Mulino 54 (2): 308–319.

Sciortino, G. 2002. Islamofobia all'italiana. Polis: Ricerche e studi su società e politica in Italia 1:103–126.

Semi, G. 2004. Il multiculturalismo quotidiano: Porta Palazzo tra commercio e conflitto. Ph.D. dissertation, Università di Torino, Italy.

Tietze, N. 2002. Jeunes musulmans de France et d'Allemagne: Les constructions subjectives de l'identité. Paris: L'Harmattan.

Venel, N. 2004. Musulmans et citoyens. Paris: P.U.F.-Le Monde.

Willaime, J. P. 2000. L'enseignement religieux à l'école publique dans l'Est de la France. Social Compass 3:383–395.

Welmoet Boender

FROM MIGRANT TO CITIZEN: THE ROLE OF THE ISLAMIC UNIVERSITY OF ROTTERDAM IN THE FORMULATION OF DUTCH CITIZENSHIP[1]

Introduction

The establishment of Islamic educational institutions is an important way for Muslims to manifest their position as a religious minority. Although young Muslims living in Europe have expressed a clear need to gain knowledge of Islam, few Islamic educational institutions exist in European countries. At present, the vast majority of Muslim religious leaders who have completed religious training come from Muslim countries. Many imams were trained in educational institutions based in Muslim countries, and often reside in Europe only on a temporary basis. As is the case elsewhere in Europe, young Muslims in the Netherlands are searching for their religion's roots and for Islamic norms and Islamic solutions to social and individual problems in the European context (see Amiraux 2000; Lesthaeghe 2000; Roy 2000; Vertovec 1998; Waardenburg 2000).

In 1997 an interesting initiative was taken by a group of first-generation Dutch-speaking Sunni Muslims from various ethnic and cultural backgrounds: they established the Islamic University of Rotterdam (IUR). The IUR's main aims are, first, to be an academic institution that conveys and deepens knowledge of Islam to Muslims living in Europe, in particular the Netherlands, and, second, to inform non-Muslims about the religion and culture of the Islamic world on an academic level. It also offers training for imams. At present, the IUR is not formally recognized by the Dutch government as a university or as a center for training imams. The university's board is eager to have the institution obtain official status.

In defining the strategy for making their religion visible in the Dutch public sphere, the initiators of this Islamic university and its students must deal with complex political, ideological, and legal structures. As a consequence of their social empowerment, Muslim organizations increasingly fill the space

---

1 This chapter forms part of my PhD research at the International Institute for the Study of Islam in the Modern World (ISIM), which examines the role of imams in Turkish and Moroccan mosque communities in the Netherlands and Flanders. I would like to thank Valérie Amiraux and Frank Peter for their helpful comments, and Elena Fiddian Mendez for making corrections to this English version.

that exists between the state and its citizens: collectively, by establishing religious organizations and, individually, by enabling processes of identity-seeking. The Netherlands has a long tradition of religious pluralism on this intermediate level between the state and its citizens. However, both a strong process of secularization and an internationally fed distrust of Islam are undermining the process whereby Muslims can establish their position in civil society.

As a religious academic institution, the IUR aims to provide Dutch society at large with a clear position on subjects that lie at the core of the normative definition of national and social belonging to Dutch society. Such subjects include the nature of gender relations, the separation of religion and politics, democracy, and attitudes towards homosexuality. As the IUR navigates the process of acquiring a recognized position in the Dutch public sphere, a few questions arise: Will the IUR be accepted and recognized as an intermediate institution in civil society? Furthermore, how can the IUR obtain its recognition, both as a university and as a religious institution, and on what conditions?

To understand the IUR's position, it is important to review the twenty-five-year debate on the establishment of imam training in the Netherlands. In so doing, I show how the legal possibilities for the accreditation of Islamic educational institutions are embedded in a historical tradition of religious pluralism, and outline the social and political fields in which the IUR must maneuver. After this introductory analysis, I look more closely at the IUR and examine the motivations and needs of the students searching for answers to their questions of faith. In the fourth section, I discuss some dynamics that are central to the constitution of the IUR. At this point it becomes evident that the IUR's room for maneuvering in the public sphere is restricted.

Yasemin Nuhoglu Soysal explores the ways in which the customary parameters of the European debate on the formation of an Islamic community are often defined as either a divisive and antidemocratic threat or as a positive contribution to Europe's political and cultural pluralism. "At issue," she states, "is the compatibility of Islam—its organizational culture and practice—with European categories of democratic participation and citizenship" (Soysal 1997, 509–510). In this chapter I outline the ways in which this question of compatibility results in a paradoxical situation in which the IUR can claim its right to orthodoxy in a liberal democracy, yet wishes to avoid putting itself in an alienated position, "foreign to the normative categories of European democracy" (Soysal 1997, 510).

Imam Training: The Public Debate

Imams working in European societies find themselves at the crossroads of a complex interplay between local, national, and transnational contexts in which Islamic knowledge is produced and transmitted. Their tasks in local mosques are more extensive than those of imams in the local mosques of countries with a Muslim majority. Historically, imams have been, together with other religious scholars, individuals who have had a certain degree of access to sacred texts. In the diaspora, however, they become both representatives of the normative Islam that is configured from such texts and the ones who form a link between diasporic communities and the cultural and socio-linguistic traditions of their countries of origin. In addition, imams are responsible for interpreting Islamic norms and values within the context of a secular, non-Islamic society. Partly because a substantial proportion of imams do not know European society from within, this process is particularly difficult and is looked upon with suspicion throughout Europe. At the same time, the second and third generations often find it difficult to understand the imam's teachings and hesitate to share their problems with the imams.

A vast majority of the estimated four-hundred salaried imams working in Dutch mosques are recruited by mosque boards in their countries of origin (Turkey, Morocco, and some other Muslim countries). For example, about one hundred and fifty Turkish imams from Diyanet mosques have been sent from Turkey as civil servants.[2] A substantial number of imams therefore have little or no proficiency in Dutch; they preach in Arabic or Turkish upon their arrival in the Netherlands. Since the 1980s, the possibility of establishing a training program for imams has been consistently raised, and as of January 2002 all alien imams entering the country have been required to complete specially designed courses that provide an introduction to the Dutch language and Dutch customs.

Although the precise role and influence of imams in the Netherlands remain unclear, particularly with respect to their influence through sermons to the younger generation, imams are thought to play a key role throughout the process of Muslims' integration into Dutch society. They are thought to play a key role because mosques and imams not only fulfill a religious but also a sociocultural role in the diaspora. Indeed, analogous to priests and ministers, imams were expected to be the obvious figures to assume the role of spiritual caretakers in government-provided prisons and hospitals (Boender and Kanmaz 2002; Rath et al. 1996; Shadid and Van Koningsveld 1997). However, imams did not appear to be trained for these new tasks of the pastoral caretaker. No new, strong Muslim intellectual elite (like those in France or Britain), which can authoritatively speak out on ethical matters and religious affairs in the public debate, has yet to emerge. The 1998 report of the Netherlands' integration policy on imams stressed:

"The government considers it of high importance that the leaders of the philosophical associations and organizations, including those which attract especially ethnic minorities, can communicate fluently in their Dutch surroundings and that they are well acquainted with the social structures and cultural characteristics of Dutch society. Here the government pays special attention to the social skills of imams, as

---

2   The Diyanet is the Turkish Presidium for Religious Affairs.

they belong to the largest philosophical stream among the ethnic minorities. The present practice of recruiting imams from Turkey and Morocco should come to an end." ("Integratiebeleid" 1998, 17; my translation)

Dutch imam training, as promoted by the government, would be aimed at substituting the current generation of imams with a "homegrown" generation. Imams trained in the Netherlands would obtain a thorough education in the Dutch language and Dutch society, both of which would be necessary for counseling Muslims who ask an imam for advice on problems emerging in the Dutch context. Furthermore, it is argued, this change would prevent the possibility of ideological and political (state) interference by Muslim countries (e.g., Rath et al. 1996, 246) and would thereby help preclude the imam-led radicalization of Muslim youth. Indeed, it would lead to the formation of a "Dutch Islam." Time and again, imam training is proposed as a solution to the problems that arise in the formulation of citizenship of first-, second-, and third-generation Muslims, as well as a means, in essence, of making "the Other" look more like "the Self" (cf. Amir-Moazami, 2001, 324–325, for the French context).

The Legal Right to Establish Imam Training

In its efforts to establish a separation of church and state in the Netherlands, the state historically has financed the academic education of the clergy, both at public and confessional universities and at seminaries. In the "pillar system" in place between 1900 and 1960, religion was strongly integrated in the public sphere, and religious diversity was institutionalized in four pillars: Protestant, Catholic, socialist, and liberal. Each pillar had the right to establish its own schools; these schools were granted the same legal status as public schools and were also financed by the state. At present, the government must provide equally for the prerequisites of all religious groups, without interfering in those groups' internal affairs. Since the formal policy on minorities was implemented in 1983, it has been recognized that religion plays a central role in the development and reinforcement of the self-esteem of members of an ethnic group as well as a considerable role in their equality and full participation in society (Minderhedennota 1983, 110). This implies that if these prerequisites in the public sphere have not been established, the government should help to provide them (Hirsch Ballin 1988). For their part, Muslim organizations are entitled to establish imam training courses if they fulfill the legal requirements.

There are three main ways that government-financed imam training can take place. The first way is to join pre-existing institutions. The second is to have the general education of professional clergy provided by a public faculty of religion, whereas clergy-specific education is provided by the religious organization itself.[3] The third way, which is the path chosen by the IUR, is that of allocation (aanwijzing; Adviescommissie Imamopleidingen 2003, 14–16). At present the IUR offers higher education that is not financed by the state, and it is unable to offer either recognized titles for graduates or scholarships for students (Adviescommissie Imamopleidingen 2003, 14). The IUR is not the only institution that functions in this way: the Islamic University of Europe, which split from the IUR in 2001 and is based at Schiedam, also opted for the allocation method and is organized in a similar way.[4]

Practical and Ideological Obstacles to the Establishment of Imam Training

Despite the existence of a number of privately run initiatives,[5] a formally recognized Islamic academic institution has not yet been created in the Netherlands. On one level this is because there are clear rules for allocation, and the institutions opting for allocation have not yet fulfilled the legal requirements. There are, however, several other factors currently impeding the successful recognition of imam training. For instance, although consensus on the importance of imam training exists among Muslims, politicians, policymakers, and opinion leaders, opinions on feasibility, need, effectiveness, content, and financing differ. Practical obstacles range from a lack of qualified teachers with a Muslim background who can teach in Dutch, to the confessional heterogeneity of Muslims in the Netherlands. Indeed, if imam training in the Netherlands is to be instituted, the religiously and ethnically divided Muslim organizations will have to reach compromises. Such compromises would relate, for example, to the length and content of the training program and the separation of theological and societal subjects. If imam education is not supported by a number of Muslim mosque organizations, there is a considerable risk that graduates will not be accepted as imams in the affiliated mosques.

---

3   This is called "duplex ordo" and is treated in Articles XIII and XIV of the law on higher education and scientific research.

4   Although the Islamic University of Europe acts in the same social, political, and legal spheres, a discussion of this institution and the reasons underlying the split are not within the scope of this chapter.

5   Some private imam training exists in the Netherlands. Organized along doctrinal lines and ethnic background, these are financed by Muslim organizations. They have not shown interest in accreditation by the government. The Jamia Madinatul-Islam of the World Islamic Mission (WIM) Netherlands instructs imams for Surinamese, Hindustani, and Pakistani mosques in the Netherlands (Karagül and Wagtendonk 1994, 22). Graduates work as imams in various Dutch WIM mosques. This traditional training focuses on the memorization of the Quran. The Ahmadiyyah federation trains "assistant imams," who can continue their education in Lahore, Pakistan. Furthermore, the Turkish Süleymanlı have their own education (see Landman 1992, 269–270).

Apart from these practical obstacles, the representation of imams in the public debate carries much weight. Three recent events which have caused a great deal of moral commotion and unrest in Dutch society illustrate this point: the so-called El-Moumni affair, about homosexuality (2001); the "Nova imams," about political enemies and domestic violence (2002); and the murder of Theo van Gogh, after a provocative film on the abuse of women (2004).[6] Each incident renewed interest in the debate on imams' roles, influence, and ideological backgrounds. In the "post-9/11 era," there has been an increasing emphasis on secularism in Dutch political culture, in the sense of *laïcité* in France, where a strong differentiation between the political and the religious is made. This interpretation of secularism is extended to the marginalization of religion to the private sphere (Casanova 1994). This tendency, however, has not prevented the state from actively interfering in the question of imam training. Since 2002, the creation of formally recognized imam training has become the spearhead of the policies espoused by the minister of alien affairs and integration.

The El-Moumni Affair

In May 2001, a Moroccan imam from a mosque in Rotterdam, Khalil El-Moumni, expressed in a television interview that "homosexuality is harmful for society" and that "if the disease spreads into Dutch multicultural society, everyone can be infected." Although his remarks caused great moral commotion in society, and charges were brought against him, the imam was cleared of the charges on the basis of freedom of religion. It was the first time that a traditional Moroccan imam had given his opinion publicly, and El-Moumni soon came to exemplify the problematic relations between Muslims and non-Muslims in Dutch society, and in particular the problematic position of imams. Imam El-Moumni unintentionally paved the way for opinion-makers to state that Islam was antimodern and antidemocratic.

The El-Moumni affair provided the framework for the continuation of discussion about the relationship between the constitutionally guaranteed freedom of religion, freedom of expression, and the limits of tolerance. Key questions were duly re-evaluated, including the questions of whether freedom of religion should still take precedence over freedom of expression and how a liberal democracy should react towards oppression in the name of a religion.

Until the end of the 1990s, the motto associated with the formal integration policy had been that citizens should be able to "integrate while preserving one's own religious and cultural identity." With El-Moumni, however, the key question became: Should the normative definition of citizenship be redefined, if it turns out that the central values of "Muslims" collide with the central, hard-won values, norms, and rights of "the Dutch"? Further, what

---

6 For explanations of the image of imams in the public debate, see Shadid and Van Koningsveld, 1999, and Boender and Kanmaz, 2002.

does integration mean? Is it assimilation into the dominant culture, or participation as a citizen in all aspects of society while preserving one's (religious) identity? What should the state's role be in dealing with religious groups in general, and with Muslim communities in particular?

"Nova Imams"

The role played by imams in processes of (deviant) normative orientation again became apparent in June 2002. On the basis of secretly taped sermons that subsequently were broadcast on television, it appeared that five Salafi imams operating from Dutch mosques called for the destruction of U.S. President George Bush and Israeli Prime Minister Ariel Sharon, proclaimed that adulterous wives should be stoned, and approved of wives being slapped by their husbands. Public anxiety about these imams' influence over their audiences coincided with a strongly growing concern about the increasing radicalization of Muslim youth; recruitment for jihad in Kashmir, Afghanistan, and Chechnya; and alleged ties between al-Qaeda and mosques in the Netherlands. Through these antidemocratic and antiliberal statements, with their message derived from political Islam, these imams crossed the boundaries of the private religious sphere and propelled themselves into the center of general public debate.

Theo van Gogh

The polarization between Muslims and non-Muslims further increased following the murder of Theo van Gogh, a controversial filmmaker and publicist who spoke in crude terms against Islam as a religion and a culture. He had made a film about the abuse of women in the name of Islam. The film showed veiled women with lines from the Quran written on their bare skin. The murder suspect was a 26-year-old Muslim man of Moroccan descent, Mohammed B., who left a note on the deceased in which he threatened Europe with a war in the name of Islam. Following this murder, which took place on November 2, 2004, there were further questions posed about why and how young men like Mohammed B. feel attracted to radical and extremist views, where they acquire their knowledge, and which mosques and imams preach this form of radical thought. Moreover, the question of how other imams react to this trend towards radicalization, and what they can do to prevent its escalation, surfaced once again. What was particularly confusing for politicians, journalists, opinion-makers, and scholars, however, was that the murder suspect had grown up in the Netherlands, spoke Dutch fluently, and was not a regular visitor of any mosque in particular (although he had been spotted in one of the Salafi mosques in Amsterdam).

109

Political pressure to establish Dutch imam training increased when, shortly after the murder of Theo Van Gogh, a motion submitted by the Social Democrats, the Liberals, the Christian Democrats, and the Green Party was successfully adopted (Motie Bos c.s. 29 854, nt 10). In this motion, Parliament requested that the government stop issuing residence permits to imams as of 2008. In this manner mosques would be forced to recruit "homegrown" imams. A second motion urged the government to oblige imams to complete their training in the Netherlands.

In February 2005, the Free University in Amsterdam received a government subsidy to start a training course on spiritual caretaking. In its prospectus, the Free University does not indicate cooperation with Muslim organizations. The applications to establish imam training presented by Leiden University, Groningen University, and the University for Humanistics at Utrecht were not granted by the minister of education and the minister of alien affairs and integration. Leiden's application was not accepted because it proposed to admit only students who had completed extensive training in Islamic sciences in the Muslim world. One of the reasons behind Groningen's rejection was its isolated location. In reaction to the rejection of these universities' proposed courses of study, the main Sunni and Shi'a umbrella organizations (Contactorgaan Moslims en Overheid and Sjiietische Islamitische Raad) announced that they intend to establish their own imam training, but have not mentioned any possible cooperation with the IUR.

Young Muslims and the IUR

The University

The IUR's main aims are twofold: first, to be an academic institution that provides and deepens knowledge of Islam to Muslims living in Europe and in particular the Netherlands and, second, to inform non-Muslims about the religion and culture of the Islamic world on an academic level. The university has created an extensive study program in Islamic sciences such as Quran recitation, *tafsir*, hadith, and *fiqh*; theology; courses in sociology and comparative religion, Islam in the modern world and Islam in the Netherlands, and Christianity; and *ney* lessons (a Turkish flute). The IUR also provides intensive language courses in Arabic. There are three faculties within the IUR: the Faculty of Islamic Sciences, the Faculty of Languages and Civilizations, and the Faculty of Islamic Arts. Courses of study leading to a BA or an MA are offered. The MA consists of imam training and training for spiritual caretakers and includes a research component. The three PhD projects currently being completed are on Turkish imams in Dutch mosques and their opinions on modern religious matters; halal food; and Ottoman-Dutch historic relations. A fatwa commission has been installed, but is not yet active.

Although the university was founded by an interethnic group, after the split in 2001 from the Islamic University of Europe the IUR's orientation became decidedly Turkish, because the board consists of Turkish professors. However, the twenty-eight male teachers are in actuality quite diverse in both ethnic and "confessional" terms. As Sunni and Shi'a, they have received their training in the Muslim world at different Turkish universities, al-Azhar, the Islamic University of Medina, and Baghdad University. There are also a few non-Muslim Dutch teachers. The board never tires of stressing that "the IUR is not the spokesman of any particular Islamic religious sect or political/ideological party or any other group" and that "the IUR is truly committed not only to Islamic values and the cultural values of the Netherlands but also the principles of Dutch higher education" (Islamic University of Rotterdam [IUR] 2002, 76). In their teachings they do not follow one particular *madhhab* (Sunni law school) or one religious current. The languages of instruction are Arabic, English, and, increasingly, Dutch.

The 428-page study guide for 2003–2004, which outlines as many as 193 courses accompanied by extensive reading lists, illustrates their high ambitions. Critics argue that their ambitions are, in fact, unrealistically high. Another point of criticism is that they have called themselves a university. A number of reasons lie behind this decision: other Dutch colleges of higher education became universities in the 1970s; the IUR wishes to connect to the Dutch law on higher education; and the designation of university opens up connections in the Islamic world. Status and prestige are also key factors in their decision to call themselves a university.

There are many challenges to the university's ambitions. One is the enormous variety in the students' backgrounds and their existing qualifications. A second, very significant obstacle stems from the language deficiencies of both teachers and students. The university is "modestly satisfied with the students' linguistic and academic profile" (IUR 2002, 33). Both teachers' and students' language deficiencies in Dutch in particular, but also in Arabic, form a "weak point in the agenda of the university" (IUR 2002, 33). Other obstacles relate to the IUR's overall financial position, the teachers' salaries, and working conditions. As a private institution it has been financed thus far by subsidies (10 %), tuition fees (30 %), and donations from various private sources, most of whom are Turkish businessmen in the Netherlands, Germany, and Turkey (Tahaparij 2005).

The Students

According to the IUR, in 2005 there were 147 full-time students and 170 part-time students. In practice, there is a relatively large percentage of "drop-in, drop-out" students. There is also staggering variety in the backgrounds of the students. They vary widely in their linguistic, ethnic, and sociocultural backgrounds as well as in age; their former educational profiles and profi-

ciency outcomes are very diverse; and they have different educational attitudes and objectives (IUR 2002, 71). The male-to-female ratio is approximately 45 to 55.

Two main motivations to study at the IUR can be identified. The first
group is formed by young, postmigrant students who are searching for
knowledge of Islam through a critical examination of the religious sources,
independent of parents and the imam. They are guided by the Islamic pre-
scription to learn as much as possible about one's religion during one's entire
life. Mehmet, Fatma, and Emine belong to this first group.[7] Mehmet was born
in the Netherlands in 1971, completed a PhD in physics at a Dutch university,
and is currently unemployed. For him, study at the IUR is not only a good
way to fill his time between jobs. More important, he started at the IUR after
completing several years of Arabic lessons with an imam in Utrecht.

"The reason I came here was that I just wanted to learn the source of Islam better. I
wanted to know why we do things the way we do them. So, to learn the real source,
to be able to hold on better to the faith. Because I am a practicing Muslim. So much
is said in society, by Muslims. And so much is based on false information. Thus, I
thought this might be a good opportunity to get things clear, to list all the
points." (Mehmet)

This personal search for knowledge about "real Islam," aimed mostly at the
enrichment of personal knowledge, was also a priority for Fatma (born in
Turkey in 1969, migrated in 1970) and Emine (born in Turkey in 1960,
migrated in 1986). They are both inspired by the teachings of Said Nursi, and
both followed a few years of Islamic high school, *imam-hatip-lisesi,* in
Turkey.

Not only at the IUR, but in Dutch society as a whole, young believing
Muslims express a great need to acquire a substantial knowledge of their
religion. With this knowledge they try to legitimate, in a religious manner,
their particular way of living. Apart from searching for the spiritual values of
Islam, they are eager to find information about Islamic norms, about what is
halal and *haram* and everything in between. In their interethnic meetings in
non-Islamic, secular society, they are confronted with the singularities of their
parents' religious practices. In providing answers about such practices, they
differentiate between what they call "real Islam" and "cultural Islam." As
Emine explained, "the problem is that Muslims are different here. They say
'this is Islam,' but it is not Islam. Their behavior is a result of their culture,
not Islam. [...] The university must provide information and be very active."

---

7   In order to ensure confidentiality, I have used pseudonyms for the students. The
    interviews referred to throughout this chapter took place in September and Octo-
    ber of 2003 as part of my PhD research. I visited the IUR approximately fifteen
    times between September 2003 and November 2004, attending seminars and
    openings of the academic year, and speaking with the rector, the vice rector, the
    secretary general, and several teachers.

This stress on defining what is "real Islam" helps to dispel interethnic differences in the interpretation of Islam. By emphasizing "real Islam," Muslim youth also hope to clear the barriers that exist between their parents' world and their own.

"Our parents were satisfied with a brief explanation about how something should be done. We, the youngsters, are educated at school to ask questions like, 'Why or why not?' We are more curious. And we have learned to think in a certain manner. I used to ask my mother about the reason behind something like, 'Why can't we see God?' And then she reacted with 'Oh, you should not even ask that!' But I was always looking for reasons. That was the beginning of a search for my own identity, while I was already Muslim. With us it is: From birth you are Muslim and after that as well, but you only learn from your own initiative what Islam means exactly. One's parents think: We have taught them enough, as we have sent them to the mosque. But that is not enough. For me, that has been the reason to study here at the IUR." (Fatma)

At school, young people have learned to critically discuss the material and subjects that are taught. They thus treat religion differently than their parents do. This difference is also evident in the changing attitude towards imams in the local mosque. Language is not the only barrier that exists, for the way in which an imam communicates his views to the young is clearly also important. Young people want to know the background to certain norms. They regard such knowledge as a modern way of explaining Islam. A recurring criticism of imams and other classical authorities is that they only speak of what is allowed or forbidden, without explaining the reasons behind these norms and rules.

However, throughout this process, which is visible in other European countries as well, the second and third generations are left to find their own resources. Indeed, those resources are very limited, because they often do not possess the key to the sources of Islam: a knowledge of Arabic. The youngsters often have strikingly limited tools and insight into the historical traditions of interpretation and religious currents. For many, the Internet has become a major source of information. As a Muslim initiative, the IUR can be regarded as a response to young people's needs.[8] Not surprisingly, many students are still at a preliminary stage of training. These students are very eager to learn Arabic, a language that enables them to study the sources for themselves. As Fatma pointed out, "the teacher must communicate the contents of the Quran and hadith to me. However, he should not interpret it himself. I'll do that. I'll find it out myself."

In this quotation we see how Fatma aspires to obtain intellectual autonomy in moral and spiritual matters. Furthermore, through knowledge of "real Islam," young Muslims can defend their religion in a seemingly hostile environment. "It is not Islam that is wrong, it is just that Muslims sometimes give the wrong image," is an oft-heard explanation given by young believing

---

8   Other Muslim responses to this need are the aforementioned Islamic University of Europe and Dar-al-Ilm, which provides short courses on Islam in Dutch.

Muslims. For Emine, this is one of the reasons she studies at the IUR: "I would like to see the Dutch and the Muslim communities cooperate, reaching out for each other's hands. I want to change the ideas of people who equate Islam with terrorism. I would really like to change that idea."

The second of the two groups consists of students who migrated at a later age, due to circumstances of family formation and reunion or because they were asylum seekers. Members of this group see it as a logical, and often as the only possible, step to continue the education that they began in their Islamic country of origin. Hawa (born in Syria in 1958) studied at Damascus University and worked as an English teacher in Syria. She greatly regrets that her work experience is not valued in the Netherlands. Since her arrival in the Netherlands, she has undertaken voluntary work in a Dutch home for the elderly, but was unable to continue there due to language barriers. She has now found part-time work at the mail distribution office and also teaches Arabic to Dutch individuals. "I have time; I have no full-time job," she explains. "I can study here and perhaps get a job in the future. That is my objective. And besides that, there are some people, not all, who think, 'Islam equals the headscarf.' But Islam is more, Islam is deeper than that."

Mohammed, born in Morocco in 1975, migrated in 2001 and is now in his final year of studies. Having studied theology at Qarawiyyin, Tétouan, Mohammed was able to skip several years of study upon his enrollment at the IUR. Although he speaks Dutch reasonably well, study at the IUR presented him with a good opportunity to receive a higher education. He hopes it will enable him to pursue an MA at a Dutch university. For students like Mohammed and Hawa, who have a language deficiency in Dutch and sometimes in English as well, the IUR may provide the only opportunity to receive a higher education, although the university's policy is to focus increasingly on becoming a Dutch-speaking institution.

New Religious Discourse

In his 1996 book, Felice Dassetto predicted that the leadership of the Muslim community would be transferred from first-generation Muslims to the second generation, newcomers, and converts. Furthermore, he foresaw a passage of leadership from the local to the national level, to which we can now add, as a further step, the transnational level (Roy 2003). Dassetto was forced to leave open the question of whether the new Islamic centers—which "a bit pompously call themselves 'universities'"—would be among those to produce these new leaders (1996, 158). His question can now be directed to the IUR, but cannot yet be answered. The ambition to contribute to the building of an elite is indeed expressed by the IUR's board. Concrete examples of contributions to the Dutch public debate are the seminars and lectures organized by the IUR over the past years. Topics covered during these seminars and lectures include interreligious dialogue, honor killings, female circumcision, and Islam and democracy. IUR professors outlined the different points of view in relation to these issues from the perspective of various schools of law (including the Shi'a Jafari school). These seminars were attended not only by IUR students but also by Dutch representatives from social organizations. Referring to the conference on female circumcision held in December 2003, Edien Bartels remarked that

"this conference at the Islamic University of Rotterdam was particularly significant. Muslims in the Netherlands that fall under Islamic schools of religious law in which circumcision of girls is not addressed—and who have actually never been involved in circumcising girls and reject the practice—are nevertheless trying to be clear about the rejection of this custom from the Islamic point of view. In so doing, they are taking responsibility for each other. Discussion is now underway about the development of a 'Dutch' Islam." (Bartels 2004, 397)

Through these seminars, the IUR provides normative information about the compatibility of Islam and the West.

The IUR's students take up a modest position: they regard their knowledge as still rather limited and not authoritative. Male and female students often are active in small, local discussion groups, women's associations, and peer groups, and they spread their knowledge through these groups. Some provide lessons for children and teenagers, with male students concentrating on communicating with other males, females with females, and both genders with younger children. One of the few Dutch-speaking Muslim lecturers, a young man of Pakistani origin who speaks at debates on Islam organized by Muslim student associations, also followed the lectures at the IUR.

Although their influence is mostly limited, the formation of a group of educated individuals with a strong Muslim identity will have an impact on the strengthening of Muslim identity at the community level. According to the interviewees, this process of strengthening religious identity and engagement as a citizen should take place not only start in the university but also in the family, in local Muslim organizations, and in mosques. But the university, as Mehmet points out, can play a special role in this process: "What I see is an estrangement from Islam. And I am pessimistic if that increases, for the Netherlands, for Islam. Little by little, people move away from Islam. Maybe the university can play a role in changing that process, I don't know." According to Mehmet, a reinforcement of identity promoted by the IUR might help to stop the secularization process taking place among young people who are loosening their ties to their original home countries and thus losing their religious and moral "nourishment."

Hawa, on the other hand, describes how she sees the Islamic university fitting into modern life, maintaining that it is important precisely because it offers the individual believer the opportunity to choose between options. "I think that the Islamic university fits well into modern life. It is not conservative. It accepts all people. It does not look at what is the *madhhab*, what is

115

Sunni, what is Shi'a. Many teachers here are Sh'ia and many are Sunni ... That is good: choose what you like."

Could we consequently say that the IUR is an educational institution that strengthens individualization by offering a place for students to gain intellectual and spiritual autonomy? Or does it offer a counterweight against the individualization and strong bricolage of believing youngsters' religious practices? It does both. As I have shown, the main motivations to study at the IUR fit with the tendency towards individualization in the former sense. But the IUR also offers a counterweight against individual bricolage, since it stimulates its students to study the *usul al-fiqh*, the sources of Islamic law, instead of being satisfied with a "copy-paste Islam," individually constructed from the Internet and (translated) books.

In response to a question about his understanding of the role played by the IUR, Mohammed answered:

"If someone comes here who is bad, but wants to find the way back to Allah, he does not go to this university. He goes to people who are a bit extremist or radical. They provide other things to him, things which are not in Islam, you see. And then he and they become more evil. But if it is someone who wants to know Islam well, he comes to this university, where there is an academic level and where people analyze things, who proceed with time and know what is correct and what is not. If they come here, they learn the right Islam and they can help other people outside. Then they can get good jobs, such as spiritual caretaking." (Mohammed)

Mohammed has distinguished for himself between "true" and "false" Islam, and it is clear that he believes the IUR provides him with access to greater knowledge about the former.

Conflicting Expectations

On the one hand, the IUR tries to make use of the legal remnants of the pillar system referred to above, as well as the importance placed in the constitution on the equality of religious and philosophical groups. It should be noted that I am not arguing that this emancipatory process is similar to that experienced by the Catholics and the Protestants as they negotiated the Dutch pillar system of the twentieth century. The ethnic and religious backgrounds of the Muslim communities are heterogeneous, and consequently the internal power dynamics are characterized by division and struggle. The economic, social, and political position of Muslims is weak, and the support from Muslim organizations of the IUR is in essence extremely limited. Some of the Turkish teachers and students are inspired by the teachings of Said Nursi, and the perception of being Nurcu, or Fethullah Gülen, is a considerable hindrance to becoming accepted as an authority by other Muslim organizations, whether of Turkish or non-Turkish origin. In addition to these factors, the split giving birth to two separate Islamic universities (the IUR and the Islamic University of Europe) further complicates the situation. The relevant question is whether IUR graduates will be accepted as imams if the IUR is not supported by the umbrella organizations and the individual mosque boards.

On the other hand, the IUR makes use of the opportunities that arise in the debates on the creation of imam training, presenting itself as in the race to be an appointed provider of imam training both to the ministries of education and of alien affairs and integration and to the relevant Muslim umbrella organizations. Although imam training as such is not its central focus, it is in the IUR's interest to emphasize that it can provide the imam training currently in demand. Indeed, it has applied for a "starters' subsidy" in order to expand its present imam training facilities.

This potential opportunity created by demand raises the question of whether the IUR should focus primarily on the study of Islam or on imam training. The students' descriptions of their main motivations to study at the IUR make clear that the institution answers their need for the study of Islam. The IUR is a place where people can learn to develop their knowledge autonomously, independent of the imam. According to my research, there are only a handful of students following the imam training course specifically. Women are not interested in imam training, as this is a male domain.[9] Mehmet and Mohammed were not interested in obtaining a position as formal imams at a Dutch mosque, and provided several reasons for this decision. First, they do not believe that imams are best positioned to change society. Second, they do not want to be cornered between the mosque board and the believers who come to the imam, twenty-four hours a day, with their personal problems. Third, the financial standing of an imam is very low, given that the mosque community is responsible for raising the funds to cover his salary. In addition to these points, Mehmet and Mohammed do not consider the mosque to be the only location from which one can change things and reach people. Not only among the respondents, but also among higher educated Muslim youth in general, I have failed to detect much enthusiasm for the profession of imam. It is possible, however, that individuals did not consider it appropriate to indicate that they do in fact wish to become an imam, as such a claim could be perceived as awarding themselves religious authority in advance.

Many of the IUR's problems are related to the fact that the university is not yet recognized and thus not financed by the state. The students hope that the institution will soon acquire a recognized status, and this hope is often connected to their financial position, as Fatma explains: "Since it is not recognized, there are not many students. Everyone must work: how could you otherwise afford it?"

The students also expect that if the IUR is recognized, they will be taken seriously as Muslims, and be able, Mohammed pointed out, "to contribute to the position of Muslims in the Netherlands." According to Mehmet, this will be possible "because people will be able to find a job which has to do with

---

9   This fact seems to be inadequately taken into account in the public debate on imam training.

Islam, like spiritual caretaker, teacher, or imam." "If we are recognized," Mohammed explained, "people will have to take our opinions into account. They must look at our theses, at what subjects we studied, at who we are. Then we can show that the university brings something that does not yet exist: imams." Their position as citizens would change, leading to their inclusion in the normative framework of Dutch citizenship.

Limited Elbowroom

Despite the aforementioned successful public seminars held over the past years, the IUR's elbowroom in the Dutch sociopolitical context seems to be rather limited. This became clear when the newly appointed rector, Professor Ahmed Akgündüz, explained in a newspaper interview that the prescriptions of the Quran and Sunna will remain valid forever. In the interview, he gave the following examples: a Muslim woman is not permitted to marry a non-Muslim man; a Muslim daughter receives half of the inheritance that a son receives; and a Muslim husband is allowed to slap his wife—provided that the woman is responsible for the marital conflict, that the man is unable to make her see reason in other ways, and that slapping will not physically harm her (Trouw, November 7, 2000). The headline "Rector IUR: You May Hit Your Wife, but not Regularly" caused moral commotion. Reactions came from all directions, including Parliament; some Muslim organizations, which took the opportunity to express their distrust towards the IUR; and the IUR itself. The former rector, Süleyman Damra, who is familiar with the Dutch language and Dutch sensitivities, tried to make the best of it by ensuring that the "alma mater advocates an Islam that fits into liberal Holland" (Trouw, November 8, 2000). Several specialists on Islam stated that the declaration of the un-changeability of the Quran and Sunna showed the rector's conservative, orthodox attitude, and would alienate him from the generation of young Muslims who are looking for flexible and liberal outlooks on Islam (e.g., Leila Jordens in Trouw, November 9, 2000).

Since this incident, the IUR has been reluctant to comment on "hot" social issues when there is a conflict between Dutch and Islamic norms and values.[10]

---

10 This does not mean that they do not give any public reactions. They have issued press releases on the following: Ayaan Hirsi Ali (January 27, 2003); the announcement of the vision and mission book (June 19, 2002); Dutch Islamic schools and relations with fundamentalist movements (February 25, 2002); information on Id al-Adha (February 22, 2002; in English); statements made by Pim Fortuyn (February 11, 2002); information on Ramadan (November 16, 2001; in English); the announcement of the project "Imams: Conditions and Functions" (November 5, 2001; in English); "A Terrorist Cannot Be a Muslim, Nor Can a True Muslim Be a Terrorist" (September 13, 2001; in English); the opening of the fourth academic year and announcement of the new board (September 3, 2001). See the university's Web site: www.islamicuniversity.nl (January 2004).

In their reactions to the El-Moumni affair (e.g., in a television interview by a group of older male students; Nova, May 17, 2001), they condemned homosexual *deeds* as being against Islam. However, the IUR's board realized that a condemnation of homosexuality itself would cause a great deal of resistance from society at large and would only further discredit the university's position as a liberal Islamic institution. Since the El-Moumni affair, an individual's position on the issue of homosexuality has become a symbolic criterion for one's integration as a Muslim. An official IUR statement on homosexuality would only have gained acceptance in wider society if it contained some form of disagreement with El-Moumni's statements and a permission of both homosexuality and homosexual deeds on Islamic grounds.

"Real" Islam or "Dutch" Islam?

In the public debate on Islam and on imam training, some people seriously question whether Islam can function as an emancipatory force in the context of present-day Dutch society.[11] According to this view, Islamic culture is backward, antidemocratic, and nourished by the political ideologies of Muslim countries, particularly by Wahhabi Islam. This construction of the Muslim as "the other," which began in colonial times, intensified in the 1990s and became even stronger after 9/11. As elsewhere in Europe, in the Netherlands "questions increasingly concentrate on issues regarding 'real' and 'good' Islam as opposed to supposedly less constructive readings of Islam" (Douwes 2003, 4).

The students interviewed in the course of my research appear to be aware of this tension and discuss relevant issues accordingly. What should the rector have done, in their opinion? Hold firm to his explanations and beliefs, or change his opinion under pressure from dominant society? "If he had done the latter, I would consider that weak of him," Fatma stressed. "But you must show society that the values are similar, but that the norms can be different sometimes. That is dialogue, isn't it, that we recognize that."

Mehmet referred to the IUR's task of bringing back Muslims who have strayed too far from the sources. According to him, some Muslim spokesmen are too flexible in their interpretations of Islam. He doubts "if the IUR can say that formally, I don't know, because you can burn your fingers on it," and continued by mentioning the incident with the rector's statement and the commotion that it evoked. He stressed, however, that while Muslims must live according to Dutch laws, a Muslim cannot ignore or modify the shari'a itself, even if the two are conflicting.

---

11 In 1991, the liberal politician Frits Bolkestein was one of the first politicians to express his doubts about the compatibility of Islam and the West (see Douwes, De Koning, and Boender 2005).

"One must think, we live in a non-Islamic country. And Islam is what it is. You must accept it the way it is. Being Muslim, you cannot adopt the Islamic shari'a in the Netherlands. But you should not say that the shari'a is different from what it is. You must take it as it is. And then you must just live according to the laws in the Netherlands. But whatever conflicts with the Dutch, or Western culture, those things are being treated as primitive. I think that is a bit nasty. Then you cannot have an open discussion and people won't say what they really think. Then you do not have transparency. That is a bit what is happening now."

This excerpt shows that Mehmet realizes that when one acknowledges this constraint, one cannot easily enter the public debate. The way Islam really is should not be changed under pressure from the outside. He summarized his concerns as follows:

"I think that the Dutch government wants Islam to adapt to the norms and values of Dutch society. And if the IUR is recognized, it will only be in that sense, I think. Only if the university fully adapts itself, only then it will be recognized, I think. No sooner than that. And then it won't be totally independent, I reckon."

If they enter the public debate and adapt to the Dutch context, they may be obliged to make concessions on what they consider to be "real Islam." It appears that the IUR "is caught in the dilemma of being recognised as a legitimate minority culture, while escaping the predicament of being a minority to watch and monitor, continuously needing to prove its loyalty" (Salvatore 2004, 1027).

Concluding Remarks

The IUR is involved in a process of acquiring autonomous religious space for both socioreligious life and participation in the normative affairs of wider society. This process is contentious (Salvatore 2004). Much can be said about the opportunities and obstacles it has met on the "road to coexistence," a path that rector Akgündüz describes as "something of a minefield."[12] Through collective action, the IUR has attempted to use existing legal and constitutional opportunities granting equal rights to every religious group. As part of a religious minority, it wishes to manifest itself in a certain way in society. In this process, it claims a right to establish an educational institution as a means to practice its right to religious expression. At the same time, emancipation also means that one is entitled to claim one's religious identity, in confrontation with the dominant society, in order to acquire a place in the public realm.

It has been my intention to show the connection between the establishment of the IUR and the public debate on imam training. The government is searching for Muslim representatives and is focusing in this process on the

---

12 From Rector Akgündüz's speech at the opening of the academic year in September 2003.

building of a new generation of homegrown imams. For the IUR, this quest for new imams is a way to access the public realm. However, the imam training debate is structured by the government's expectations of what a Dutch imam should be and do. These expectations appear to be difficult to fulfill. Through my interviews with several male and female students, I have identified the main constraints at present. First, the students, particularly the women, do not seem to be interested in becoming imams in a local mosque, and, second, the students have constructed a clear picture of what they regard as "real" or "authentic" Islam. However, they are aware that what they say in public affects the way in which Muslims are perceived in the public sphere. To be fully recognized as contributors in the normative debate on Dutch citizenship, the IUR must not only fulfill certain objective legal criteria but also convince society at large that "their Islam" can be "trusted."

References

Adviescommissie Imamopleidingen. 2003. Imams in Nederland: wie leidt ze op? Rapport van de Adviescommissie Imamopleidingen. The Hague: Ministerie van Onderwijs, Cultuur en Wetenschap.

Amiraux, V. 2000. Jeunes musulmanes turques d'Allemagne: Voix et voies de l'individuation. In Paroles d'islam. Individus, sociétés et discours dans l'islam européen contemporain/Islamic words: Individuals, societies and discourse in contemporary European Islam, ed. F. Dassetto, 101–123. Paris: Maisonneuve et Larose.

Amir-Moazami, S. 2001. Hybridity and anti-hybridity: The Islamic headscarf and its opponents in the French public sphere. In Muslim traditions and modern techniques of power (Yearbook of the Sociology of Islam 3), ed. A. Salvatore, 309–329. Piscataway, NJ: Transaction.

Bartels, E. 2004. Female circumcision among immigrant Muslim communities: Public debate in the Netherlands. Journal of Muslim Minority Affairs 2 (2): 393–399.

Boender, W., and M. Kanmaz. 2002. Imams in the Netherlands and Islam teachers in Flanders. In Intercultural relations and religious authorities: Muslims in the European Union, ed. W. A. R. Shadid and P. S. van Koningsveld, 169–180. Leuven, Belgium: Peeters.

Casanova, J. 1994. Public religions in the modern world. Chicago: University of Chicago Press.

Dassetto, F. 1996. La construction de l'islam Européen; approche socio-anthropologique. Paris: l'Harmattan.

Douwes, D. 2003. Editorial. ISIM Newsletter 13:4.

Douwes, D., M. de Koning, and W. Boender, ed. 2005. Nederlandse moslims. Van migrant tot burger. Amsterdam: Amsterdam University Press/Salomé.

Hirsch Ballin, E. 1988. Overheid, godsdienst en levensovertuiging; eindrapport van de commissie van advies inzake de criteria voor steunverlening aan kerkgenootschappen en andere genootschappen op geestelijke grondslag. The Hague: Ministerie van Binnenlandse Zaken.

Integratiebeleid. 1998. Nota van de minister van Binnenlandse Zaken en staatssecretaris Netelenbos van Onderwijs, Cultuur en Wetenschappen, Het integratiebeleid betreffende etnische minderheden in relatie tot hun geestelijke bedienaren. The Hague: Ministerie van Binnenlandse Zaken.

Islamic University of Rotterdam (IUR). 2002. The Islamic University of Rotterdam into the third millennium. Rotterdam: IUR.

Karagül, A., and K. Wagtendonk. 1994. De Imâms. Hun taak, hun functie en hun opleiding. The Hague: Islamitische Raad Nederland.

Landman, N. 1992. Van mat tot minaret. Amsterdam: VU uitgeverij.

Lesthaeghe, R., ed. 2000. Communities and generations: Turkish and Moroccan populations in Belgium. Brussels: VUB University Press.

Minderhedennota. 1983. Tweede Kamer, zitting 1982–1983, 16102 nrs 20–21. The Hague: Ministerie van Binnenlandse Zaken.

Rath, J., R. Penninx, K. Groenendijk, and A. Meijer. 1996. Nederland en zijn Islam. Een ontzuilende samenleving reageert op het ontstaan van een geloofsgemeenschap. Amsterdam: Het Spinhuis.

Roy, O. 2000. L'individualisation dans l'islam européen contemporain. In Paroles d'islam. Individus, sociétés et discours dans l'islam européen contemporain/Islamic words: Individuals, societies and discourse in contemporary European Islam, ed. F. Dassetto, 69–84. Paris: Maisonneuve et Larose.

———. 2003. De globalisering van de Islam [L'Islam mondialisé]. Amsterdam: Van Gennep.

Salvatore, A. 2004. Making public space: Opportunities and limits of collective action among Muslims in Europe. Journal of Ethnic and Migration Studies 30 (5): 1013–1031.

Shadid, W. A. R., and P. S. van Koningsveld. 1997. Moslims in Nederland. Minderheden en religie in een multiculturele samenleving. Houten, the Netherlands: Bohn, Stafleu, Van Loghum.

———. 1999. Beeldvorming over de imam in Nederland. In Religie, cultuur en minderheden. Historische en maatschappelijke aspecten van beeldvorming, ed. W. A. R. Shadid and P. S. van Koningsveld, 55–77. Tilburg, the Netherlands: Tilburg University Press.

Soysal, Y. N. 1997. Changing parameters of citizenship and claims-making: Organized Islam in European public spheres. Theory and Society 26:509–527.

Tahaparij, H. 2005. Islamitische universiteit zoekt de weg naar de dialoog. Op weg naar erkenning. Erasmus Magazine, March 1. http://erasmus magazine.nl/default.aspx?artID=1212.

Vertovec, S., and A. Rogers, eds. 1998. Muslim European youth: Reproducing ethnicity, religion, culture. Aldershot, UK: Ashgate.

Waardenburg, J. 2000. Normative Islam in Europe. In Paroles d'islam. Individus, sociétés et discours dans l'islam européen contemporain/Islamic words: Individuals, societies and discourse in contemporary European Islam, ed. F. Dassetto, 49–68. Paris: Maisonneuve et Larose.

Gerdien Jonker

ISLAMIST OR PIETIST?
MUSLIM RESPONSES TO THE GERMAN
SECURITY FRAMEWORK

Is German society ready to digest religious "offerings" (*da'wa*) that aim at solving its problems from a Muslim point of view? Can it recognize these for what they are? Or has the distinction between religion and politics now become a "no-go area" in this time of international terrorist threat? In this contribution, I cross-reference the political discourse in Germany *on* Muslims with the religious discourse *in* different Muslim communities. Between these two worlds there exists a remarkable asymmetry that can be conveyed through two observations: First, policymakers consider the phenomenon of Muslim terrorists to be a consequence of the Islamic religious tradition and to be part of Muslim identity. The majority of Muslims in Germany have furiously denied this imputation. Second, policymakers demand answers from the Muslim communities that could help to enforce security. These Muslim communities have not responded in a direct way, but instead have resorted to issues of religious conduct and ethics.

Since the attacks on New York and Washington, an alternating current exists between policymakers and Muslim communities in Germany. The former responded to imminent threat with security measures that took all Muslims in Germany into consideration. The latter denied the perpetrators the right to call themselves Muslims and protested that the security measures were unjust because they focused on the wrong actors. It is my argument that the resultant interaction took the form of a process of translation. Muslim communities rendered political signals into religious ones, and policymakers (re-)translated religious gestures and other expressions into the language of politics. In the highly sensitive climate that currently surrounds Muslims and Islam, the borders between religion and politics are being redefined. Some hundred years ago, Max Weber pointed out the basic tensions between politics and religion. The question now is how, in the present situation, this tension is given shape.

To outline the scope of these tensions I focused on two Turkish religious communities. One is the Jamaatunnur, a pious Sufi lay community that embraces a politics of improving European society through the reformulation of Muslim conduct as a universal value. The other is the Islamic Community of Milli Görüş, an Islamist organization that tries to realize its social concerns through legal and political claims-making (see also the chapter by Gökçe Yurdakul in this volume).

Several reasons back up this choice. A focus on Turkish communities that settled down in the 1960s and look back on a history of some forty years allowed me to weigh continuity against change. It also enabled me to depict the religious framework and to lay out the diversity of religious propositions that respond, however indirectly, to the pressure and demands from outside the community. The choice of two Turkish rather than, for instance, two Arabic communities is not haphazard. Muslim organizations in Germany are dominated by Turks (75 %) and characterized by an intense struggle between laic and religiously organized Turks, on the one hand, and between (Turkish) state-controlled and independent religious organizations, on the other.

The two communities have in common that they organize independently of the Turkish state and over the last thirty years have developed their own Western European profile. For that reason they are attractive to young Turks. The anguish that laic Turks in Germany experience vis-à-vis their religious compatriots accounts for the fact that religious Turks attract negative attention more readily than do Muslims in other religious organizations.

Both Milli Görüş and Jamaatunnur members shape their personal conduct with the help of shari'a rules and regulations. What they share is the attempt to consolidate strict religious conduct while observing the German constitution, for example by holding on to gender segregation and the covering of women—to mention only the most visible aspects of a social order based on shari'a. However, Jamaatunnur translates the keyword of Muslim religious participation, jihad, into a process of inner discovery and a culture of ascetic religious conduct, whereas Milli Görüş translates this keyword into political engagement. Due to these different aims, the two differ dramatically in the way they make their entrance on the public stage. Jamaatunnur opts for a religious politics that aims at the implementation of Muslim ethics and addresses colleagues, neighbors, and the workplace. Milli Görüş opts for a religious politics that aims at political change and addresses actors in the legal and political spheres. Their different politics have made Jamaatunnur almost imperceptible. By contrast, they have rendered Milli Görüş glaringly visible.

The interaction between policymakers and Muslim communities will be set against the backdrop of the violent events that, over the last few years, have influenced the public perception of Muslims and "Islam." Focusing on Germany, I first recount the particular scenario in which young Arab students in Hamburg planned "the legitimate defense" of the Islamic moral and legal order, which culminated in the massacre of 9/11. I then outline the German political reaction that introduced a new discourse on Islam. The bulk of this chapter then describes the different strategies with which young people in the Islamic Community of Milli Görüş and in Jamaatunnur presently counteract both policymakers and jihadis. Finally, I sum up the reciprocities between terrorism, political pressure, and the recent changes in the two communities and draw a number of conclusions. These conclusions touch upon internal differentiation and the tension between religion and politics, the diversity of Muslim views on the "secular world," and the task that young Muslims have set for themselves.

Several questions helped me to select my material and to think through the details of my narrative. For example, what do young believers do when they represent a religious tradition which, in another corner of the world than they happen to be in, sanctions and generates violence? How do they measure the distance? How do they advance their own religious vision? Which *voices* become audible? Which *faces* represent the promotion of the religious vision? Who opts for what, and why?

Jihad as "Legitimate Defense"

The German scholar of religious studies Hans G. Kippenberg recently advanced the theory that free global markets diminish the power of the nation-state and stimulate new forms of religious solidarity (Kippenberg 2005; Kippenberg and Seidensticker 2004, 85). Islamic organizations such as Muslim Brothers, Hezbollah, Hamas, and al-Qaeda must be viewed as outcomes of this development. Combining a high level of solidarity with the inside—even the willingness to sacrifice oneself for one's community—with a rigorous and violent policy of separation from the outside, these organizations regard violence as a necessary form of defense that is supported by the Quran and a long political history (Krämer 2005; Malik 2005)[1] In their particular worldview, non-Islamic values and norms presently beleaguer the Islamic world: a threatening situation resembling the *jahiliyya* of the time of the Prophet has arisen. Therefore, they have taken it upon themselves to "free" Islamic norms and values. This scenario also legitimized the attacks on New York and Washington. The documents that the perpetrators left behind prove beyond a doubt, Kippenberg argues, that the attacks were religiously motivated.

His analysis is based on the contents of the so-called spiritual manual, a document that was found in the luggage of the perpetrators and that apparently guided them through the different stages of preparation. The text makes abundantly clear that the attacks were considered a *ghazwa,* a "raid," and were staged as a meticulous imitation of the historical raid that Muhammad once fought at Badr. Without ever mentioning the deed itself, the stages that led to its performance were embedded in asceticism. They involved purity of

---

1 Jihad means "effort on the road to God." The Quran uses the term thirty-five times, twice with the meaning of "peaceful struggle" and twenty-nine times as "warfare." Beginning in the eleventh century, the Sufi tradition gave the term the spiritual dimension of "inner struggle, inner growth" (Malik 2005). The history of Islamic political governance is rich with examples in which the concept of jihad is used as a political instrument to justify military attacks, predominantly against "unbelievers" (Krämer 2005).

intention, worldly denial, sincerity, and the high consciousness of ritual re-enactment, ritual cleansing, fasting, and the constant recitation of prayers. The instructions were designed to turn "ordinary young Muslims into warriors and martyrs" (Kippenberg 2005, 30), convinced of the need to perform a legitimate jihad, a military act for the benefit of the Muslim community. In accordance with this logic, the young men were to neither feel hatred nor turn their raid into an act of personal vengeance. Rather, their role was to be that of the seclusive executor, soberly performing a painful but necessary deed. The result of this painstaking preparation was that, on the morning of September 11, seventeen young men simultaneously boarded three planes in Boston in order to in all probability cut the throats of the flight personnel and to aim themselves as flying bombs at their targets, causing the death of some thirty-five hundred people. The careful instructions in the "spiritual manual" indicate that the ascetic preparation was not simple embellishment but a central component of the perpetrators' activities. Their aim was to turn the massacre into an act of worship (Kippenberg 2004; Scheffler 2004).

Although in the course of 2002 it was firmly established that, of the 3.2 million Muslims in Germany, fewer than three hundred were in some way or another involved in the al-Qaeda network, the perpetrators conferred a terrible heritage on the remaining Muslims. Their response took the form of the asymmetry that is the subject of the following pages.

Political Perceptions

On Tuesday, September 11, 2001, when the planes crashed into the twin towers in New York City and the media images of their collapse caused a global chain of reactions, a sequence of events also was set off in Germany. It pushed the political perception of who Muslims are and what they stand for in the direction of security. Observers were quick to notice that the change in perception caused "a general suspicion of Islam."[2] However, it was not the suspicion but the acute interest that was new. A climate of mutual indifference had characterized the relations between Muslims and non-Muslims in Germany. German policymakers took no great interest in migrant groups and for a long time did not attempt to integrate them. Most scientific studies in the field of Islam concentrated on historical and philological research. Whenever media attention turned to the Muslim world, it employed the old binary construction of "Oriental (Muslim) culture" versus "Western enlightenment" (Rotter 1992).[3] For their part, Turkish and other Muslim migrants did not take much interest in their host country. Most of the migrants came from rural

---

2   Matthias Geis, "Vom Gastarbeiter zum Schläfer," *Die Zeit*, April 15, 2004; "Eine Religion unter Verdacht," *Stern*, April 8, 2004.

3   In 1992, the German Islam specialist Gernot Rotter (1992) analyzed the way in which the media, with the help of the Middle East "specialist" Rainer Konzelmann, produced distorted images of the Islamic world.

areas and had had very little education; they had to struggle to make a living in Germany and, for the most part, were content to live their lives according to their own rules. In terms of visibility, neither German society nor Muslim migrants took much notice of each other.

This state of affairs changed radically after 9/11. The absence of reliable data—for instance on the number of organized Muslims or the way they were represented—caused an information vacuum. Yet information was the first commodity that policymakers were in need of. As long as this vacuum existed, it caused a structural uncertainty that had to be dealt with. Speculations and suspicions emerged as the natural mechanisms to fill the gap. They offered, at least, answers in a situation in which previously no questions had been asked.

Actual information on Muslims in Germany was also substituted by the stream of information on violence, mismanagement, and terrorism in the Islamic world. Together with the media coverage of the actions of terrorist organizations, this indeed conveyed a threatening picture of Muslims and their religious traditions. Through this change of perspective, Muslims in Germany, who for so long had remained invisible, were suddenly set in a blazing light. Having allowed them to develop religious structures in Europe was soon judged to be "a deadly tolerance."[4] Consequently, Islam became "a religion under suspicion."[5] With each attack on the global stage, fear of the three million Muslims in Germany grew.

Rabei Osman Sayed Ahmed, the Egyptian who is said to have been responsible for the "raid" in Madrid on March 11, 2004, accurately identified that fear and used it in the global battle on Islamic visibility. In a telephone call to a young recruit shortly before the deed, he toyed with its more worldly options:

"We are migrants of God. We believe in God and [therefore] everything is permitted to us, also that we marry Christian women, because the papers are useful. We have to be present everywhere, in Germany, in Holland, in London. We dominate Europe with our presence. The women find us the necessary documents because we represent God's business." (lead article, *Frankfurter Allgemeine Zeitung*, March 18, 2004)

This is not the voice of asceticism. Rather, the speaker shrewdly mixes the religious and the political realm. In his narrative, "migrants" become divine messengers: "migrants of God" who are freed from legal forces and given religious authority instead, through which "everything is permitted." The mixture of religion and political claims-making encourages deception: "we marry Christian women" as a means to reach the ultimate goal, to "dominate Europe with our presence." The mass murder in Madrid which followed one

---

4 Mechtild Küpper, "Worte zum Opferfest," *Frankfurter Allgemeine Zeitung*, January 23, 2005; "Eine Religion unter Verdacht," *Stern*, April 8, 2004.

5 "Eine Religion unter Verdacht," *Stern*, April 8, 2004, 49.

week later drove the message home. It also functioned as yet another piece in the security puzzle about "what Muslims think." The merging of religion, migration, and infiltration was exactly what scared the German public most. The spelling out of key elements of infiltration—the misleading of women, unlawful access to documents, and domination—provoked deep fears about fifth columns. Osman Ahmed's justification of the murder of hundreds of people by declaring "we believe in God," "we are migrants of God," and "we represent God's business" conjured up the image of a ruthless religious activist. His words were considered to be yet another indication of the type of covert political activities that Islamic organizations were suspected of.

In an interview on the state of security, granted some days after the attack on Madrid, the German minister of the interior, Otto Schily, expressed this sentiment: "All Muslims living in our country must ask themselves why their communities produce such furious fanatics."[6] With these words he implicitly expressed security agencies' beliefs about Islamic communities in Germany: "their communities" produce terrorists—"such furious fanatics." Neither the media nor policymakers questioned the equation. In the absence of information other than the current news items, they had associated Islam with a dangerous form of political Islam, so-called Islamism. As a consequence, the insufficient transparency of Islamic organizational structures, the absence of Muslim spokesmen, the insistence on wearing headscarves, and the institutionalization of Muslim conduct through German legislation were all read as signs of the same persuasion that had engendered al-Qaeda cells and death pilots (Breuer 2003).[7]

These are the components, then, which in recent years have framed the visibility of young Muslim men and women making their entry in the German public agora: acts of global Islamic terrorism, demands for clarification, and a political discourse that equates Islamic religious diversity with Islamism. To enable the development of appropriate political responses, policymakers adopted a well-known German rhetoric of connecting the present security threat with earlier periods of crisis. They recalled the popular student protests of the 1960s and 1970s, which culminated in isolated terrorist acts against the German state. As will be shown, this rhetoric heightened the political perception of Muslim activists as belonging to the extreme right and of Islam as a right-wing ideology. The presence of a strong Turkish political Islam, embodied by the Islamic Community of Milli Görüş, made people in Germany aware of the potential politicization of Islam. It functioned as a *pars pro toto*, as a part that, in the eyes of the general public, represented the whole. In line

---

6   Konrad Schuller, "Wir leben in Zeiten epochaler Bedrohung," *Frankfurter Allgemeine Zeitung*, March 21, 2004.
7   In September 2003, in line with this development, public opinion polls reported that 93 % of the German population thought of "oppressed women" upon hearing the word "Islam"; 83 % associated the word with "terror"; and 82 % thought that Muslims were "fanatical and radical."

with this perception, Muslim visibility itself already functioned as a sign of threat.

One did not have to go all that far to understand how this master narrative was adapted to the German context. It was enough to read the dailies in the morning and zap through the many talk shows at night. On these well-visited German stages, now paralyzed by fear of international terrorists, phrases popped up that reminded Germany of its own terrorist past. It did not take long before a scenario had been set up in which "terrorist cells," "sleepers," a "milieu of sympathizers," and "naive do-gooders" played the main roles. The vocabulary evoked the German past: some of it went back to the crisis of the 1970s, when student protests rocked the country; some of it went further back to the Nazi period. The chain of associations itself was hardly a subject for contemplation; rather, it offered a quick and therefore welcome means to identify the enemy within and launch upon a well-trodden political path of action.[8]

One particular occurrence helped to set the train in motion. Soon after the airplanes had crashed into the twin towers, it was discovered that one of the traces left behind by the suicide pilots led to Hamburg. Here, unnoticed by security forces, scholars, neighbors, church dialogue partners, or anyone who had been in regular contact with the Muslim community in Hamburg, an *'ashira*, a cell belonging to al-Qaeda, had been formed. The leader of the group, Muhammad Atta, even appeared to have been a well-respected student at the Technical University of Hamburg.[9] From this city, more traces led to inconspicuous provincial towns such as Bochum and Osnabrück, where equally young and unsuspected Arab students had been preparing for the attack. To its horror, the German population realized that the terrorists of New York and Washington had been planning in its midst without attracting the least attention. As long as they did not commit any crimes, these young men had been literally invisible.

To grasp this extraordinary fact, the term *Schläfer* (sleepers) made its (re-) entry.[10] Originally, the term had been used in bacteriology to indicate carriers of infectious diseases. Nazi Germany borrowed it to label "asocial elements"—men and women who acted against the ruling ideology (Briese 2003). In the 1970s, it was again used to describe the cells of leftist activists.[11] Schläfer called up the image of a hidden threat "sleeping" in the bowels of society. It suggested the presence of an invisible enemy within, waiting for its chance to strike. It also aptly conveyed people's feelings of helplessness.

---

8 Peter Homann, "Terrorismus und RAF," *Der Spiegel*, February 21, 2002.

9 Niklas Maak, "In einer kleinen Stadt," *Frankfurter Allgemeine Zeitung*, September 19, 2001.

10 "Behörden kündigen gezielte Suche nach 'Schläfern' an," *Frankfurter Allgemeine Zeitung*, September 21, 2001; Anne Zielke, "Import, Export, Mord: War Mohambedou Ould Slahi der Mann, der die Schläfer weckte?" *Frankfurter Allgemeine Zeitung*, October 30, 2001. .

11 Peter Homann, "Terrorismus und RAF," *Der Spiegel*, February 21, 2002.

Several markers helped to identify the new "sleepers." The first set combined "male," "Muslim," and "student." For some time, the application of this set of markers turned a substantial portion of the male Muslim population into potential suspects.[12] The next marker to be added was "religious," rerouting the search to Germany's twenty-four hundred mosque organizations. Excerpts from the "spiritual manual" and the testament of Muhammad Atta appeared in the papers.[13] From these could be gleaned that Muhammad Atta and his crew apparently had been pious Muslims who turned to a rigorous form of asceticism in order to fulfill their death mission. The trail they left behind seemed to indicate that "religious" would be the most promising marker.

In line with Germany's recollections of the Rote-Armee-Fraktion (the Red Army Faction), in which sleepers had entertained stable connections with a "milieu of sympathizers," the Hamburg mosques came under suspicion. But suspicion did not limit itself to Hamburg alone. Unlike the German terrorists of the 1970s, who had maintained connections to a limited number of supporters only, the Muslim terrorists appeared to be backed up by masses of people all around the world. Television viewers could witness, in the first media images after the attack, large crowds in Indonesia, the Middle East, and some African countries applauding the suicide bombers. A story emerged that in a Milli Görüş mosque in Berlin spontaneous applause broke out during Friday congregation and sweets had been handed around to celebrate.[14] Whether fact or rumor, this story awakened another misgiving that took hold of politicians, opinion-makers, and the general public: Muslims all over the world apparently rejoiced in the death of thousands of people. From here, the transition to a general suspicion of all mosque organizations in Germany was no longer all that great. Muslim organizations were accused of cooperating with the extreme-right neo-Nazi scene. Although there was a lack of proof and the accusation was dropped after some time, the accusation pushed the perception of religious Muslims into a corner from which German politicians and journalists necessarily had to distance themselves.[15]

---

12 Lutz Schnedelmann, Franziska Köhn, and Christine Richter, "Nach den Terror-Anschlägen: Polizei überprüft arabische Studenten," *Berliner Zeitung*, September 19, 2001.

13 "'Leben im unendlichen Paradies': Der in Boston gefundene Leitfaden für die Attentäter," *Frankfurter Allgemeine Zeitung*, September 29, 2001; "'Beten, daß ich bei den Engeln bin': Das in Boston aufgefundene Testament des mutmaßlichen Terroristen Atta," *Frankfurter Allgemeine Zeitung*, October 1, 2001.

14 A German convert and imam of the German-speaking Muslim community in Berlin broadcast the story. In an interview with the *Berliner Zeitung* (September 20, 2001), he stated, "I have been a Muslim for twenty-one years; I am familiar with the scene and know where the terrorists are." Other witnesses still maintain that an old man gave sweets to some children to keep them quiet during sermon.

15 "The World Crisis," *Focus*, September 21, 2001; "Islam – Eine Religion im Visier," *Stern*, September 17, 2001; Anne Zielke, "Allah ist mit den Springerstiefeln," *Frankfurter Allgemeine Zeitung*, September 15, 2001.

As stated earlier, suspicion as such was not a novelty. In some ways the public had always observed Muslims through the frame of Orientalism: exotic at its best, untrustworthy at its worst. In the past, however, this suspicion was coupled with indifference, in the sense of "we don't care what they do." New was the vehemence with which the old binary construction of "Oriental culture" and "Western modernity" was expanded into a narrative that held Islam to be a threat to the constitution. New also was the polarization that marked off religious Muslims in Germany as right-wing and legitimized the full force of the state. The phrases and metaphors that were used to identify them helped to accelerate this process.

The spotlight on sleepers incidentally illuminated another group of persons, the so-called *Gutmenschen* (do-gooders), who were accused of being blauäugig (literally, "blue-eyed"; figuratively, "naive"). The word Gutmenschen carries with it a complex nexus of accusation and self-hatred and betrays an instance of suppressed German collective memory.[16] First, it conjures up memories of blond and blue-eyed Nazi soldiers and denotes people who seemingly are all right but in the end prove to be malicious. In reference to this usage, the term has been used, in the context of the protest movement of the 1960s and 1970s, to accuse leftist students of "naive" phantasmagoria. Applied in connection with Muslim "sleepers," Gutmenschen comprised a group of professionals, scholars, churchmen, and social workers who had had regular dealings with Muslims. They were scolded as Gutmenschen because they, whenever dealing with Muslims, supposedly had ignored "the dark sides of Islam." In retrospect, it seemed almost incredible that these men and women had not noticed any impending danger. They were suspected of both "shutting their eyes" and being dangerously "naive," that is, of talking something straight that was very clearly wrong. Above all, they were considered "door openers" because their work had provided Islamists and terrorists with a large window of opportunities (Kandel 2002).

The political decision-makers reacted with extensive security measures and with a political redefinition of Muslims and their religious traditions which equated Islam with Islamism (Bundesministerium des Innern 2003). This step entailed the homogenization of a group of people with an otherwise high level of differentiation. It also set into motion a polarization between "us" and "them" which turned Muslims—whether migrants or converts, religious or laic, pious or politically oriented—into suspect outsiders and potential troublemakers. Islam was declared "potentially dangerous" and

---

16 Dictionaries point to two different origins. One is the dictum of Friedrich Nietzsche that "perhaps there is no ideology more dangerous, no mischief in psychological matters more grave than the intention to be good: it has engendered the most repulsive type of human being, the toady" (Nietzsche 1873, part 3, 798; my translation). The other goes back to the Nazis' corruption of the Yiddish expression "a gutt Mensch" in order to ridicule German church officials who opposed their euthanasia program (Droste and Bittermann 1998; Schmidt 2004).

young women with headscarves "political weapons" (Haug and Reimer 2005; Kandel 2004).

Not only religious activists but also Turkish laic Muslims opposed the sweeping gesture with which their religion was condemned and their integrity questioned. Muslim members of Parliament, trade unionists, writers, and scholars wrote vociferous letters of protest to the papers.[17] Mehmet Daimagüler, a German politician of Turkish descent and a member of the executive board of the liberal party (the Freie Demokratische Partei), summarized the situation thus:

"All of us, more than three million Muslims in Germany, are held in suspicion. This is not just a vague feeling but harsh experience: I was born and raised in this country; nonetheless, the word 'sleeper' is being written all over my election posters. Most of us came from Turkey, and we have lived here for forty years or more. By comparison, the Hamburg terrorists were all Arab students, not really at home in this country. But nobody seems to notice the difference. We pay for the crimes of others and we are powerless." (Daimagüler, "Wort zum Freitag," *Frankfurter Allgemeine Zeitung*, June 23, 2004)

Daimagüler, a laic Turk who is a fully active citizen in German society, is light years removed from that little group of Arabic students in Hamburg that secretly planned a terrorist act. Yet he too became part of the vicious circle that associated Muslims with internal foreigners, with sleepers, with hidden threats, with extremists, and with terrorist deeds. The adoption of a rhetoric that called up old fears from the German past helped to set the wheel in motion. With the help of "sleepers," "do-gooders," "sympathizers," and "terrorist cells," the political perception managed to reduce a large and highly differentiated group of people to a mere security risk.

One circumstance that favored this change in perspective was the lack of representation on the side of Muslims. On October 3, 2001, during the official act of national celebration, and for the first time since migration started, a religious Muslim representative spoke in public and was listened to by millions of people. Contrary to official expectations, however, Dr. Nadeem Elyas, president of the Central Council of Muslims in Germany (Zentralrat der Muslime in Deutschland), did not represent all religious Muslims in Germany but only his organization, which counted some twenty thousand members. Here, then, was another point of irritation that the new visibility of Muslims revealed. It had been expected that, in line with civil society, one representative would now step forward and gain visibility on behalf of all others. But the organization of Islamic devotion was scattered, or so it appeared. If anyone ventured to speak out at all, Muslim actors acted on behalf of small factions or as individuals, speaking just for themselves. In this

---

17 Mehmet Daimagüler, "Wort zum Freitag," *Frankfurter Allgemeine Zeitung*, June 23, 2004; Navid Kermani, "Feindliche Übernahme," *Tageszeitung*, October 9, 2003.

respect, too, the political demand and the Muslim supply did not fit. A politician skilled in returning the inquisitive gaze, Daimagüler chose the word "powerless" to capture the situation.

For the two religious communities discussed in the following sections, the discourse of security sets the stage for asymmetrical communication. Whereas policymakers claimed that "the whole of Islam is a mistake,"[18] and treated Muslim activists as "a potential threat," the two communities contrasted their strategies in order to find acceptance for their own interpretation of jihad.

"Like Greenpeace": Milli Görüş and German Society

In the course of 2002, a young spokesman of the Islamic Community of Milli Görüş—I shall call him Mehmet—started to notice severe changes in the way he felt treated in public. For years, Mehmet had represented his organization at public occasions, and because he was a pleasant, communicative fellow he had been treated with respect. In September 2002, he related to me the details of a roundtable that for some time had already been dealing with plans for Islamic religious instruction in public schools.[19] Although the curriculum had been discussed in great detail and had already been agreed upon, the participating policymakers suddenly expressed severe misgivings about the hidden intentions of his organization, Milli Görüş. Refusing to acknowledge the difference between his person and his organization, he reacted pretty much like Susanna in *Les Noces di Figaro* and took their doubt for personal defamation. Referring to his discussion partners, he remarked to me, "How long have we already been speaking with one another? Five years? Seven years? Why should they cast old doubts over and over again?" A churchman present at the same meeting recalled him exclaiming, "If I have explained my view on a subject, say ten times or a hundred times, that must be enough. When do you start to believe me, then? Always you hark back!"[20]

Glimpses like this one illustrate a clash of entirely different frameworks. The young man still counted on the commitment that springs from personal involvement. He called up as his witnesses his personal integrity and the sheer length of time that he had discussed his plans with policymakers. Against their professional doubts he employed the experience of shared communication and the context of everyday trust. He realized that "the other side" possessed a power of definition against which his personal weight could not compete. Instead of acknowledging the trouble that his local Milli Görüş peers had been provoking at that time (see below), he reacted with a generali-

---

18 In an interview with the journalist Konrad Schuller, Otto Schily, the minister of the interior, stated, "To our understanding of religious freedom must belong the possibility to argue that the whole of Islam is a mistake" (Schuller, "Wir leben in Zeiten epochaler Bedrohung," *Frankfurter Allgemeine Zeitung*, March 21, 2004).
19 Interview with M. T., September 17, 2002.
20 Telephone call with H.–H. W., September 20, 2002.

zation: "Somehow it is like this. If one holds onto a different view, one is sure to be chopped up in this city."[21] Mehmet presents one aspect of the Milli Görüş relationship with the outside world, but presently not the one that dominates. To understand the community's predominant view of—and its communication with—the world around, it is helpful to first consider the internal communication of the movement.

Mehmet's career resembles that of many young men in the Milli Görüş organization. As a child left to himself for the larger part of the day, the Milli Görüş youth organization took care of him, provided him with a view on the world, and gave him something to do for the weekend. The community supported him in school and organized a grant for him, enabling him to go to university. After finishing his studies at the age of 26, he was already considered one of Milli Görüş's elite and given a responsible post. Back then, I knew him as a humorous fellow who believed in the force of personal encounter and always looked at the bright side of things. Seven years later—and the same goes for many of his peers—he made the sickly impression of being just short of a heart attack.

The Milli Görüş community started as a social movement that catered to poor, uprooted, and illiterate Turkish peasants (Seufert 1997; Hermann 1996). This was back in the 1960s, when Turkey's rural inhabitants started to move to the big cities and challenged the city dwellers with their conservative outlook. The name Milli Görüş itself is a pun that blends a national with a religious view and, moreover, mixes religious with political interests. What the movement proposed to the Turkish nation was a religious alternative. It preferred the fruits of Islamic civilization over those of Western modernity and proclaimed the fusion of religion and the state (*din ve dawla*) in opposition to the Turkish secular order, which actually keeps religion tightly under control.

From the start, Turkey's policymakers and elite suspected that these demands threatened the republic's principles. And, indeed, the emerging religious-political movement pushed towards a conception of society with a revolutionary potential, one that had to be realized here and now. In the early 1990s, its political claims-making culminated in the manifesto "The Right Order" (*Adil Düzen*), a mixture of communist and religious ideals to realize social justice with the help of religious rule based on shari'a. In the manifesto, "the right order" was contrasted sharply with the Western or "the wrong order" (*batil düzen*). The manifesto also contained outspoken anti-Western sentiments.

The shift of generations began in Hamburg in the late 1990s.[22] The aftermath of 9/11 accelerated the retreat of the founding generation; the national

---

21 Interview with M. T., September 17, 2002.
22 The following is based on a series of interviews and informal conversations in the period between October 2001 and March 2005. Among the interviewees and discussion partners were Ali Kizilkaya, secretary general of the organization at the time of the interview and around thirty years old; Mustafa Yeneroglu, head of

steering group in Cologne was restructured and revitalized, and other cities soon followed suit. However, many features typifying the old community structure remained. The organization continued to be dominated by men, for instance. As before, there exists a national women's organization that caters to the religious needs of women, and locally one can find large women's congregations that engage in prayer sessions and handicrafts. All the decision-makers, however, are male (Jonker 2003a, 2003b). The new elite also consciously held on to the distinguishing features of a social movement. In this respect, they stayed in line with the founding generation as well. In 2004, the secretary general acknowledged:

"We are a movement, no question! We insist on personal responsibility. That's what we stand for. That makes us different from [other Turkish communities such as] Süleymanci and Nurcu. [...] One should leave the people their freedom. That's how we can reach more people than we have members. What we do, we set out a general direction and leave it up to them to take responsibility." (interview with Oguz Üçüncü, May 7, 2004)

In their refusal to exercise control and to instead stress personal responsibility, in their preference to set out "a general direction" for like-minded people who are not necessarily a member, the younger generation follows in the footsteps of its fathers. By holding on to the distinguishing features of a socioreligious movement, the community is guaranteed a dynamic character. Like all social movements, it aims to create a strong collective identity, a broad network, and a strong potential for mobilization. Various initiatives "from below" that do not fall under the leadership's responsibility should follow from these efforts. The new leaders opened up new avenues for others to take up, avenues that the founding fathers had not even fathomed would exist. One of these is the introduction of new legal interpretations of shari'a that have the capacity to "zip up" Islamic law with the German constitution:

"If one begins to take this seriously—integration, to become integrated—then we want to be taken seriously as partners as well. We represent the largest Islamic community in this country. If we want to succeed, we have to find new interpretations for shari'a regulations, not only for those that make Islamic life possible but also for the hard spots [*hudud* punishments for *fitna*, theft, and adultery]. We want to become accepted with our rough edges and likewise build up solidarity with the whole *umma*. We want to become a partner of the state." (interview with Mehmet Yeneroglu, April 16, 2004)

---

the legal department, and Oguz Üçüncü, secretary general, both in their late twenties and members of the steering committee at the time of the interviews; Mustafa Yoldash and Ramazan Yazici, both in their thirties and responsible for the Hamburg community at the time of the interviews; Mehmet Gül, head of the local community in Berlin and 61 years old at the time of the interview; Nail Dural, head imam of the Berlin community and in his late fifties at the time of the interviews. In addition, I regularly spoke with younger members and activists holding lower positions. I cite them with their initials only for several reasons.

The speaker, who is head of the legal department, demanded integration through partnership. This approach must be understood in two ways. The notion of "partners" implies a claim to the legal status of a "Church," the so-called corporation of public law, which in Germany only the churches and the Jewish community possess—none of the Islamic organizations possess this status (Jonker 2002). It also lays claim to the right to political participation, with or without that status. The word "partners" indicates a shift between religion and politics, one that is to be realized through existing legal means. For the movement, this discourse signaled a new self-confidence. In passing, it broke with the conservative spirit of the older generation. What his legal department tried to discover, my discussion partner explained to me, were brand new possibilities for the legal interpretation of shari'a that could be accepted by German legislators. His department was busy adapting central shari'a regulations to a secular framework: "In Germany, Islamic law has been interpreted within the context of German law for a long time already. All we want is to smooth up the process a bit." Central religious regulations that secured an Islamic life in Germany included halal slaughtering, Islamic cemeteries, the wearing of headscarves in state-run institutions, access to religious education in public schools, and the aforementioned status of a corporation of public law. At the time, these regulations were still treated under Article 4 of the constitution, freedom of religion. In the future, or so my discussion partner speculated, they would be reinterpreted in the context of different constitutional articles:

"Take the headscarf. Right now it is being treated [in court] in the context of an individual right. Or take slaughtering: it also touches upon articles that deal with the protection of animals. If we succeed in its transference, Muslim concerns can be better understood by secular society." (interview with Mehmet Yeneroglu, April 16, 2004)

The key term on which everything hinges is "secular society." By transferring religious concerns into central values, Milli Görüş tries to "zip up" with German society. It aims to convince others that its concept of "jihad equals political engagement" is a general concern comparable with other forms of participation:

"What matters is that one does more than the daily prayers and the *zakat*. That's what everybody does. What matters to us is engagement. To engage is the same as jihad. Jihad includes just about everything; it means that one engages politically, like Greenpeace." (interview with Mustafa Yeneroglu and Oguz Üçüncü, May 7, 2004)

"Like Greenpeace." This approach is at the core of Milli Görüş's response to security measures and political pressure exactly because it promises understanding. My discussion partner felt certain that, some day, even the "hard" bits of shari'a—the hudud punishments in the case of adultery, theft, or anarchy—could receive some new interpretation in the context of German law and become recognized as a "secular" (universal) concern. But that, he acknowledged, was still a long way off.

For the moment, this approach was difficult to stomach for at least part of the community. When, in June 2003, the new head of the European community of Milli Görüş, Yavuz Karahan, spoke in front of the general assembly in Cologne for the first time, he bluntly stated, "The Quran and Sunna present no obstacle to our integration into the existent [German] juridical system." In reaction, around half of the imams and other representatives rose from their seats and left the meeting hall in protest.[23] Karahan's words were judged an intolerable provocation. The protest made clear that, within the organization, reformers stood against conservatives and both sides could count supporters from all generations. However, the demonstration did not split the organization. Political participation being the ultimate aim, the very last thing anyone wanted was a cleavage. The younger generation had taken over and continued in ways that were far more challenging than the revolutionary ideas of the older generation, which had, after all, produced nothing but ideas.

What made an impression was the fact that the new generation had begun to employ legal means to defend the organization against critics. In 2002 and 2003, the legal department of the Milli Görüş organization deluged administrators, policymakers, and the federal agency for internal security with legal charges. Anyone who wrote or spoke about the Milli Görüş community in a derogatory manner, or who distorted the image nurtured by the community, could reckon with charges. The charges against the agencies for internal security in Bavaria, Baden-Württemberg, and North Rhine-Westphalia especially caused commotion.[24] In 2002, for instance, the North Rhine-Westphalia report on Milli Görüş appeared under the heading "Extremism of Foreigners." It quoted from the revolutionary manifesto *Adil Düzen* and suggested that this organization was based on authority and obedience, that members nursed undemocratic and anti-Zionist sentiments, that the organization intended to Islamize Germany, and that, for these reasons, it presented a natural habitat for extremists (Verfassungsbericht NRW 2002, 167–175). Through the use of legal charges, the Milli Görüş steering group tried to break the federal agencies' power of definition. The charges were also intended to rid the organization of close observation by the authorities as soon as possible. In reality, however, scrutiny of the organization had just begun in earnest. In the years to come, although the charges of extremism or of relations with terrorists were withdrawn, the federal agencies continued to make accusations against the organization. Structures that were not sufficiently transparent,

---

23 Konrad Schuller, "Von der Demokratie verführt? Die Islamisten von Milli Görüş erwägen eine Abkehr von ihrer strikt antiwestlichen Linie," *Frankfurter Allgemeine Zeitung*, April 18, 2004.

24 On September 12, 2002, against the federal agency of Bavaria; on February 5, 2003, against North Rhine-Westphalia; and on April 12, 2003, against Baden-Württemberg (VG Stuttgart 18 K 41 79/02).

attempts to legalize shari'a rule, and proof of anti-German sentiment were considered sufficient to justify the accusations.

The Islamic Organization of Milli Görüş in Germany is currently in trouble. It has been under constant surveillance by the federal agencies for internal security since the 1980s. The social seclusion, the revolutionary sympathies, and the hostile language of the parent generation gave rise to serious doubts about its intentions. The strategy embraced by the present generation has strengthened the suspicions of the security agencies. The employment of legal means to sanction religious conduct and ward off unwanted critics has invited even more observation. The youngest generation is already objecting to this treatment and showing signs of impatience: "When can we finally say what we think in this country?" they asked Mehmet.[25] The old men, less concerned that they might be overheard, vent their emotions in public. Yakup Tashi, who has been a preacher in one of the Milli Görüş mosques in Berlin since 1979, remembered in one of his Friday sermons in November 2004:

"When we came here, these Germans gave us no toilets. There were no toilets in the apartments when we came. One had to go five flights down to use a bucket. They had put together four or five boards for us to use as a toilet." (Verwaltungsgericht 2005, 4)

In that sermon, knowing that he was touching upon a shared sentiment, the preacher expressed his frustrations. What he told his audience came down to this: Some Germans are all right, but most stink because they do not shave under their armpits; they are atheists, good-for-nothing. Eventually, they will end up in hell (Verwaltungsgericht 2005, 4). These words were taped in secret and broadcast on television some days later. Policymakers considered the animosity of his words to be "hate speech." In the trial that followed, security agents also brought proof of the preacher's sympathy with "Iraqi martyrs" and his conviction that the death of a martyr ranked among the most beautiful. In actuality, he expressed this sentiment not in a sermon but in a prayer that was recited at the end of a pro-Iraq demonstration. The prayer contained the word "ghazi" (freedom fighter), which erroneously was translated as "martyr" (Schiffauer 2005). But this is a detail. Anti-German sentiments linked to sympathies with suicide bombers proved to be too much. The events fuelled public suspicions that Milli Görüş, despite its repeated denials, shared the worldview of terrorists. After reflection on the consequences of such leadership, the city of Berlin started a procedure to obtain a deportation order and have him expelled.

---

25 The questions were posed in educational courses that Mehmet currently organizes. The aim of these courses is to introduce teenagers to Islamic thinkers like Qutb and Mauwdudi and to explain to them how "the West" thinks (informal conversation, February 3, 2005).

Having considered these different voices, it is time to ask what the Islamic Organization of Milli Görüş chooses. What is its religious framework, and what does it perceive through it? Having grown up as children of immigrant families in Germany, my discussion partners, once in power, started to turn the revolutionary Milli Görüş ideals into concrete demands for political, social, and legal incorporation. Words like *hizmet* and jihad became rites of passage from religious mobilization to political participation and legal partnership. What connects the new generation with the founder generation is a demand for social justice. In line with the older members, in line also with other protest and socioreligious movements, they want to inspire and mobilize people whom they do not necessarily know. The general aim should be democratic involvement, not acts of illegal resistance. Yet although the line between the two sometimes seems dangerously thin, they also know that creating control mechanisms and transparency would lead to a loss of mobilization capacity.

Unlike the experience of the founding fathers, the upbringing and self-image of the new generation suggested that it might be possible after all to be both a German and a Muslim. Nevertheless, at the back of their minds they held on to a deep resentment of German society, which, under the security pressures of the last three years, they increasingly referred to as "the West." Distrust of it remains an integral part of the Milli Görüş identity.

In this transition, the instructions that shari'a issues for personal conduct act as a compass for identity politics. "Zipping up" shari'a with the German constitution is presently considered a guarantee of partnership, political participation, and group rights. In the eyes of my discussion partners, the private religious conduct that other Islamic communities profess simply cannot be enough. What they wish to accomplish is the incorporation of Islamic regulations—those that "guarantee" a collective Islamic life—into the foundations of German legislation. It brings them into competition with politics: "Gaining political acceptance in Germany comes down to overcoming the legal system," is how the head of the legal department put it.[26]

His formulation holds the key to the lock. Like their fathers, this generation links political demands for social justice with religious revolutionary zeal; but unlike their fathers, they do this in the context of a nonreligious European society that currently feels threatened by Muslim terrorism. The founding generation still demanded *din ve dawla*, the fusion of faith and politics, in Turkey. The younger generation in Germany has modified this demand: it now seeks a fusion of religious law with secular law. It wants its concerns to be understood as a universal interest, something for the common good that transcends national borders.

In its attempt to make itself understood, the new steering committee began the transfer from religious to secular rights with the help of legal means. In other words, Milli Görüş responded to the political pressures telling them to

---

26 Interview with Mehmet Yeneroglu, April 16, 2004.

distance themselves from terrorist activism with a totally different kind of activism, namely, that of political claims-making. This strategy brought the organization into a deadlock with security agencies.

The ideal profile of a Milli Görüş activist, then, includes elements of social engagement, the voice of the oppressed, distrust, and a readiness to claim power. My interview partners denied having any association or sympathies with the worldview of hijackers and suicide bombers ("we cannot break with people we do not know"). Instead, they urged policymakers to accept them as partners with legitimate claims. As a result, they managed to make Milli Görüş glaringly visible.

"The Need for Translation": Jamaatunnur Reflects on Secular Society

In order to illustrate the breadth and scope of Muslim religious responses to German security pressures, in this section I provide a brief depiction of the Jamaatunnur, or "Nur community." This is a Turkish Muslim organization that shares the same religious compass as their Milli Görüş compatriots, but that embraces an entirely different approach to the public sphere. Its general direction is engaged asceticism, which is a combination of ascetic conduct and the introduction of ethical standards in the workplace.

The Nur community was founded on the writings of the Turkish philosopher and theologian Bediüzzaman Said Nursi (1878–1960; Mardin 1989; Vahide 2000; Abu-Rabi 2003). Unlike the founders of the Milli Görüş movement, who appeared in the public arena some forty years after the founding of the Turkish republic, Said Nursi opposed Kemal Atatürk's republican reforms from the very start. He inspired peaceful resistance that especially caught on among rural Turks. In the course of his life, he became the republic's most prominent religious opponent and certainly the most prolific: Said Nursi wrote sixty-five hundred pages of free Quranic interpretation (*tafsir manevi*, the so-called *Risale-i Nur*, or "Letters of Light," which were smuggled across the country and secretly copied by hand hundreds and thousands of times). Imprisoned by the republic for most of his life, he attained a level of popularity that was matched only by the founder Kemal Atatürk himself. Fear of his reputation ran so high that, when Said Nursi died, his body was abducted by the military in a covert action and buried in an unknown spot. Although he had appeared in public only to defend himself in one of his many trials, Said Nursi became the most visible and, because of his nonviolent resistance, most respected Muslim of the early Turkish republic.

Today his students still gather to study his writings. Said Nursi had claimed that every Quran reflection should also include the study of nature. He believed that the contemplation of nature provided a safe way to discover the miracles of God in the universe. It encourages students to fuse religious with scientific knowledge and to simply feel enchanted with the world

(Nereid 1997; Reed 1999). On a more practical level, Nur students search for ethical inroads into European society. They look for ways to share their brimming enthusiasm with others, both Muslims and non-Muslims, on an individual level. Editing and printing Said Nursi's words and furthering their reflection is considered the most important road towards that aim.[27]

From the start, the emerging community focused on collective reading as well as the interpretation of the *Risale-i Nur*. Because of the exegesis involved, this approach led to many competing groups (Yavuz 1997). Jamaatunnur claims to safeguard the core and manages to include a wide spectrum of followers, ranging from "traditionalists" who still copy the *Risale-i Nur* by hand to international scholars who compare Said Nursi's theology with relevant Christian thinkers. Up to now, only the Turkish preacher Fethullah Gülen, once a companion of Said Nursi, could seriously challenge this claim (Yavuz and Esposito 2003).

Community life centers first on the collective study of Said Nursi's texts and second on the discovery of new knowledge. Like Said Qutb and Hassan al-Banna, Nur students claim that all knowledge must be discovered rather than constructed. This means that the production of knowledge is considered a process in which the truth dawns upon one rather than a result of deconstruction or reconstruction. But unlike Qutb and al-Banna, who pursued the Islamization of science, Nur students fuse Western scholarship with love of nature, "the great book of the universe," which to them is the quickest road towards the discovery of divine love. All knowledge of the world, including the one that has not yet been discovered, has in principle been described in the Quran. They compare its text with seeds from which everything emanates. A correct Quranic interpretation occurs when the mind, the heart, and the spirit blend and infuse the reader with a range of intellectual and emotional insights. Said Nursi's inspired Quranic commentary serves as a compass in achieving such interpretation.

Nur philosophy is about localization. Like Milli Görüş, it deals with "communities of feeling" (Appadurai 1996) that try to create localities in a shifting world. Like Milli Görüş, Nur students in Germany struggle to make their religious concerns understood by "secular society." But unlike the former, they cultivate a culture of individual, peaceful conduct that is designed to be shared with people who do not belong to the Nur community or even to the Muslim community.

In 2003, I was invited to participate in a youth seminar in which Nur students from different cities of Western Europe meet.[28] It is called the International Seminar Group and was first held in 2000. Over the last five years

---

27 Printed in the 1950s for the first time, the collection was translated into fourteen languages. There are thirteen publishers and distributors of the *Risale-i Nur*. I also counted seventy-three Web sites in twenty-two languages; see http://www. Ahmetberk.tripod.com/ and click on the "Risale-i nur" link.

28 On October 4–5, 2003, the International Seminar Group met in Ludwigshafen, Germany.

students have met every other month. The group is an outcome of a different effort to mobilize the Nur community, the so-called international symposia, which since 1991 have taken place in Istanbul.[29] Whereas the organizers of the symposia try to interest renowned Arabic and Western scholars in the writings of Said Nursi, the organizers of the seminar group encourage students to take steps on the path to intellectual independence—while staying within the religious framework set by their founder. In some cases, they are being prepared to join in the international scholarly exchange.

A word on my entrance in the Nur community: over the last ten years, I had known of the existence of the Jamaatunnur but had never succeeded in making any contact. Among Muslims in Germany, the community was disparaged as being of the intellectual type and renowned for minding its own business. It was my impression that this community shunned public debate related to Muslims to a degree that made it invisible. If it had any strategy for visibility, I had concluded, it must be the private politics of not being noticed at all. The first time I encountered the Jamaatunnur in public, it was in the form of a press release issued shortly after 9/11. It stated, among other things, the following:

"We call upon the responsibility of the general public with a basic principle from the Quran: 'Partners, families, or their communities cannot be blamed for the faults and crimes of individuals or small groups.' Therefore, one should not confound a world religion, whose members sharply condemn these abominable terrorist acts, with those who misuse the name of this religion." (press release on September 13, 2001)

Here was the first explicit sign of a religiously based refusal to answer to the challenge of 9/11. When, in September 2003, the leader of the community approached me with a request for research, I was intrigued. Where did this community position itself? The answer I brought away from the meeting was that Nur students were changing their approach. Without so much as mentioning the "jihad equals legitimate defense" approach of their violent coreligionists, they actively promoted another view of jihad, one that equated it with intellectual discovery and spiritual growth.

Approximately fifty persons attended the seminar, and the majority seemed to be younger than thirty years old. Of the thirty men present, twelve worked in finance management, consultancy, or banking professions, six claimed to be scholars in the technical sciences (three professors among them), and the others were still university students. I counted sixteen women,

---

29 International symposia took place in 1991, 1992, 1995, 1998, 1999, 2001, and 2004 in Istanbul. The scholarly output is impressive: the organizers already have published ten thousand pages both in English and in Arabic. See, for instance, the proceedings of the 1995 symposium: The Third International Symposium on Bediüzzaman Said Nursi: The Reconstruction of Islamic Thought in the Twentieth Century and Bediüzzaman Said Nursi, ed. Nesil Foundation (Istanbul: Sözler Publications, 1997), which comprises some one thousand pages. All proceedings are printed in Istanbul and are widely distributed.

among them two doctors, one theologian, two business managers, two teachers, and a range of students in computer science and business information management. Men and women sat in the same room but kept different sides. All of the women had their heads covered.

The main subject of the seminars is the adaptation of *ahlaq*, Islamic ethics, to different professional situations. The working language is Turkish, but during break country representatives stood together and preferred to discuss the proceedings in their own European language. It struck me that the delegation from Holland had something unmistakably Dutch in the way they were dressed and in their facial expressions and body language. Looking around, I saw that the Swiss, the German, the Austrian, the French, and the English delegations equally bore a whiff of their respective European country.

On this particular weekend, the seminar concentrated on *hizmetkar liderlik*, or "leadership as a religious task." Important qualities such as mentorship, responsibility, and empathy were discussed, and the participants spoke at length about the necessity of showing one's spiritual roots and of "being different." As a matter of course, a *Risale-i Nur* text formed the basis for discussion. Said Nursi's free poetic style allowed the seminar participants to reflect together. From all sides of the room ideas were offered and new thoughts were developed quickly. Although the teacher remained standing on the male side of the room, the women freely and frequently contributed with questions and objections.

Later that day, a brainstorming on how to continue best in the near future took place. Suggestions included the encouragement of dissertations, the preparation of short PowerPoint presentations, and, above all, a selection of thoughts from the *Risale* that could answer to the pressing problems of European reality. The group especially stressed "the need to find translations." More important than anything else, Said Nursi's ideas should be made accessible to the larger public and "translated" into nonreligious thinking.

The Jamaatunnur does not want to impress with numbers but with quality.[30] As one of the more prominent participants remarked, "We are the yeast that makes the dough rise."[31] I came home with the impression that these

---

30 There seems to be an average of three Nurcu-run study centers or dormitories (*dershanes*) in fifteen German cities as well as in London, Vienna, Rotterdam, Luxembourg, Zurich, Brussels, Paris, Metz, and Strasbourg. Together, they add up to approximately sixty Nur centers in Europe. Each receives some one hundred participants on a regular basis (two to four times a week). Adding these numbers together, I count no more than six thousand active Nur students in Europe. As for the competition, most interviewees mentioned two to three centers in their town or its vicinity in which the writings of the preacher Fethüllah Gülen dominate. None of them, however, possessed a full overview of all Nur activities in Europe (results of a questionnaire issued to the participants of the seminar group in October 2003).

31 Faris Kaya, organizer of the international symposia in Istanbul and himself one of the original companions of Said Nursi.

people challenged the defensive and violent interpretation of jihad through the active promotion of a view that preached nonviolence and spirituality instead. They were, moreover, convinced that Said Nursi's writings held something in store for their Christian and nonreligious colleagues. But where were the words that might fit the lock?

There is still a large distance to be crossed from the local Nur study center in Europe to the international symposia in Istanbul. Local discussion circles revolve around Muslim devotion, enchanted visions of nature, questions of private conduct, and, above all, the desire "to look behind the curtain and realize, 'Ah, that's how it is!'"[32] The international symposia cater to the international standards of the scientific community while introducing a set of ethical standards. As one of the organizers, a philosophy professor, explained to me, "Our jihad is a jihad of pen and paper"[33] The material with which the Nur community wants to build a bridge is made of something far more comprehensive than the local political claims-making, partnership, or group rights of their Milli Görüş brethren: a universal language that touches upon matters of insight, inspiration, and a common, universal ethics.

The Jamaatunnur is, however, by no means a sect. Milli Görüş members view it as an orthodox and devoted community that does far more than is strictly necessary. As they see it, Nur members pray more, they pray longer prayers, and they meet more often to study religious texts. In the eyes of religious Muslims, Nurcus are religious virtuosi. The latter's efforts to translate Quranic values into universal values seems to escape them. During Ramadan I regularly saw Milli Görüş members make a "crossover" to join in the extra-long evening prayers of the Nur community. But, as these people told me, this was just to do something extra in an extraordinary time. To them, during the rest of the year, five times a day was more than enough.

These few glimpses must suffice to answer the question of what framework the Jamaatunnur employs and what it allows the community to see. How does it answer to the present situation, which is dominated by violence legitimized with the Islamic tradition and oppressive security politics? In comparison to Milli Görüş, Jamaatunnur does not present the fuzzy territory with unclear borders that typifies social movements. The community does not care about political claims-making. To the contrary, its borders are clearly defined by a corpus of texts and a method to deal with them. The Nur community is first of all a community that consumes meaningful texts. It busies itself with the copying, reading, interpreting, editing, printing, and distributing of the immense oeuvre of its founder. Moreover, the Nur community is a text-producing community. With the help of the international symposia in Istanbul, some ten thousand pages of commentary on the founder's oeuvre already have been published, and more is expected in the future. Their occupation with meaningful text also creates the framework for the mobiliza-

---

32 Group interview at the Islamic University of Rotterdam, January 8, 2003.
33 Group interview at the Islamic University of Rotterdam, January 8, 2003.

tion of that heady human potential located somewhere between enthusiasm, inspiration, and love. The expression that the heritage of Sufi devotion takes in this community comes close to the Pentecostal experience. Nur students brim with enthusiasm and they are willing to share it. But who is willing to be a recipient? At this point, Europe, or, more precisely, European nonreligious society, comes into view. What Nur students seem to perceive is a world that must do without inner experiences, a disenchanted and demoralized society that is badly in need of a spiritual infusion. To view Europe as a place for da'wa, as a place to bring the good message to those who are in need, is not unique to Nur students. But what sets them apart from other Muslim endeavors is their refusal to proselytize. Instead, they want to share universal essence, reaped from the Quran, discovered with the help of Said Nursi's inspired commentary, and processed through texts and individual encounters.

The profile of the ideal Nur activist, then, is that of the intellectual, well-trained, highly ethical, and engaged colleague and neighbor. Nur students want to convince through personal conduct. Its perception of German society, and the strategies that were found to cope with it, keeps the Nur community outside the spotlights of policy-making agencies, although not outside those of the media. Meanwhile, though still in need of finer translations, it already has managed to translate the current political signals—suspicion and pressure—into a pressing need on the part of "secular" society, to which it responds from its religious point of view.

Summary and Conclusions

In the course of 2000 and 2001, a small group of Arab students prepared to execute a massacre. Hamburg was the center of their preparations, New York and Washington their ultimate stage. From the documents left behind by the students, it can be concluded that they considered the massacre a necessity to free Muslim norms and values from what they deemed intolerable oppression. Among the documents left behind was a "spiritual manual," which the students in all probability used. The manual gave instructions for a rigorous asceticism that prepared them for and guided them through the deed. The careful ritual setting and the ritual re-enactment of a raid that the Prophet had once staged indicate that the perpetrators acted within a religious framework and that they were religiously motivated, deliberately turning the massacre into an act of worship.

The hijack bombers of 9/11 shocked German policymakers out of their disinterest in Muslims. They suddenly realized that Muslims also lived in Germany, but, in the absence of other information, they could not—or could only with great difficulty—distinguish them from Muslims all around the world. As a result, all Muslims were perceived through a security framework. What this framework allowed them to see was an amorphous group that shared religious claims, organizations without any transparency or representation, and individuals who seemed to sympathize with terrorists. Their response was a standard reaction that came out of Germany's historical experience with left- and right-wing terrorists, ranging from student protests to the extermination politics of the National Socialists. Part of this collective memory was recalled with the use of words like sleepers, sympathizers, and do-gooders. The rhetoric helped to shape a political response that seemed appropriate in similar situations. Whether the current situation was really comparable with those of the German past was a question that did not receive much attention. The approach simply pushed the perception of Muslims, in particular religious Muslims, into the corner of right-wing activism, from which German politicians necessarily had to distance themselves. Observed from this angle, Muslim holy texts seemed to speak against the basic rights as guaranteed by the constitution, in particular that of equality between the sexes. Islam appeared to embody a particular political interest that threatened democracy. It was thus equated with Islamism, which in its turn was considered a fertile ground for terrorists. At this turning point, the lack of transparency and representation of the religious organizations started to serve as proof that they indeed had something to hide. The accusation of being sleepers, of undermining and threatening the democratic order, was aspersed like dew on all 3.2 million Muslims in Germany.

The Muslim community in Germany reacted with repulsion and apprehension. Secular Muslim members of Parliament and writers admitted that they were "powerless," meaning that they were not able to turn the tide with the same means on the same level. Religious organizations denied that they shared a religious tradition with hijackers and suicide bombers. They felt that the ensuing political pressure had been wrongly addressed. Then, in a second step, they began a complicated shift in strategies that revealed a new scale of tension between religion and politics: first, within a few years' time, the younger generation replaced the older one; second, "powerless" was reformulated as "inner strength"; and third, the dominant perception of "Islam equals politics" was challenged with a view of Islam that underlined its divine origin and universal value. In a third step, different Muslim religious actors embraced different strategies to become accepted as a group. The two religious organizations that I have discussed, Milli Görüş and Jamaatunnur, are positioned at opposite ends of the scale. The former launched into political claims-making; the latter placed its trust in ethical involvement and the power of inspired words. The former wound up in a headlong clash with political interests; the latter escaped any specific political attention. Their different strategies brought Milli Görüş all the limelight that political Germany could muster. The Jamaatunnur managed to stay more or less out of focus.

What do young Muslim believers do when confronted with the fact that their religious tradition also sanctions and engenders shocking instances of violence, although they themselves do not? How do they counter the political pressure? How do they communicate their version of their religious tradition? In this chapter, I have tried to capture the reciprocity between terrorism, political pressure, and the change of generations in two communities. To sum up my conclusions:

1. The groups under study positioned themselves in the German context differently. The distinction proposed by Max Weber can be applied: Milli Görüş actors moved towards the political sphere, whereas Nurcus laid claim to a shared professional sphere. Milli Görüş adherents, once they had taken over the positions of their fathers, intensified their political claims-making. Nur students reacted by linking spirituality with concrete instances of personal involvement. As a result, the former clashed with policymakers whereas the latter did not. These clashes, however, proved to be the decisive factor in gaining visibility.

2. This difference in approaches allows us to perceive Islamic groups that nurse distinct religious interpretations and embark upon divergent courses. This insight is of particular importance because the Islamic tradition allows for a multitude of interpretations, courses, and organizational forms, all of them considered to be equal to each other. It does not, however, allow for standardization—neither through a hierarchy nor through terrorist acts. Muslims who try to bomb themselves to the top count on achieving high visibility through the global media, something that is then counteracted with the silence of nonviolent Muslims.

3. Both groups are very much aware of the multitude of possible interpretations and the limits that this multiplicity sets on their own interpretation. Terrorist acts in the name of Islam forced them to act in a global context, but they rejected the idea of a theological discussion or direct confrontation with their extremist competitors. The terrorist attacks challenged them to actively promote a different interpretation of the Islamic tradition and to act out their beliefs in the German context. Both communities fostered a discourse on Islam which was based on nonviolence and social engagement, hoping that one day it would gain dominance again. In their local context, their respective discourse brought both groups only negative visibility: the signals that Milli Görüş sends are perceived as "dangerously close" to the worldview of extremists; the signals that Jamaatunnur sends are considered to be "missionary."

4. In both communities, the German context was captured with the word "secular," secular being the keyword with which the new generation perceives and reacts to its surroundings. For the one it stood for atheist and good-for-nothing, for the other it meant disenchantment. "Secular" also stood for the power to define values, to anchor them in the constitution, and to declare them universal. "Secular society" as perceived by young Muslims born and raised in Germany calls for the need to be different, to show one's religious roots, and to translate Muslim values into understandable principles that are equally universal.

5. For Nur students, the tension between religion and the world involves the entire social world. For Milli Görüş, it is limited to the political world.

The new Milli Görüş generation formulated the task of finding a compromise as a legal matter, transferring religious claims to secular rights as guaranteed by the constitution. Nur students formulated their religious claims in philosophical terms, embarking upon a translation of Muslim conduct as universal ethics.

6. In the highly tense political situation, their religious views on Germany offered both groups a means to translate political pressure into a basic human need. They drew their impulse from this change of frameworks. For the younger generation, it finally made Germany visible as a promising field to make oneself understood and to gain respect.

References

Abu-Rabi, I. M. 2003. Islam at the crossroads: On the life and thought of Bediüzzaman Said Nursi. Albany, NY: State University of New York Press.

Appadurai, A. 1996. Modernity at large: Cultural dimensions of globalization. Minneapolis: University of Minnesota Press.

Breuer, R. 2003. Grundlagen der Scharia und ihre Anwendung im 21. Jahrhundert. In Islamismus: Texte zur inneren Sicherheit, ed. Bundesministerium des Innern, 100–101. Berlin: Bundesministerium des Innern.

Briese, O. 2003. "Schläfer" und "Rasterfahndung": Kochs Konzept gesunder Keimträger. In Rasterfahndungen: Darstellungstechniken, Normierungsverfahren, Wahrnehmungs-konstitution, ed. T. Nusser and E. Strowick, 181–199. Bielefeld, Germany: transcript.

Bundesministerium des Innern, ed. 2003. Islamismus: Texte zur inneren Sicherheit. Berlin: Bundesministerium des Innern.

Droste, W., and K. Bittermann, eds. 1998. Wörterbuch des Gutmenschen. 2 vols. Berlin: Edition Tiamat.

Haug, F., and K. Reimer, eds. 2005. Politik ums Kopftuch. Hamburg: Argument.

Hermann, R. 1996. Die drei Versionen des politischen Islam in der Türkei. Orient 96 (1): 35–37.

Jonker, G. 2002. Konsensbildung und Beschlußfassung: Im Kräftefeld islamischer Interessen in der Bundesrepublik. In Adaption des Deutschen Recht und Islam, ed. J. Oebbecke, 1–24. Münster: Fink Verlag.

———. 2003a. Islamic knowledge through a woman's lens: Education, power and belief. Social Compass 50 (1): 35–47.

———. 2003b. Vor den Toren: Bildung, Macht und Glauben aus der Sicht religiöser muslimischer Frauen. In Facetten islamischer Welten: Geschlechterordnungen, Frauen- und Menschenrechte in der Diskussion, ed. M. Rumpf, U. Gerhard, and M. M. Jansen, 219–242. Bielefeld, Germany: transcript.

Kandel, J. 2002. Lieber blauäugig als Blind? Anmerkungen zum "Dialog" mit dem Islam. Berlin: Friedrich-Ebert Stiftung.

———. 2004. Auf dem Kopf und in dem Kopf: Der "Kopftuchstreit" und die Muslime. Berlin: Friedrich-Ebert Stiftung.

Kippenberg, H. G. 2004. Terror als Gottesdienst. In Terror im Dienste Gottes: Die "geistliche Anleitung" der Attentäter des 11. September 2001, ed. H. G. Kippenberg and T. Seidensticker, 67–85. Frankfurt: Campus.

———. 2005. "Consider that it is a raid on the path of God": The spiritual manual of the attackers of 9/11. Numen 52: 29–58.

Kippenberg, H. G., and T. Seidensticker, eds. 2004. Terror im Dienste Gottes: Die "geistliche Anleitung" der Attentäter des 11. September 2001. Frankfurt: Campus.

Krämer, G. 2005. Geschichte des Islam. Munich: Beck.

Malik, J. 2005. Gewalt und Gewaltverzicht im Islam. In Religion–Christentum–Gewalt: Einblicke und Perspektiven, ed. W. Ratzmann, 57–73. Leipzig: Evangelische Verlagsanstalt.

Mardin, S. 1989. Religion and social change in Turkey: The case of Bediüzzaman Said Nursi. Albany, NY: State University of New York Press.

Nereid, C. T. 1997. In the light of Said Nursi: Turkish nationalism and the religious alternative. Bergen, Norway: Centre for Middle Eastern and Islamic Studies.

Nietzsche, F. 1873. Unzeitgemäße Betrachtungen. Ed. G. Colli and M. Montinai. Berlin: De Gruyter.

Reed, F. A. 1999. Anatolia junction: A journey in hidden Turkey. Toronto: Talon Books.

Rotter, G. 1992. Allah's Plagiator: Die publizistische Raubzüge des Nahostexperten. Heidelberg: Palmyra.

Scheffler, T. 2004. Zur Gegenwartsdiagnose Bin Ladens. In Terror im Dienste Gottes: Die "geistliche Anleitung" der Attentäter des 11. September 2001, ed. H. G. Kippenberg and T. Seidensticker, 87–105. Frankfurt: Campus.

Schiffauer, W. 2005. Gutachten [expert opinion], dated January 5, attached to the Verwaltungsgericht Berlin VG 25 A 6.05 Beschluß (February 22, 2005), 28–33.

Schmidt, M. G., ed. 2004. Wörterbuch zur Politik. Munich: Kröner Verlag.

Seufert, G. 1997. Politische Islam in der Türkei: Islamismus als symbolische Repräsentation einer sich modernisierenden islamischen Gesellschaft. Munich: Franz Steiner.

Vahide, S. 2000. Bediüzzaman Said Nursi. Istanbul: Sözler Publications.

Verfassungsbericht NRW. 2002. Verfassungsbericht des Landes Nordrhein Westfalen 2002. Düsseldorf: Land Nordrhein Westfalen.

Verwaltungsgericht Berlin. 2005. Verwaltungsgericht Berlin VG 25 A 6.05 Beschluß [legal decision of the administrative court], February 22.

Yavuz, H. 1997. Print-based Islamic discourse and modernity: The Nur movement. In The Third International Symposium on Bediüzzaman Said

Nursi: The reconstruction of Islamic thought in the twentieth century and Bediüzzaman Said Nursi, ed. Nesil Foundation, 324–350. Istanbul: Sözler Publications.

Yavuz, H. M., and J. L. Esposito, eds. 2003. Turkish Islam and the secular state: The Gülen movement. Syracuse, NY: Syracuse University Press.

Gökce Yurdakul

SECULAR VERSUS ISLAMIST:
THE HEADSCARF DEBATE IN GERMANY[1]

Two opposing voices from Turkish communities emerge in public space in Germany.[2] One argues that Muslim teachers should be allowed to wear headscarves in public service:

"The religious freedom of Muslim teachers who wear headscarves is restricted, and their free entrance to jobs in public service, which is their right according to constitutional law, becomes impossible. This cultivates prejudices against Muslims, encourages continued discrimination against Muslims in all social spheres, and negatively affects the integration efforts of Muslims. The essence of the judgment is that the state would have to declare neutrality. This principle of government action is incompatible with a Muslim teacher who wishes to wear a headscarf while teaching. Obviously, the judge is proceeding from an incorrect understanding of the principle of neutrality." (Oguz Ücüncü, secretary general, Islamische Gemeinschaft Milli Görüş; see Ücüncü 2002)

The other one argues that this is an "Islamist trap":

"Have they forgotten that fundamentalist claims mean real discrimination against girls and women? The Türkischer Bund in Berlin-Brandenburg warns against falling into the Islamist trap, which connects the 'ban on headscarves' to 'professional exclusion' and then to 'discrimination against women.'" (Türkischer Bund in Berlin-Brandenburg, press release, December 1, 2003)

It may seem unusual that I wish to explore how Turkish social democratic associations compete with religiously oriented Turkish Muslim associations

---

1 I would like to thank Gerdien Jonker and Valérie Amiraux for their encouragement and support in my pre- and post-natal months, and my daughter Daphne Yudit for her patience while I was writing this chapter. I also would like to acknowledge the intellectual contribution of Michal Bodemann and Pascale Fournier to the research and writing process.

2 A number of terms are used to describe Turkish immigrants and their children in Germany (Caglar 2001). In this chapter I use the term "Turkish communities" to refer to the Turkish immigrants and their children who live in Germany. "Turkish Muslims" is used to refer to the Turkish immigrants and their children who strongly associate with Islam.

for political representation in Germany.[3] Many of the studies on Muslims in Europe and North America fail to discuss the heterogeneity of these communities. They focus on Muslim communities as only a homogeneous group. By focusing on Turkish social democrats as well as Muslim associations, I aim to bring the heterogeneity of immigrant communities into the discourse. I present comparative case studies of the Türkischer Bund in Berlin-Brandenburg (the Turkish Union in Berlin-Brandenburg; hereafter "TBB"), a secular, social-democratic immigrant association, and the Islamische Gemeinschaft Milli Görüş (hereafter "Milli Görüş"), a religiously oriented Turkish immigrant association with ties to Islamic fundamentalism.[4]

The third voice in this debate is that of German political actors. They have formed the context for the TBB spokespersons and Milli Görüş representatives during the headscarf debate. Specifically, in the aftermath of 9/11, the German police and the mass media started to focus on Islam and Muslim communities. The gathering places of Muslims, such as mosques and religious associations, became the targets of state inspections and the subjects of flashy newspaper headlines, both of which viewed them as possible shelters for terrorists.[5] Muslims from different backgrounds—from Moroccans to Turks, Egyptians to Pakistanis—became the victims of the same anti-Muslim discourse, which portrayed them as foreigners posing a threat to European democracy and society (Amiraux 2003; Bodemann 2004; Kastoryano 2004; Fournier and Yurdakul, forthcoming). I chose the headscarf debate as one example among many discussions about Muslim practices in Germany because the differences between the discourses of Turkish social democrats and of Muslims became clearer and more explicit in this debate than in any other public debate. Various explanations can account for this development, but one thing is clear: although the headscarf debate in Germany occurred in a different legal, social, and political system, it had similarities to the headscarf debate in Turkey. Therefore, the echoes sounding from the Turkish context may have played a central role in dividing the Turkish communities in Germany. In Germany, as in Turkey, this Muslim community was considered

---

3   It is important to note that the Milli Görüş and the Türkischer Bund in Berlin-Brandenburg (TBB) are not competing for the same kind of political representation. Whereas the Milli Görüş emphasizes that the social and political differences of Muslim practices should be recognized (these practices are defined in the "Islamische Charta"), the TBB argues for erasing social and religious differences from the public sphere. As a result, these associations have different political representations and appeal to different constituencies.

4   Of course, the Turkish Muslim community in Germany is not limited to these two groups. It is also divided along lines of ethnic, religious, and gender difference. In this chapter, however, I intentionally focus on the TBB and the Milli Görüş and the different political perspectives and stances they represent.

5   Islamische Gemeinschaft Milli Görüş, "Münchener Polizei tritt den Rechtsstaat mit den Füßen," September 30, 2004, on their Web site "Das islamische Portal": http://www.igmg.de/index.php?module=ContentExpress&func=display&ceid=12 77&itmid=1.

homogeneous; other features, such as the leftist, social democratic, and pro-integration characteristics of some Muslim immigrant communities, as well as class, gender, and ethnic differences, were mostly ignored (Yurdakul, forthcoming).

I shall first briefly introduce the TBB and the Milli Görüş, two political immigrant associations that compete for representation in the German political context. I then discuss the different discourses that emerged during the heated debate over Muslim women's headscarves in public places in Germany. In this section I map the different positions of the German political actors and the immigrant associations. I explore how the discourses of the social democratic and the religiously oriented associations competed during the headscarf debates in Germany. Drawing on this debate, I then consider what these discourses tell us about immigrants' political representation in Germany today.

The TBB and the Milli Görüş

The TBB is a social-democratic immigrant association that claims to represent the Turkish communities in the Berlin-Brandenburg region. The core organization of the TBB was originally the BTBTM (Berlin Türk Bilim ve Teknoloji Merkezi, or the "Turkish Science and Technology Center Berlin"). This student organization was founded by Turkish students at the Technical University of Berlin in 1977. The BTBTM defended the rights of immigrant workers and also fought for equal rights for international students, in particular Turkish students. From its beginnings, the association had a strong social democratic tendency, which was deeply affected by the rising tensions between left- and right-wing political parties in Turkey in the late 1970s, which resulted in the abolishment of all nongovernmental associations after a military coup d'état in 1980. In fact, the official letterhead of the BTBTM in 1977 bluntly revealed the political leanings of this student organization: "The Turkish Science and Technology Center Berlin; Political Tendency: Democratic Left."

According to its early archives of 1977, the BTBTM openly showed solidarity with the JungsozialistInnen (Young Socialists), the youth organization of the Sozialdemokratische Partei Deutschlands (Social Democratic Party; hereafter "SPD"), by attending common events such as student meetings. However, in the late 1970s, the BTBTM's major focus was its ties with the social-democratic Turkish political parties, specifically with Bülent Ecevit, the founder of the Demokratik Sol Parti (Democratic Left Party). In various documents, such as annual reports and press releases, two main themes were expressed: the BTBTM's strong political support for the social democrats in Turkey and the attempts to find solutions for the problems of Turkish workers in Germany.

By 1992, the Turkish students of the BTBTM had begun to welcome second-generation Turks in Germany: the children of guest workers were grown up, had started to attend German universities, and had joined Turkish students' political movements. In the early 1990s, the executive committee of the BTBTM started discussions about an umbrella organization that would bring all Turkish immigrant associations together. This organization developed from the BTBTM to the Federation of Immigrants from Turkey (Bund der EinwanderInnen aus der Türkei) and finally to the TBB in 1995.

The current political tendency of the TBB is still social democratic; however, it now emphasizes equality for immigrants, specifically Turkish immigrants. Eren Ünsal, a spokeswoman of the TBB, described the association's goals and constituency as follows:

"The political aim of the TBB is based on the thesis that immigrants do not have equal rights [with Germans]. Our aim is to ensure that they have equal rights. And we organize our campaigns according to this aim. [Our campaigns are] directed not only at Turks; they are directed at everyone who is not German. But the TBB appeals more to Turks. Turkish people feel sympathetic to us and become our members. But our campaigns and projects are directed at all people who are not European, who are not German." (interview with Ünsal on October 24, 2002)

In general, Ünsal is relatively accurate about the aim and the constituency of the TBB. However, the TBB's aim is not solely to defend immigrants' rights; in fact, the TBB's major aim is to organize political mobilization against all sorts of discrimination against immigrants and foreigners in Germany. In this sense, the TBB has redefined its previous role as the Federation of Immigrants from Turkey, which had attempted to defend only Turkish immigrants' rights.

Although the TBB was founded to defend the rights of immigrants at large, it is in fact a technocratic and top-down elitist body (Göle 1986). The founders of the TBB are traditional intellectuals in the Gramscian sense: they have been educated in the best schools in Turkey. A spokesman of the TBB also heads the foreigners' commission of the German Federation of Trade Unions in the Land of Berlin-Brandenburg (Ausländerberatungsstelle des Deutschen Gewerkschaftsbundes, Landesbezirk Berlin-Brandenburg). The other members also come from privileged backgrounds and occupy high positions in state institutions or private enterprises. They thus are not like the immigrants whom they claim to represent, who own an *Imbiss* (a snack bar or *döner kebab* stand) or work shifts in a German factory.

Many German political authorities refer to the TBB as the supporter and guardian of "immigrant integration." In return, the TBB keeps close contact with parliament members and political parties. Although the spokespeople of the TBB strongly emphasize that they have good relations with all of the political parties, there is an obvious affiliation of the TBB's executive committee with the SPD. TBB's executive director serves as the chair of the Migration Working Group (Arbeitsgemeinschaft Migration) within the SPD.

The working group specializes in immigrants' issues, presenting reports to the party authorities. The treasurer of the TBB is a member of the SPD, serving on the commission for women's issues.

Although there are many indications of the close ties between the TBB and the SPD, a spokesman of the TBB, Safter Cınar, denies that this is the case. It is the TBB's duty, he explains, to mobilize German Turks to vote in the elections; the TBB should not, however, encourage German Turks to vote for a specific party. He claims that the TBB is a nongovernmental association; hence, a specific political ideology would not be imposed on its members.

Having said this, who is the constituency of the TBB? The TBB is made up of nineteen member associations. It appeals to associations that have social-democratic political tendencies, such as the Türkischer Elternverein (Turkish Parents Association), as well as some individual members who are in politically powerful positions, such as Mehmet Eksi, a politically active teacher and researcher in the Aziz Nesin Europäische Schule (Aziz Nesin European School),[6] and Mustafa Yeni, who is the chair of the foreigners' commission in one of the most powerful unions in Germany, IG Metall.

In sum, the TBB appeals to people with a social-democratic and middle-class background who have settled down in Berlin. The main concerns of this constituency are immigrant integration, political representation, and antidiscrimination campaigns. Through a statistical analysis of a random sample of fifty topics from the TBB newsletters published between 2002 and 2004, I found that the most popular topics were the integration of immigrants (nine cases), campaigns against racism and discrimination (seven cases), the education of immigrant children (seven cases), and political lobbying for Turkey's candidacy to the European Union (eight cases). The least popular topics were environmental consciousness (one case) and campaigns against homophobia (one case), which do surface on the TBB's agenda, though rarely.[7]

Like the TBB, the Milli Görüş also frequently campaigns about discrimination, though exclusively about discrimination against Muslims. In fact, the historical background of the Milli Görüş in Germany is characterized by this emphasis on Muslim mobilization. The Milli Görüş was present as an informal network in Europe even in the early 1970s. In Germany, it emerged as a diasporic association of the members of Milli Selamet Partisi (National Salvation Party), the banned party of Necmettin Erbakan, a former prime minister of Turkey and the spiritual leader of Milli Görüş ideology.

The name Milli Görüş refers to the political ideology created by the Milli Nizam Partisi (the National Order Party) in Turkey during the 1970s. The ideology of the Milli Görüş has been represented in the Turkish political arena by a series of religiously oriented political parties, such as the National Order Party (founded in 1970 and banned from politics by the Constitutional

---

6   Aziz Nesin Europäische Schule was the first school to introduce bilingual education in Turkish and German.

7   There may be a time-specific bias.

Court in 1971), Milli Selamet Partisi (the National Salvation Party, founded in 1972 and banned after the 1980 coup), Refah Partisi (the Welfare Party, founded in 1983 and banned in 1998), Fazilet Partisi (the Virtue Party, founded in 1997 and banned in 2001), and, finally, Saadet Partisi (the Felicity Party, founded in 2001). During these various bans from political activities and subsequent re-establishment of the party under different names, the Milli Görüş was strengthened as a diasporic network of Turkish Muslims in Europe, and particularly in Germany.[8]

The Milli Görüş is listed by the Bundesverfassungsschutz (Germany's federal office for the protection of the constitution) as a "threat" to German democracy (Schiffauer 2004). The main reason for the inclusion of the Milli Görüş on this list is that it is considered to be Islamic fundamentalist, preventing the immigrants concerned from full political participation in German society. The report states that the Milli Görüş pursues anti-integrative efforts, especially with respect to the Islamic education of children. Moreover, the report provides many examples of defamatory statements made in Milli Görüş publications, in particular anti-German and anti-Semitic statements in the *Milli Gazete*.[9] The label of "threat" to German democracy largely restricts Milli Görüş activities and campaigns and makes Milli Görüş members objects of suspicion (Schiffauer 2004; Bodemann 2004). German political actors, in particular, consider the Milli Görüş to be an illegitimate discussion partner.[10]

Because the association is included on the list of the Bundesverfassungsschutz, Milli Görüş leaders are not able to find supporters among German politicians and state authorities. Although they are represented as a threat to German society, they still make claims on the German state in order to create sociopolitical space for Muslims in Germany. However, because the Milli Görüş has no credibility among German politicians, they use different channels, different associations, and other kinds of representatives. One of these associations is the Islamische Föderation in Berlin (Islamic Federation of Berlin), which has been granted permission to teach Islam courses in German secondary education in the German language.[11]

---

8 The Milli Görüş is a diasporic network in many countries in Europe as well as in North America. The networks in Germany, the Netherlands, and France are the most well known.

9 The daily newspaper *Milli Gazete* is considered to be the major publication of Milli Görüş supporters. Its anti-Semitic and anti-German statements have provoked many negative reactions from the German state authorities. The Milli Görüş in Germany has published different German periodicals that are not affiliated with the *Milli Gazete*, such as *Perspektive*.

10 The Milli Görüş has an organic relationship with the current governing party, Adalet ve Kalkınma Partisi, in Turkey. Even this relationship is not sufficient to clear its name from the list of the Bundesverfassungsschutz.

11 See "Milli Görüşe John Destegi," *Sabah*, July 10, 1999; "Geld für Islam-Unterricht," *Berliner Morgenpost*, September 21, 2002; Häußler 2001. In the school year 2002/2003, 1,607 students in Berlin (852 girls, 805 boys) took Islam as a religion course in Berlin; 74 % of them were of Turkish nationality, 21 %

In addition to cases involving educational rights, the following legal cases have been introduced by the Milli Görüş to the German courts: the right to ritual slaughtering (affirmed by the courts in 2002), Muslim teachers' right to wear religious attire in schools (denied in 2003), the right to have religious education (affirmed in 1984), Muslim girls' right to withdraw from swimming courses when both sexes are present (affirmed in 1993), the right to add Muslim names in conversion to Islam (affirmed in 1992), the right to the availability of Muslim services in social and medical institutions (still in consideration), and the right to burial according to Muslim rituals (still in consideration). The right to the announcement of Islamic prayer (*ezan*) with speakers and the right to receive permission from the employer for daily prayer times (*namaz*) and for religious holidays (*dini bayram*) have not been brought to the courts yet.[12]

Of these court cases, the most controversial was the one on Muslim women's wearing of religious headscarves in public places. Although women have rarely been in a position to demonstrate their strengths in the Milli Görüş movement, in the headscarf debate the Milli Görüş appeared to be the pioneering organization for defending women's right to wear the headscarf in public places. Mustafa Yoldas, chairman of the Schura, Rat der Islamischen Gemeinschaften (Schura, the Council of Islamic Communities), explained the strong position of the Milli Görüş in the headscarf debate:

"If you force people, saying 'this is the only way,' then people will do the opposite. Many young girls began to cover their heads as a reaction. If you treat [Muslims] like this, and if we have to make a choice, then we have to choose the people of our own religion. This is what we are experiencing after September 11." (Interview with Yoldas on August 10, 2004)

During the court cases on wearing the headscarf while in public service, the Milli Görüş supported the teacher, Fereshta Ludin. Eventually, Ludin began work as a teacher in an Islamic primary school in Berlin that is affiliated with the Milli Görüş.

The Headscarf Debate in Germany

In late 2003 there was renewed controversial public debate in Germany about whether Muslim women teachers could attend their classes wearing the traditional headscarf. The debate was re-ignited when a German schoolteacher of Afghan origin, Fereshta Ludin, insisted on wearing the hijab in

---

were Arabs (see Islamische Föderation in Berlin, "Aktuelle Daten über den IRU für das Schuljahr," http://www.islamische-foederation.de/IRU.htm; "Die Kopftuch Schule," *Die Tageszeitung*, June 24, 2004).

12 See "Das islamische Portal," the Web site of the Islamische Gemeinschaft Milli Görüş: http://www.igmg.de.

school. Ludin was subsequently dismissed from her teaching job, and she in turn complained that she was being discriminated against on the grounds of her religious beliefs. When her case was brought before the Bundesverfassungsgericht (Germany's Federal Constitutional Court),[13] the court ruled that "Germany's constitutional law did not explicitly forbid the wearing of headscarves in the classroom in state-run schools" (the German station Deutsche Welle, September 25, 2003). However, the courts expressed fear that the headscarf, as a religious symbol, would in and of itself threaten the educational mission:[14]

"If teachers introduce religious or ideological references at school, this may adversely affect the state's duty to provide education which is to be carried out in neutrality … It at least opens up the possibility of influence on the pupils and of conflicts with parents that may lead to a disturbance of the peace of the school and may *endanger* the carrying out of the school's duty to provide education. The dress of teachers that is religiously motivated and that is to be interpreted as the profession of a religious conviction may also have these effects […]."

"If a teacher wore a headscarf in lessons, this could lead to religious influence on the students and to conflicts within the class in question, even if the subject of complaint had credibly denied any intention of recruitment or proselytizing. The only decisive factor was the effect created in students by the sight of the headscarf. The headscarf motivated by Islam was a plainly visible religious symbol that the onlooker could not escape."[15] (Fournier and Yurdakul, forthcoming)

Presented as creating a "potential situation of danger" in the classroom,[16] the headscarf is regarded by the court as an expression of Islamic fundamentalism: "Most recently, it is seen increasingly as a political symbol of Islamic fundamentalism that expresses the separation from values of Western society" (Fournier and Yurdakul, forthcoming).[17] In a final step, the court let the individual *Länder* decide whether to legally enact a ban on wearing the headscarf in school:

"However, the *Land* legislature responsible is at liberty to create the statutory basis that until now has been lacking, for example by newly laying down the permissible

---

13 During the court case, it was believed that Ludin was supported by the lawyers of the Milli Görüş to bring out the headscarf issue and challenge the incorporation policies for Muslims; this point, however, has not been publicly confirmed.

14 The following two paragraphs were written exclusively by Pascale Fournier in our co-authored article "Unveiling Distribution: Muslim Women with Headscarves in France and Germany," in Migration, Citizenship, Ethnos, ed. Michal Bodemann and Gökce Yurdakul (New York: Palgrave Macmillan, forthcoming).

15 BVerfGe, 2BvR, 1436/02, Judgment of the Second Senate of September 24, 2003, on the basis of the oral hearing of June 3, 2003, Supra, note 24, at Par. I (6).

16 Ibid., at Par. III (1).

17 Ibid., at Par. II (5) a).

degree of religious references in schools within the limits of the constitutional requirements. In doing this, the legislature must take into reasonable account the freedom of faith of the teachers and of the pupils affected, the parents' right of education, and the state's duty of ideological and religious neutrality."[18]

Most German *Länder* were in favor of the ban, particularly those states governed by the conservative Christian Democratic Union and Christian Social Union parties, such as Baden-Württemberg. They supported the ban by stating that the German "constitution is based on a Christian Occidental tradition and [that] they would begin to draw up legislation to ban headscarves in the classroom as soon as possible" (Deutsche Welle, September 25, 2003). According to this argument, nuns who obviously come from the aforementioned Christian tradition are allowed to wear headscarves while teaching. Muslim women, however, are not allowed to wear their headscarves because their Oriental religious attire is not compatible with the "cultural homogeneity" of majority society (Schieck 2004, 71).

Since then, the Stuttgart school authority—the school district for which Ludin used to work—argued with respect to the state's obligation to religious neutrality that it views "the headscarf [as] symbolizing a desire for cultural disintegration that was irreconcilable with the state's obligation to neutrality" (Schieck 2004, 70). Referring to the court's statements about religious neutrality, the school authority revision board (Oberschulamt Stuttgart) carried the topic further to the conflicting religious beliefs of parents and teachers. It argued that the students will be influenced by the teacher's headscarf, viewing it as a religious statement. As the debate shifted to the issues of state neutrality, the "common good" of the society, religious freedom, and gender inequality, Ludin had to give up her hopes of teaching in her previous school. She moved to Berlin and took a job at the Islamische Gesamtschule, a private school where she can wear her headscarf while teaching.[19]

At the peak of the headscarf discussions, leftist politicians were divided on the issue, and the political climate in Germany dramatically changed. Supporters of multiculturalism (e.g., *Integrationsbeauftragte* ["government representatives for integration"] and Marieluise Beck, a member of the Green Party) stood behind religious immigrant organizations in their efforts to defend multicultural rights, whereas supporters of state neutrality (e.g., Lale Akgün, parliament member from the SPD) were in the same camp as mainstream Christian Democrats, arguing against the politicization of Islam.

The Green Party, and especially Marieluise Beck, defended the supporters of the headscarf by emphasizing multiculturalism and, therefore, a respect for diversity. In fact, the leading German women of immigration politics, such as Marieluise Beck, Barbara John, and Rita Süssmuth, stated in an open letter on the banning of the headscarf from public places:

---

18 Ibid., at Par. 72.
19 "Die Kopftuch Schule," *Die Tageszeitung*, June 24, 2004.

"Whether or not one should opt for a more strictly secular school system, we want to make religious plurality in our society visible. The equal treatment of all religions is mandated by the constitution. A different treatment of Islamic symbols as opposed to Christian or Jewish ones is problematic from the viewpoint of integration and exacerbates conflicts instead of reducing them."[20]

The former president of Germany, Johannes Rau, also addressed the headscarf issue:

"I am firmly convinced that we cannot prohibit the symbol of a religion—and the headscarf is one such—and can still believe we could leave everything else the way things are. This cannot be reconciled with freedom of religion, guaranteed to all by our constitution. It would open the door to a development which most proponents of the prohibition of the headscarf surely would not want." (speech by President Johannes Rau in 2003; my translation)

Whereas the president of Germany was openly against the headscarf ban, Lale Akgün, a parliament member from the SPD and an immigrant of Turkish background, presented arguments similar to those of mainstream Christian Democrats and launched a campaign against the wearing of the headscarf in public places. In addition, an open letter in response to Beck's call for the headscarf was signed by many pioneering women academics, politicians, artists, doctors, and teachers:

"Who within the Muslim population would feel marginalized if the headscarf were prohibited in school? Only those who are under the influence of the Islamists and for whom wearing the headscarf is a sine qua non not only in the private sphere, but also in public service. All those for whom religion is a private matter and all those who are indifferent to religious precepts know and accept without problem the constitutional principle of neutrality in the school system."[21]

At the same time, immigrant organizations were competing for space in the public sphere to promote and defend their views. Turkish Muslim immigrant organizations in particular, such as the Milli Görüş, argued that religious and cultural differences should be regarded as constitutional rights and that, consequently, Muslim women should not be prevented from practicing their religion in the public sphere. In contrast, the immigrant organizations with social democratic leanings, such as the TBB, supported the ban of all religious symbols from the public sphere, a position that is in line with the Turkish state's secularism.[22]

---

20 "Religious Plurality Instead of Forced Emancipation: An Appeal Against the Headscarf Law," open letter published in *Die Tageszeitung*, December 15, 2003.
21 "Für Neutralität in der Schule," open letter published in *Die Tageszeitung*, February 14/15, 2004.
22 The tension between these opposing views should be viewed in relation to the headscarf debate in Turkey (Göle 1997; Göcek 1999; Cizre and Cinar 2003). Currently, it is forbidden for students to wear headscarves in Turkish universi-

The TBB issued a press release informing Germans about the differences between the regular headscarf and the Islamic fundamentalist headscarf and warning the public about the evils of the latter. The traditional headscarf, the association explained, has a loose knot under the chin and leaves some of the front hair out, whereas the political headscarf, also known as a turban or hijab, is a conservative covering of the head which leaves no hair out and wraps tightly around the neck. The former is eligible to "cross the border" from the immigrant society to the mainstream host society, whereas the latter, the political headscarf, must be eliminated from the public sphere. The TBB accused the religious immigrant organizations of being Islamic fundamentalists, and Marieluise Beck and her supporters of being naive.

"When [...] the headscarf, veil, and burka are 'instruments for the oppression of women and when they represent basic political symbols,' then this naiveté [Beck and her supporters] is incomprehensible especially in a time of stronger fundamentalist activities." (TBB press release, December 1, 2003)

Launching a campaign in support of parliament member Lale Akgün, the TBB took a public stance against the Green Party's policy on the headscarf. The standpoint of the TBB—an association that represents Turks in Berlin—put the Green Party in a strange position: in spite of the reaction from Turkish immigrants favoring social democracy, the Greens were trying to force multiculturalist values down immigrants' throats. In fact, the TBB warned Germans about Islamic fundamentalism:

"The people who signed this letter stress that the banning of the headscarf from public services would concern only women (and therefore be discriminatory). Have they forgotten that fundamentalist claims mean real discrimination against girls and women? The Türkischer Bund in Berlin-Brandenburg warns against falling into the Islamist trap, which connects the 'ban on headscarves' to 'professional exclusion' and then to 'discrimination against women.'" (TBB press release, December 1, 2003)

On every occasion involving the headscarf debate in Germany, the TBB supported the idea that religion is a private matter and discouraged the idea of wearing religious symbols in public service. In order to prove its point, the TBB drew on various assumptions, the most common of which actually mirror many Germans' conceptions of Islam "the headscarf is a symbol of women's oppression in the Muslim world," "it is the symbol of Muslim

---

ties. A university student, Leyla Sahin, who wanted to wear her headscarf in the university brought her case to the European Court of Human Rights in Strasbourg. The court decided in favor of the Turkish state and declared that it is the state's right to protect public order. For more information on this case, see the European Court of Human Rights, Case of Leyla Sahin versus Turkey, Strasbourg, June 29, 2004 (available online).

fundamentalism," and, most important, "the Muslim headscarf is a threat to the German state's religious neutrality."

As a cultural interpreter of Turkish Islam, which is unfamiliar to many Germans, the TBB warned the German public that the wearing of religious symbols in public service would hinder immigrant assimilation. Moreover, by emphasizing that the Muslim headscarf is a threat to the religious neutrality of the German state, the TBB argued that one of the most important principles of German democracy is under scrutiny by Muslim communities (Schieck 2004; Yeneroglu 2004).

The position of the Milli Görüş in the headscarf debate was fundamentally different from that of the TBB. When the spokespeople of the TBB warned Germans about the rise of Islamic fundamentalism, they were referring to religiously oriented immigrant groups such as the Milli Görüş (interview with Safter Cınar in April 2005). In contrast to the TBB, Milli Görüş representatives and related associations argued that women should be allowed to wear headscarves in public places.[23] Legal permission to wear the Muslim headscarf in public places had been discussed in Milli Görüş publications, such as the German association's magazine *Milli Görüş Perspektive*. Oguz Ücüncü, the secretary general of the Milli Görüş in Germany, explained:

"The religious freedom of Muslim teachers who wear headscarves is restricted, and their free entrance to jobs in public service, which is their right according to constitutional law, becomes impossible. This cultivates prejudices against Muslims, encourages continued discrimination against Muslims in all social spheres, and negatively affects the integration efforts of Muslims. The essence of the judgment is that the state would have to declare neutrality. This principle of government action is incompatible with a Muslim teacher who wishes to wear a headscarf while teaching. Obviously, the judge is proceeding from an incorrect understanding of the principle of neutrality." (Ücüncü 2002)

In this publication, Ücüncü stresses that the headscarf ban will exacerbate discrimination against Muslim women and hinder efforts to integrate Muslims. Moreover, he juxtaposes the two important concepts of the democratic state, freedom of religion and state neutrality, and argues that the judge misinterpreted the neutrality of the state in religious matters. Contrary to what Akgün and her supporters argue (that wearing the headscarf in public places threatens the state's neutrality), Ücüncü stresses that state neutrality in religious matters is to encourage religious plurality.

In opposition to the court's statement (i.e., "If a teacher wore a headscarf in lessons, this could lead to religious influence on the students and to conflicts within the class in question, even if the subject of complaint had credibly denied any intention of recruitment or proselytizing"), Ücüncü (2002) argues the following:

---

23 Associations such as Islamische Föderation Berlin and SCHURA Hamburg.

"One of the aims of education is to make students think about other cultures and religion. This aim would be supported by a Muslim teacher who is wearing a headscarf. Through this, she could help weaken prejudices and provide better understanding."

Mustafa Yeneroglu, the lawyer of the Milli Görüş in Cologne, takes a fiercer and more defensive position. In an interview, he brought up the controversial connection between the headscarf and Islamic terror:

"The decision of the Constitutional Court on the headscarf is wrong. Although it seems like the decision is in favor [of wearing the headscarf in public places], when you look at other decisions of the Constitutional Court in religious matters, this one is wrong. The court left the freedom of religion, a matter of basic freedom, to the decision of *Land*-level parliaments. It left it to political initiatives ... Whatever I say, in all the reports of the constitutional institutions, it is stated that 'these are fundamentalists, Islamists, radicals, extremists ... they are terrorists.' This is how it is perceived." (Interview with Mustafa Yeneroglu, head of the legal office for the Milli Görüş in Cologne, July 27, 2004)

In all of these statements by Milli Görüş representatives, the main aim of the Milli Görüş is to bring some exclusively Muslim practice, such as wearing the headscarf, into German political discussions.[24] The TBB, on the other hand, have made Muslim immigrant associations the main target of their accusations, warning against "Islamic fundamentalism" in their press releases. Therefore, whereas the Milli Görüş brings Muslim practices into the debate, the TBB accuses Muslim associations of being Islamic fundamentalists and threats to German society.

Muslim Debates in the German Context

What do the competing discourses of the TBB and the Milli Görüş on the headscarf debate tell us about the political representation of immigrants in Germany today? In consideration of the many themes and concepts that emerged during the headscarf debate, such as discrimination against Muslim women and teacher conflicts with parents' right of education, it is remarkable that "state neutrality in religious matters" and "freedom of religion" consistently appeared as two controversial topics.

"State neutrality in religious matters" originates from the idea that in Western liberal societies, nation-states are "culturally homogeneous." According to the cultural principle of constitutive justice, "the political community should consist of a group of like-minded members who band together to

---

24 These Muslim practices are listed in the "Islamische Charta," from the Zentralrat der Muslime in Deutschland (2002); see the Web site of the Zentralrat der Muslime: http://www.islam.de/3035.php.

nurture their own common identity and who reserve the right to accept or reject new members" (Barbieri 2004, 17). This principle assumes cultural homogeneity as the basis for democracy and gives minorities and immigrants three options: assimilate, live in social exclusion, or leave the country.

As Gavin A. Smith (1999) argues, cultural homogeneity is intrinsic in the Marshallian concept of citizenship, which derives from "deeply middle-class, English, male and white" cultural values. It does not take individual subjectivities and cultural differences into account (Benhabib 2002). Most important, the different experiences of state rules and regulations have not been addressed in the discussions on citizenship. Nevertheless, immigrants are still subjected to the law of the state even though they have not rationally and officially consented to be ruled in this way. The cultural homogeneity principle assumes that the culture of the majority is neutral and that it forms the norm for all members of society.[25]

However, neutrality is a problematic concept of liberal democracy and has been widely criticized in political philosophy literature (Ackerman 1983). Critiques of the supposed neutrality of the liberal state argue that neutrality is built on the "necessity of having a secure culture" (Kymlicka 1989, 896). Will Kymlicka argues that in those cases in which a "collectively determined ranking of the value of different conceptions of good" do not exist, then the state authorities may take action to "formulate and defend the conception of good" (1989, 900). As he points out, this action may not be desirable, because state authorities would give priority to predominant ways of life and exclude the values and practices of marginalized and disadvantaged groups. Minority groups would be "convinced" to transform their values, norms, and practices to the majority's conceptions of good. According to Kymlicka, this process reinforces the cultural conservatism of the dominant group over the minority.

An example of such a process is the headscarf debate in Germany, which brought up issues of state neutrality. The case of Fereshta Ludin shows how cultural conflict is discussed in different ways by the state authorities, such as the Constitutional Court, by politicians, such as Marieluise Beck and Lale Akgün, and by immigrant associations, such as the TBB and the Milli Görüş. The ambiguous definitions of the state's obligation to neutrality make these

---

25 For a discussion about immigrant and minority consent to state regulations, please see Will Kymlicka's argument in *Politics in the Vernacular* (2001) and its critique in Sujit Choudhry's article in the *Journal of Political Philosophy* (2002). According to Kymlicka's argument (2001), immigrants become part of the country as permanent residents or full citizens; that is, through voluntary immigration. As such, they are expected to learn the language of the majority, conform to its values and norms, and assimilate into the host society. In his article, Choudhry referred to Kymlicka's assertion that "immigrants have waived their right to live in accordance with their own cultures through the decision to immigrate to a society which they knew that they would constitute a minority" and has provided his critique against Kymlicka's assumptions (2002: 60–61).

different expressions possible. As Kymlicka has argued, when there is ambiguity about the collectively determined notions of common "good," the state authorities define these notions and give priority to the predominant values. Consequently, the conflict will lead either to the forced assimilation of the minority groups or to their social exclusion, as in the case of the conflicts over the headscarf issue.

The headscarf debate between German political actors, social-democratic immigrant associations, and religiously oriented immigrant associations illustrates that concepts central to the German nation-state are redefined by immigrant groups. Whereas Muslim immigrant groups challenge the state's neutrality by making claims to religious plurality, others redefine its function for immigrant groups. In both cases, the fundamental values of Western democratic societies become major subjects for discussion, and immigrant groups become important actors in the German political arena.

Conclusion

In this chapter I attempted to show how a social democratic association, the TBB, campaigns against the promotion of wearing the headscarf in public places in Germany, unlike the Milli Görüş, which protests against the headscarf ban. I also elucidated and discussed the TBB's major aim, which is to erase the ethnic and religious differences between Turks and Germans so that German Turks can enjoy equal rights as German citizens.[26] The TBB represents the Turkish immigrant as a "good citizen" who views religion and ethnonational identity as private matters. This representation fits very well with the preference for cultural homogeneity in the German nation-state.[27]

For the TBB, immigrants who challenge the idea of homogeneity by wearing headscarves, by insisting on holding Turkish passports, and by frequenting mosques are threats to immigrant integration. Seyla Benhabib (2002) has argued that, "just as German Jews, German Turks should make their religion a private issue, so that they would be assimilated into the majority and would not be threatened by the occidental civic traditions." This policy of making religion a private issue is quite evident in the example of the TBB and its stance in the headscarf debate in Germany.

However, the positions of the TBB and the Milli Görüş in the headscarf debate are paradoxical. On the one hand, the TBB, whose members have a social-democratic political orientation, argue that permission to wear the

---

26 For detailed observations that explain the TBB's political stance, see Gökce Yurdakul, "Mobilizing Kreuzberg: Political Representation, Immigrant Incorporation and Turkish Associations in Berlin" (Ph.D. dissertation, University of Toronto, Department of Sociology, 2006).

27 Benhabib (2002) rightfully argues that "Germans would like to make 'good Germans' out of Turks when contemporary Germans themselves are hardly sure what their own collective identity consists of."

headscarf in public places would foster Islamic fundamentalism in Germany. Moreover, the wearing of the headscarf in schools and other government institutions would pose a threat to the state's neutrality. Therefore, the TBB, which claims to be the representative of Turkish immigrants in Berlin, was against wearing the headscarf in public places in Germany. On the other hand, the spokesman of the Milli Görüş, Oguz Ücüncü, argues that the ban on the headscarf will foster discrimination against Muslim women, because they will not be able to practice freedom of religion.

The headscarf debate between social democrats and the religious immigrant association Milli Görüş leaves us with two puzzles. The first one is about cultural conflict, state neutrality, and freedom of religion: How can the state solve the paradoxical relationship between the state's neutrality and freedom of religion, particularly with respect to immigrant communities in Germany? Should cultural differences be recognized as political rights, and would this facilitate the incorporation of immigrants into the majority society? If so, what kind of rights should be recognized? Could the German debates on the headscarf be affected by the human rights narratives of the dominant juridical framework at the European level?[28]

The second puzzle is about the future of Muslims in Germany: Which political association attracts more young people into its body and mobilizes Muslim immigrants? Are the TBB's campaigns against racism and discrimination also an appeal for Muslim youth, who are arguably one of the most discriminated groups in Germany today? Or, as Mustafa Yoldas stated in his interview, will more young women prefer to wear headscarves in reaction to the state's ban on the headscarf from public places?

Although the TBB started as a youth group at the Technical University of Berlin and clearly attracted students with social democratic leanings in the 1980s, it is questionable whether the TBB continues to be successful in recruiting young people. Safter Çınar, a spokesperson of the TBB, explained his worries about Turkish youth in Germany as follows:

"We will lose these young people if we fall into the trap of organizing only as an ethnic association. This is because we think of ourselves as ethnic immigrants. But our situation would change if we would organize around a social problem. There is a social problem [racism], and we organize around it. Then we are not different from Amnesty International, Greenpeace, or ATTAC." (interview on November 3, 2002)

Although the TBB claims to attract young Turkish people to the association, it is doubtful whether they provide an alternative to the religious associations currently attracting many of them (see the chapter by Gerdien Jonker in this volume). Contrary to what Çınar maintains, Muslim youth associations, as markers of identity, seem to appeal to many young Turks today. With more extensive research in this area, we will be able to understand what attracts the youth to religion rather than to social democratic values.

---

28 See Soysal (1994) for a related argument.

References

Ackerman, B. A. 1983. What is neutral about neutrality? Ethics 93 (2): 372–390.

Amiraux, V. 2003. Turkish political Islam and Europe: Story of an opportunistic intimacy. In Muslim networks and transnational communities in and across Europe, ed. S. Allievi and J. Nielsen, 146–169. Leiden, the Netherlands: Brill.

Barbieri, W. 2004. Multiculturalism and the bounds of civil society. In Civil society: Who belongs?, ed. W. A. Barbieri, R. Magliola, and R. Winslow, 9–24. Washington, D.C.: The Council for Research in Values and Philosophy.

Benhabib, S. 2002. The claims of culture: Equality and diversity in the global era. Princeton, NJ: Princeton University Press.

Bodemann, M. 2004. Unter Verdacht. Süddeutsche Zeitung, 30 November.

Caglar, A. 2001. Constraining metaphors and the transnationalisation of spaces in Berlin. Journal of Ethnic and Migration Studies 27 (4): 601–613.

Choudhry, S. 2002. National minorities and ethnic immigrants: Liberalism's political sociology. The Journal of Political Philosophy 10 (1): 54–78.

Cizre, Ü., and M. Cinar. 2003. Turkey 2002: Kemalism, Islamism, and politics in the light of the February 28 process. The South Atlantic Quarterly 102 (2/3): 309–332.

Fournier, P., and G. Yurdakul. Forthcoming. Unveiling distribution: Muslim women with headscarves in France and Germany. In Migration, Citizenship, Ethnos, ed. M. Bodemann and G. Yurdakul. New York: Palgrave Macmillan.

Göcek, M. 1999. To veil or not to veil: The contested location of gender in contemporary Turkey. Interventions: International Journal of Postcolonial Studies 1 (4): 521–535.

Göle, N. 1986. Mühendisler ve Ideoloji. Istanbul: Metis.

———. 1997. The forbidden modern: Civilization and veiling. Ann Arbor, MI: University of Michigan Press.

Häußler, U. 2001. Muslim dress codes in German state schools. European Journal of Migration and Law 3:457–474.

Kastoryano, R. 2004. Religion and incorporation: Islam in France and Germany. International Migration Review 38 (3): 1234–1256.

Kymlicka, W. 1989. Liberal individualism and liberal neutrality. Ethics 99 (4): 883–905.

———. 2001. Politics in the vernacular: Nationalism, multiculturalism, and citizenship. New York: Oxford University Press.

Schieck, D. 2004. Just a piece of cloth: German courts and employees with headscarves. Industrial Law Journal 33 (1): 68–73.

Schiffauer, W. 2004. Das Recht, anders zu sein. Die Zeit, 18 November.

Smith, G. A. 1999. Overlapping collectivities: Local concern, state welfare and social membership. In Confronting the present: Towards a politically engaged anthropology, 195–227. New York: Berg.

Soysal, Y. 1994. Limits of citizenship: Migrants and postnational membership in Europe. Chicago: University of Chicago Press.

Ücüncü, O. 2002. Presseerklärungen: Generalsekretär Üçüncü warnt vor Ausgrenzung muslimischer Frauen. Milli Görüş Perspektive 8 (91/92): 27.

Yeneroglu, M. 2004. Almanya Anayasasında Din Özgürlügü ve Basörtüsü Sorunu. Unpublished manuscript.

Yurdakul, G. 2006. Mobilizing Kreuzberg: Political representation, immigrant incorporation and Turkish associations in Berlin. Ph.D. dissertation, University of Toronto, Department of Sociology.

———. Forthcoming. State, political parties and immigrant elites: Turkish immigrant associations in Berlin. Journal of Ethnic and Migration Studies 32(3).

Philip Lewis

FROM SECLUSION TO INCLUSION:
BRITISH *'ULAMA* AND THE POLITICS OF SOCIAL VISIBILITY

The British State and Religion

In Britain, civil society includes civic religion with government-funded chaplaincies to parliament, the armed forces, and wherever people are vulnerable, whether in prison or hospital. The personnel and buildings of the Church of England—an established church—continue to be used for national and local rituals of celebration and mourning. Public service broadcasting continues to include religion. All state schools must give education in religion, and taxpayer money funds students who study nondenominational theology at the university level, so that the discipline is not confined to confessional colleges and maintains a conversation with academic life in all its diversity.

Because public life makes institutional space for "religion," that space has begun to make room for Islam, as it earlier had for nonestablished Christian denominations and the Jews.[1] The annual ceremony at the cenotaph in remembrance of those who died in war now includes members of all faiths. All new religious education syllabi used in schools—agreed at municipal level—have to reflect diversity and no longer can simply teach about Christianity. Many university departments of theology now include religious studies. Islamic Studies can be studied at the postgraduate level at at least sixteen universities, and a growing number of academics teaching the discipline are themselves Muslim.

Since the Labour government came to power in 1997, a range of measures have been taken to meet Muslim-specific concerns. In 1998, after a ten-year struggle, Muslims won the right to state funding of a couple of schools, a privilege hitherto only enjoyed by Christians and Jews. In September 1999, the Prison Service appointed the first Muslim Adviser. And a question on religious affiliation was included in the 2001 census in England—the first since 1851—after strenuous lobbying by Muslims. The Home Office also commissioned research to determine the extent of religious discrimination, an issue that has exercised many Muslims since the publication in 1997 of the

---

1 A new study of Muslims in Britain, France, and Germany makes clear that each nation's approach to Muslims is shaped, in part, by historically based church-state institutions (Fetzer and Soper 2005).

Runnymede Trust inquiry, entitled *Islamophobia: A Challenge for Us All* (Commission on British Muslims and Islamophobia 1997).[2]

The institutionalization of Islam also has proceeded apace. Key battles were won in the 1980s on issues such as planning permission to establish mosques; the accommodation of religious and cultural norms in schools, including the provision of halal meat in school meals; burial spaces in cemeteries; gender-specific community centers; and the right to wear Islamic dress. In a city such as Bradford, Muslims can perform the call to prayer from their mosques for three of the five daily prayers. "By the mid-1990s [in Britain], there were at least 839 mosques and a further 950 Muslim organizations, ranging from local self-help groups to nationwide 'umbrella organizations'" (Ansari 2002, 6). The most significant among the latter is the Muslim Council of Britain (MCB), founded in 1997. The MCB has its roots in Islamist protests against Salman Rushdie's book *The Satanic Verses*; the upsurge of protests indicated the pressing need for an effective national body to lobby government and liaise with statutory and public bodies.

Indeed, in Britain it is the Islamists who have pioneered an Islamic civil society with associations of Islamic doctors, lawyers, and teachers, an Islamic human rights commission, and the cleverly named FAIR, or Forum Against Islamophobia and Racism, established in 2001. The MCB is indicative of a new organizational sophistication. For its inaugural convention and accompanying glossy literature it chose the slogan "Seeking the Common Good," which deliberately echoed an influential document published a year earlier by the Catholic Bishops of England and Wales. The main weaknesses of such a movement are that it is seen as elitist, enjoys little grassroots support in the main centers of Muslim settlement, operates mainly outside traditionalist Muslim networks, and is dismissed as Wahhabi/Salafi by those in the more Sufi-oriented traditions.[3]

The Muslim communities enjoy a measure of incorporation into public and civic life. In 2001 there were more than two hundred Muslim local councilors (161 Labour, 27 Liberal Democrat, and 22 Conservative). In 1997 the first Muslim member of Parliament was returned, with another selected in 2001. The government also appointed three Muslim peers drawn from the Pakistani, Bengali, and Indian communities.

In the last few years the British state has also begun to self-consciously engage with what are dubbed "faith communities." This is most evident with the creation of a Faith Communities Unit in the Home Office in November 2003. In February 2004, in a wide-ranging report entitled "Working Together: Co-operation Between Government and Faith Communities," the government acknowledged:

---

2 A new report, *Islamophobia: Issues, Challenges and Action* (Richardson 2004), reviews progress in the last six years.

3 For an overview of Salafism in the United Kingdom, see J. Birt, 2005.

"In recent years there has been a sea-change in the consultation of faith communities. Work done, in particular through the Inner Cities Religious Council and the Inter Faith Network for the United Kingdom, has been influential in changing Government's attitude to the contributions which faith communities can make. Some areas of policy are now routinely recognised by Departments as requiring the input of the faith communities, for example as partners in urban regeneration." (Home Office Faith Communities Unit 2004, 8)

The Inner Cities Religious Council was set up in 1992 as a forum in which representatives of faith communities could work together on urban renewal and issues of social exclusion. It was an initiative born of collaboration between the Archbishop of Canterbury and a government minister. The Inter Faith Network for the UK is a nongovernmental organization that was established in 1987 to link interfaith activity and develop good relations between people of different faiths. The network has worked with a range of government agencies to develop "religious literacy": 44 % of authorities in England and Wales now have an officer responsible for liaison with faith groups (Inter Faith Network for the UK 2003, 1X).

The rationale for such collaborative activity was that faith communities were considered a good point of entry for involving local communities and, particularly in the inner city, difficult-to-reach groups. Further, it embodied "the new politics of the 'third way'": "instead of a dominating state or a minimalist state, the future is seen as a partnership between an active civil society and a modern government committed to social partnership and decentralisation [...] [with] faith communities [...] viewed as agents of social cohesion, important building blocks of civil society and valuable partners in the new frameworks and processes of local government" (Farnell et al. 2003, 7–8). It was also in line with European Union directives—the "Employment Equality (Religion or Belief) Regulations 2003"—to make reasonable accommodation for religious needs in the workplace.

The Home Secretary's rationale for establishing a Faith Communities Unit in the Home Office was clear in the Heslington lecture "One Nation, Many Faiths—Unity and Diversity in Multi-Faith Britain," which he delivered at York University in November 2003: to recognize and build on practical collaboration across different faiths, to encourage interreligious and inter-community engagement, and to incorporate moderate religious leaders in policy discussions and thereby isolate extremists.

Scrutinizing the 'ulama through a Post-9/11 Security Lens

It was important to point to the continuity of government policy pre- and post-9/11. However, it is clear that Muslims in general and imams in particular are now the object of scrutiny in a way they were not pre-9/11.[4] This should not be a source of surprise: in December 2001, Richard Reid, the shoe bomber, was apprehended during his attempt to blow up a plane on its flight from Paris to the United States; Reid, a Muslim convert, was radicalized at the now notorious Finsbury Park Mosque. In May 2003, two British-educated Pakistani Muslims were involved in suicide attacks in Israel. A Rubicon was crossed in March 2004, a couple of weeks after the Madrid massacre of 191 people, when eight British Muslims, most of them young British-born and - educated Pakistanis, were arrested after the discovery of more than half a ton of explosives and bomb-making equipment in west London. Five have since been charged. In the past, radical Muslims in London were drawn from "Arab Afghans," Egyptians such as the now notorious Abu Hamza, arrested in May 2004 and facing extradition to the United States for his alleged links with al-Qaeda. Yet here were young, British-educated Muslims drawn from the biggest ethnic group in the United Kingdom—two-thirds of Britain's 1.6 million Muslims, according to the census data for 2001, have their origins in South Asia, with the biggest group from Pakistan.[5]

Concern about the nature, character, and impact of Muslim religious leadership in the United Kingdom—a staple of Islamic publications for more than fifteen years (cf. Lewis 2002, chap. 5)—is increasingly being articulated by a variety of distinguished British Muslims in the mainstream media. Two examples illustrate this concern. Lord Ahmed, one of the three Muslim members of the House of Lords, and himself of Kashmiri origin, recently penned a long article in *The Mail On Sunday* (April 4, 2004)—a newspaper considered the voice of "middle England," whose votes Labour and other political parties carefully cultivate—under the title "Top Muslim: Ban Preachers of Hate," in which he alleged:

"[...] a significant minority of imams perpetuate the outdated notion that Muslims are the victims of British colonial oppression and encourage people to rise up against the white man. If a Church of England vicar used the kind of abusive language about Muslims that some imams habitually use about the British, they would be rightly prosecuted for inciting racial hatred. The reason the imams are not prosecuted is because the non-Muslim community has no idea what goes on inside some mosques [...] Most come from the Indian subcontinent, speak no English and have no knowledge of British culture [...] All this has a terribly damaging effect on young Muslims in Britain. They go to the mosque and hear a sermon in a foreign language

---

4   BBC news reported on July 2, 2004, that the Home Office had released figures revealing that police stop and search of "Asians" had increased threefold from 2002 to 2004, largely as a result of new antiterrorist legislation. In real terms this meant an increase per day from two to eight stop and searches. In 2004 the MCB produced a short pocket guide for Muslims entitled "Knowing Your Rights and Responsibilities," which includes sections on "stop & search powers of the police" and "vigilance and the terror threat."

5   The 2001 census gives the ethnicity of South Asian Muslims as follows: Pakistani, 42.5 %; Bangladeshi, 16.8 %; and Indian, 8.5 %.

about the past. It has no relevance to the problems they face—unemployment, racism or any of the economic and social problems affecting Muslims in Britain. At the same time, it fills them with hate and absurd notions about Britain and the British. They leave the mosque angry and confused and walk straight into the arms of extremist groups such as Al-Muhajiroun which talk to them in language they understand and offer them a way of venting their anger [...]"[6]

A young award-winning British filmmaker and radio producer, Navid Akhtar, recently underlined the seriousness of the alienation of sections of young Muslims from South Asian backgrounds in a radio program broadcast on prime time on a popular BBC radio show, *Five Live Report*. His program was cleverly entitled "Islam's Militant Tendency" and began with these words: "I am a British-born Muslim and I have always believed it is possible to practise and live a British way-of-life. But among young Muslims I am increasingly rare."[7] His program opened a window into the proliferation of radical Muslim bookshops that romanticize jihad and pump out audiotapes and videotapes by the likes of Abu Hamza—a radical Salafi message—and study circles that meet outside the mosques and are led by young British Muslim professionals. Akhtar worries that such literature and study circles, though not advocating violence, generate "an extreme and separatist version of Islam." He believes that many young British Muslims are "at odds with their parents' insular Asian culture and the mainstream British way of life. They find themselves in a vacuum with no direction, no roots and a lot of questions. 'Pure' [Salafi] Islam claims to be authentic Islam as practised at the time of the Prophet Muhammad" (BBC's *Five Live Report*, March 14, 2004).

British Muslim academics and intellectuals also have little positive to say about 'ulama. Ziauddin Sardar, who writes for the *New Statesman*, has one reference to 'ulama in the index of his much publicized *Desperately Seeking Paradise, Journeys of a Sceptical Muslim*. The reference is to an address by a preacher of an influential revivalist movement, which he characterized as "a closed circuit whose sole, obsessive concern [...] [with] ritual obligations [...] left the world and all its problems out of the equation" (Sardar 2004, 13). Dr. Humayun Ansari, in a ground-breaking history of Muslims in Britain,

---

6 Al-Muhajiroun is a splinter group that broke away from Hizb at-Tahrir; the latter had their origins in Palestine, where they had separated from the Muslim Brotherhood. Lord Ahmed also appears for the prosecution in a detailed indictment of the *'ulama* in the first of a four-part series of articles on life in Muslim Britain in *The Times* (July 26, 2004), written by young British journalist Burhan Wazir and entitled "Mosques: Sources of Spiritual Comfort or Out of Touch?"

7 Militant Tendency was a radical left-wing group that infiltrated mainstream Labour politics in the 1980s and for a while, especially in Liverpool, where they were the controlling group, brought the city's public services to a halt.

dryly describes the proliferation of mosques in Britain as "accompanied by sectarian fragmentation and ideological inflexibility" (2004, 346).[8]

The Home Office's response to these anxieties has been to render obligatory as from August 2004 a certain standard of English for any "minister of religion" wanting to work in the United Kingdom.[9] Further, it has supported the Learning and Skills Council in England to pilot some basic managerial training for Muslims active in mosques and Muslim organizations. In the longer term it intends to open a dialogue with all religious communities in order to establish basic accreditation and accrediting bodies for "ministers of religion" coming into the country.

British-Educated 'ulama: The Impact of Post-9/11

The picture offered so far of the 'ulama is, however, only partly accurate. I have worked for twenty years as an adviser on Christian-Muslim relations to Anglican Bishops in Bradford, as well as for the last four years as a university lecturer in the Department of Peace Studies at Bradford University. This experience has provided me with a range of contacts and friendships within the Muslim community, not least among some religious scholars.[10] In what follows I briefly profile a number of imams whom I have got to know. All are Sunnis who have spent much of their education and socialization in Britain and, with one exception, in Islamic *madaris* in Britain.[11]

All are seeking to connect with young British Muslims, many alienated from the mosques. All have realized that the institutions of wider society are eager to work with them on a range of initiatives, especially at city level on issues of cohesion and urban regeneration. One had developed partnerships with agencies and organizations in wider society, and his work was already marked by a new professionalism well before 9/11. Others again, in retro-

---

8 Fear of *'ulama* as bearers of South Asian sectarianism, among other things, was one reason the founders of the Bradford Council for Mosques drafted a constitution in 1981 to exclude them (Lewis 2002, 145–146).

9 British Council offices overseas will give a test to ascertain whether the applicant has reached Level 4 of an accredited system—at present graduates overseas need Level 5; nurses and doctors need Level 6. After two years they will be expected to achieve Level 6.

10 This is not to pretend that I have not been viewed at times with suspicion and variously accused of being a "spy for the church" or of working for MI5! Such "malicious gossip" has been noted by other academics working in this field (see Werbner 2002, IIX).

11 There are now at least twenty-five registered Islamic seminaries in Britain. Only three offer undergraduate or graduate courses accredited by British universities. One was established in the 1970s, three in the 1980s, eighteen in the 1990s, and three since 2000. For their history, ethos, sectarian affiliation, curriculum, and changing social roles, see J. Birt and P. Lewis (forthcoming) and S. Gilliat-Ray (forthcoming).

spect, saw 9/11 as an event forcing a conservative community to open up mosques to a range of outside agencies, however reluctantly. Another realized that post-9/11 he had to encourage Muslims to emerge from their comfort zones and begin to engage with wider society. One continues to be ambivalent about such engagement.

I do not pretend that they are typical of the majority of British imams; they are not. They do, however, indicate an emerging engagement with British society among a section of the better educated imams. Their career trajectories illuminate both the civic and public roles we might envisage more of them fulfilling in the years to come and the structural weaknesses that must be addressed if more are to follow them.

Pioneering a Multipurpose Muslim Center

Dr. Musharaf Hussain, in his early forties and of Pakistani ancestry, is the founder of and inspiration behind the Karimia Institute in Nottingham, which he established in 1990. Dr. Hussain has traversed three distinct intellectual and cultural worlds. He acquired his elementary religious education from a Pakistani imam in Bradford, then went on to earn a PhD in medical biochemistry. After some years as a research scholar at a British university, he spent a year in a traditional Islamic "seminary" in Pakistan. He rounded off his Islamic formation by obtaining a BA in Islamic Studies from al-Azhar in Cairo.

The Karimia Institute is an innovative, multipurpose center serving the local community. It includes a mosque, a new sports center, an accredited nursery, an information and technology center and a number of classrooms, and a radio station. Its private primary school is located nearby. Dr. Hussain also established a monthly magazine, *The Invitation*, which has been running for more than ten years and now has some two thousand subscribers and a Web site. The institute's most recent annual report listed seventeen projects, twenty full-time and thirty-five part-time staff, and an annual budget of some £400,000. What is striking in the report is the institute's emphasis on youth:

"At Karimia our youth work is not about tackling disaffection but more of preventative nature by providing a learning environment, recreational activities and camps. We want to inspire the young and train them to be good citizens by giving them a sense of direction and mission, so that they can be a positive force for social change. Our youth club attracts many youngsters who would otherwise be on the streets."

Another feature of the report is the willingness of staff to be involved in a range of partnerships, whether with the local education authority, urban regeneration schemes, the local further education college, or the youth service. Their work in providing tutorial classes in English, math, and science for youths under 16; a General Certificate of Secondary Education in Islamic Studies in Urdu; and homework clubs, adult classes, and youth provision all point to their success in such partnerships. In the report, they reflect on the demands of partnerships:

"It is important to emphasize the fact that the organisation's work does not only produce good in an individual's life but [...] produces many goods for the wider society. [Further] work that is funded by others may be minutely scrutinized [...] [and] such funds cannot be used for *da'wa* [an "invitation" to Islam] work [...] and [must] not discriminate against anyone [...] Most of us joined [Karimia] because [we] are driven by faith to help and serve others [...] I hope that our secular friends and agencies will notice this commitment to faith and the important role it plays in people's life."

In conversation, Dr. Hussain remarked that as he engaged with wider society and its agencies his fears and stereotypes began to be challenged. He feels that most local Muslim institutions in the United Kingdom are still in the first two stages of creation and consolidation. Few have moved into the critical third phase of "professionalism." He also was one of the pioneers of the local Muslim charity Muslim Hands, which now has sixteen paid workers and operates in thirty-five countries. In 2003 it raised some £4 million. Muslim Hands is now a professional organization and has won an "Investing in People" award: most of the staff have gone through his mosque, local schooling, and university.

He has developed many of his initiatives gradually. For seven years the institute ran extratutorial classes in a variety of subjects. This project enabled the institute to develop a pool of young trained teachers, some of whom now work in its private school. Similarly, they have been licensed by the radio authority to run a local radio station during the month of Ramadan every year since 1996. They trained a number of people during this time, three of whom have gone on to be journalists with the BBC in various capacities. This gave them the confidence to apply for one of sixteen licenses across the country for community radio. They won this license in 2002, partly because of their willingness to share it with an Asian women's group.

The ethos and concerns of Dr. Hussain are evident in his professionally produced monthly magazine, *The Invitation*. He writes the editorial; one of his Friday sermons becomes the article on the Quran; his book of hadith translations furnishes a monthly hadith reflection; and he acts as resident mufti, answering a selection of questions. His contributions breathe a Sufi humanism; indeed, he often cites from famous Sufi writers. This observation is not to charge his magazine with otherworldliness. He told me that often his editorial is a response to an article in *Newsweek*; he reads eclectically and draws from the Islamist journal *Impact International* as well as the monthly *Q-News*. There are articles on fair trade and health matters, as well as articles by local Muslim women. A recent issue of *The Invitation* includes a hard-hitting piece entitled "Why We Are Where We Are?", from which the following remarks are drawn:

"[Our] dominant chauvinism has trampled upon [women's] God given rights [...] Women have become subservient to [...] husbands [...] extra decoration pieces in their homes [...] There are few independent and progressive thinkers in contrast to the vast majority of traditionalists and ritualistic [scholars] [...] because it is an easier option as compared to requiring *ijtihad* or adaptation to the new realities of the modern world. In the absence of any clear vision, today the Muslims present themselves as victims around the world [...] [we retreat into] escapism from reality [...] [and] we blame the Jews for [all] our ills [...] [the desiderata listed include the need to] build bridges of understanding with the West [...]" (2003, 10:2, 24–25)

He is one of only two scholars in the Barelwi/Sufi tradition who sit on the central committee of the MCB. Since 9/11 he has sought to increase the range of contacts with his local community—not least a joint project with a local church—so as to challenge negative depictions of Muslims. He assumed national media prominence when, in September 2004, he and the assistant secretary general of the MCB, Dr. Daud Abdullah, went to Iraq, supported by the British Foreign and Commonwealth Office, to intercede for the life of Ken Bigley, a British hostage, who later was murdered. Dr. Hussain had already held a much publicized prayer vigil for Mr. Bigley in his local Muslim primary school. Their intervention won much praise from the British media for them personally and for the MCB. The choice of a member of the Muslim Brotherhood and a Sufi to travel together showed a good deal of wisdom, as each could appeal to different constituencies in Iraq.

Dr. Hussain is aware that if more 'ulama are to have the skills and confidence to benefit from the new openness of the local state and public bodies to Islam, there will have to be major changes in religious formation. He sets great store by the Muslim schools movement; there are now over 110 full-time private Muslim schools in the United Kingdom, most of which are affiliated with the Association of Muslim Schools (AMS), established in 1993, to which he belongs and which he used to chair. He believes that such a network will render many of the Islamic "seminaries" in Britain irrelevant in the not-too-distant future. The AMS network follows the national curriculum; thus, schools in the network do not teach Islam "out of context"—unlike in many Islamic seminaries in the United Kingdom, whose teaching still occurs in Urdu and whose curriculum still appears to be frozen in nineteenth-century India. He surmises that the Muslims will follow the Catholics and develop a tertiary college and teacher training college within the next decade. Such an institution could draw on the products of the AMS and both offer degrees and pioneer an appropriate Islamic curriculum in order to develop a new religious leadership that is at ease in Britain. Such a curriculum could include history, philosophy, and the social sciences.

We Can Kick It:
An Islamic Drug Awareness Service

In 1996 Khalil Ahmed Kazi, a Gujarati and in his early thirties, became one of the first imams appointed to prison chaplaincy work after completing his six-year *'alim* course at a "seminary" in Bury.[12] He initially assumed that his role would simply be an extension of his preaching and teaching role in the mosque, which he continues part time. He discovered that his *'alim* course had furnished him with few transferable work or social skills: he had to master the art of writing complex letters on behalf of inmates to probation officers and review boards; to organize religious festivals in the prison; to develop administrative and managerial skills enabling him to work within a complex hierarchical institution; to acquire the knowledge and confidence to relate to Christian colleagues; to perform a pastoral role for disorientated Muslim prisoners and intercede with fathers whose first response was to wash their hands of the sons who had brought shame on the extended family; and to build a network of support within the Muslim community for those released. As a chaplain he had a generic role and therefore wider responsibility for all prisoners. Initially, his role as a prison chaplain was met with incredulity within the Muslim community, which was in denial about the soaring number of Muslim prisoners.[13]

The lessons he has learned as chaplain were applied in Batley, West Yorkshire, where he is general secretary of an institute of Islamic scholars which networks some one hundred Deobandi 'ulama. His first biannual report for 2000–2002 made clear both the need for "professionalism" in the organization and the emerging patterns of interaction with wider society. The report was marked by a refreshing candor. Typical was the comment in the foreword by the chairman, who pointed to the need for

"true Islamic knowledge and wisdom [in a period] of turmoil and *fitna*. Each day brings greater challenges and requires insight into complex issues. Many a time it becomes extremely difficult to differentiate between *haq* [truth] and *batil* [falsehood], and thus a dilemma is created as to which route one should adopt."

The organization is between Dr. Hussain's second and third phases, consolidation and professionalism. This is clear from Kazi's overview as general

---

12 Bury is the "mother" house of a network of sixteen Islamic seminaries in the United Kingdom which belong to a reformist traditionalist group, Deoband, created in India in 1867. Historically, a main target for reform has been other traditionalist Muslims, especially the Barelwis, who are deemed to have made too many concessions to Hindu religiosity and customs. The Barelwis have five seminaries in the United Kingdom.

13 The census data for 2001 indicated that 2.7 % of the British population is Muslim, yet the Muslim prison population is 8.5 % (see Home Office Faith Communities Unit 2004, 96).

secretary of the institute, in which he described the shift from "ad hoc" responses to development of a formal constitution and the introduction of the apparatus of any "professional" organization—agenda, attendance registers, minutes, and even a Web site. The report indicated the extent to which they were engaging with wider society through their contacts and work with groups responsible for hospital and prison chaplaincy; local schools and colleges; a *da'wa* and publications department; lecture and youth programs; a community services network working with the police, members of Parliament, and policymakers; lectures on Islam delivered in a variety of venues, including an interfaith council; and a support group for drug and alcohol abuse.

There was also plenty of self-criticism. In the section on Islamic education the report noted that "the student, after spending a good part of the day at [state] school, comes exhausted both mentally and physically to the madrasah. If the [teacher] then conducts his lesson without any preparation, planning or using relevant methods, how would that then capture the imagination, attention and hearts of the students?" One major concern clearly articulated in the report was the limited expectations that parents have of Islamic education. "Their idea of Islamic education is no more than the ability to read the Qur'an [...] [U]nder the pretext of flimsy excuses, such as increased school workload or attending weddings," they deprive them of this basic education:

"Consequently, when pupils reach adolescence, when they are in a position to appreciate the beautiful teachings of Islam, when they need to be guided through the difficult period of teenage-hood, they are taken out of *madaris*. This great injustice is going to create an identity crisis, an ignorant rebellious Muslim."

As a prison chaplain, Kazi is well aware of the growing disaffection of a section of young Muslims from the mosque. In Batley, where he serves as a part-time imam, he has started meetings for these disenchanted young Muslims in a community center, a neutral space outside the mosque. Able to bridge the world of mosque, prison, and wider society, he has developed some innovative projects in partnership with local agencies. One that has given him considerable satisfaction was the launch at a Muslim community center in Batley in April 2004 of an Islamic drug awareness service, We Can Kick it, with an accompanying Web site.

The project, which aims to work with hard-to-reach groups in local mosques, schools, and community centers, involves all of Batley's fifty mosques and has been devised by Kazi, as Muslim consultant and project coordinator, with a number of Muslim professionals—two drug trainers from the Health Authority, a sports researcher, and a community liaison officer—who have created the material to be used in the mosque with eleven-year-olds. The material has been tested with schools and the project funded by police and drug action teams. Those who complete the two-hour course, whether in a mosque, a community center, or school, are given a certificate and access to sports training programs as an alternative to the culture of "hanging out" and drug misuse.

This is just one of many projects in which Kazi is involved. Another, the Madressah Project, aims to promote positive parenting and provides guidance on child-welfare issues. It is headed by another Bury-trained religious scholar and funded by the social services and community education and regeneration services. It has already built relationships with thirty mosques, establishing a cross-cultural dialogue in order to explain child protection, behavior management, and health and safety issues both in the home and in the mosque teaching environment. Kazi is a member of its management committee.

His latest project, which at the time of writing is awaiting Home Office approval, is an imaginative scheme to provide a community chaplaincy project in three areas from which many Muslim prisoners come. The aim is to establish a team of chaplains who will recruit, train, and supervise teams of volunteers. These volunteers will act as mentors and provide one-to-one support for ex-offenders released from prison. Services on offer will include housing advice, drugs- and alcohol-awareness training, counseling, debt counseling, benefits advice, and job-search support. The project has the full support of all the chaplains and Anglican and Catholic dioceses. Although the project will cost in excess of £800,000 over three years, it would only have to keep twenty prisoners per year from re-offending and returning to prison in order to cover its costs through the money saved by the prison services.

For Kazi the key to the success of such ventures is partnership: partnership between Muslim scholars and Muslim professionals and partnership with a variety of agencies now willing to work with religious groups. Police now go into mosques to speak about drugs awareness, something that would have been unheard of just a few years ago. The mosques used to be closed worlds, and many of the elders and 'ulama were deeply suspicious of non-Muslim society. Kazi frankly admits that the shock of 9/11 has enabled him to open up this closed world: as a respected traditionalist religious scholar, he has been able to negotiate access to such agencies and legitimize such initiatives in Islamic terms by providing Islamic support materials.

From Seclusion to Inclusion?

The activities of 'ulama like Khalil Ahmed Kazi, who have developed a new set of skills by working outside the Muslim subculture of Islamic seminary and mosque, indicate a growing awareness of the need to connect with streetwise British Muslim youth and the increasing willingness of support agencies to work with them. Two young Bradford religious scholars reflect two overlapping sets of responses to this challenge. Although their work cuts across ethnic divides, Mufti Saiful Islam, a Bangladeshi scholar, serves a largely Bangladeshi community, and Sheikh Ahmed Ali, a Pakistani, serves a largely Pakistani constituency. Both are in their early thirties and have established independent Islamic institutions, staffed and run largely by British-educated 'ulama whom they have recruited from Bury and its associate seminaries. Both continue to have good relations with local mosques.

The aim of such independent institutions is to get away from the somewhat negative associations that mosques carry for Muslim youth. Both run a range of activities for Muslim youngsters which are intended to maintain their interest through adolescence—the major gap in provision that Kazi identified. Ahmed Ali runs additional educational classes on the weekend in computing, English, and math as well as homework clubs. Everything is studied through the medium of English. In all, he and his colleagues seek to supplement and consolidate state education. In the summer Ali takes youngsters camping and organizes day trips to local theme parks. In cooperation with youth workers they arrange weekend soccer games and competitions in the summer. They take groups of young men between fifteen and thirty years of age to the annual Islamic study camp (*tarbiyya*) organized by Bury since 1998, where they listen to addresses in English delivered over a period of three days and live under canvas. Ahmed Ali states quite clearly that his Islamic academy is to be understood as a "social center" generating a wide range of activities not normally associated with a mosque.

Ahmed Ali is a charismatic speaker and has used this strength to develop an audiotape ministry. He has over sixty titles and sells between forty thousand and fifty thousand tapes a year. He does not avoid controversial issues. One of his best-selling tapes is entitled *Drugs, the Mother of All Evils*. It is clear why he is popular: he can speak the language of the street, and his tapes are larded with local phrases drawn from the drug culture. The message, however, remains very traditional: shape up or else hellfire awaits you. He is a textual scholar, not a social scientist. Another recent tape is amusingly entitled *"The IT Syndrome" (I am IT!)*; in it he parodies the "big-timers" and role models for disaffected youth in the community, with their "7-series BMWs, Mercs and mobile phones," who forget the Quran's warnings about "exalting riches and forgetting Allah." He reminds them of the Quranic punishments: amputation for theft, "80 of the best" for false accusation, stoning for adultery with a married woman. He does not spare his hearers gruesome and lengthy details about the humiliations of hell. Ali makes no concessions to Western, liberal sensibilities.

Two other tapes indicate that he is unapologetically traditional in his thinking. He addresses the issue of "forced marriage" and acknowledges that it is a widespread cultural abuse in South Asian communities: "some are blackmailed, some are threatened, some are severely beaten." Drawing on Hanafi jurisprudence, he points out that Islamic legal norms insist that the wife is not a commodity, that she has rights to a modest dowry, and that she must give her permission to marriage. Moreover, the essential factor in choosing a partner should not be her wealth, status, or beauty but her piety. Marriage, he adds, is a form of worship; unfortunately, piety is not the first concern of parents who are more preoccupied with marrying "this or that uncle's or aunt's son or daughter." Further, a guardian should take account of *kuf*, equality of status. He also is deeply critical of conspicuous consumption at weddings—what he amusingly refers to as "blow [all your savings] and show [off your supposed wealth]"—as well as of the popularity of Hindu customs. Imparting much sensible advice, he mentions that if men contemplate multiple wives—no more than four, of course—they must treat them with "equality and justice."

In two recent tapes entitled *Iraq*, Ahmed Ali shows that he is well read in classical Islamic history. The burden of his lengthy narratives is that Allah tests his people; they show patience and eventually prevail. He reminds them of the early conquests of Islam, when the mighty superpower of its day—Persia—was "humiliated" by the Muslim armies, whose faith struck "terror into the hearts of the *kuffar*." Chapters drawn from Iraq's bloody subsequent history are rehearsed to conform with this pattern: Ali is killed in vicious intra-Muslim wars, and the splendid Abbasid empire centered on Baghdad is exposed to defeat and "terrifying slaughter by the pagan Tartars." Today the Iraqis have suffered terribly from sanctions and war, but, as Ahmed Ali reminds his audience, the Tartars were eventually converted to Islam. Allah prevailed then, and Islam will prevail again. For the present, Ali suggests to his audience that, "instead of spending their money on five mobiles and three satellite TVs," they should visit Iraq, Jordan, and Palestine with an Islamic scholar in order to strengthen their faith. "Remember it is the site of your religious history ... so when the bombs drop remember this."

He is anxious about the inroads of non-Muslim cultural practices. In one of his most recent cassettes, *Tawheed and Shirk*, he reminds his audience that *shirk*—associating something or someone with Allah—is the unforgivable sin. He expresses dismay that some misguided Muslims protested against the Taliban's destruction of Buddhist statues in Afghanistan. He recounts with approval a hadith to the effect that a companion of the Prophet is commended for cleaving the head of a female seer. Yet all around Ahmed Ali sees Muslims adopting unacceptable practices: whether consulting their zodiac signs in the tabloid press—a particular weakness, he alleges, of Muslim women; celebrating Valentine's Day; or advertising the festivals of the *mushrikun* (those who commit shirk) in Islamic magazines. He also delivers an intra-Muslim polemic against practices such as praying at the tombs of Islamic saints for children. All such activities are tantamount to shirk, as only Allah has knowledge of the future and of the unseen.

Ahmed Ali, unlike the two other 'ulama discussed thus far, has not been systematically exposed to wider society, and so has not had to develop new intellectual and social skills to complement those acquired in his Islamic formation. His only openness to non-Muslim agencies has been some collaboration with Muslim youth workers and teachers. He seems content to work within a relatively closed Muslim social world. In conversation with me, he expressed some bitterness that the valuable work he does to engage with disaffected Muslim youth and raise educational standards is not recognized by teachers and the police.

Whereas Ahmed Ali's main medium of communication to a broader constituency is the audiotape, Mufti Saiful Islam prefers the popular format of the magazine, the pamphlet, and poetry. Like Ahmed Ali, he went straight into an imamate at a local mosque after completing his 'alim training. Whereas Ali went to Cairo to complete his training at al-Azhar, Saiful Islam was in the first group to complete a newly developed ifta' course begun in Bury in 1995 to train Hanafi muftis. Like Ali, he soon became aware of the limited impact of the traditional mosque on Muslim youth, who were increasingly being drawn into a range of antisocial and immoral behavior. For this reason, he too has established an independent Islamic institution.

In addition to carrying out "normal" methods of teaching, Saiful Islam runs a weekly session of Quran exposition followed by a question-and-answer session. He makes clear in his publications that simply rehearsing what the Quran and Sunna say about issues is no longer enough. In a pamphlet entitled "Alcohol, the Root of All Evil," he notes after the section on Quranic verses and hadith that "these traditions should be sufficient to display the corruption and evils of alcohol. Unfortunately in this 'advanced age' [...] one may be more influenced by medical and scientific research." He then includes material on the intellectual, physical, psychological, and social costs of alcohol, drawing on a range of popular sources, including *Reader's Digest*.

He has produced two volumes of pithy comments and articles entitled *Pearls of Wisdom* in 2001 and 2002. As with Ahmed Ali, fear of hell plays a central role in his teachings. Thus, a warning was sounded for would-be usurers when a Pakistani, well known for dealing in interest, died: "Soon after his passing away, his facial features began to change until it resembled that of a pig" (1:39).

In both volumes a traditionalist reading of the social roles of women is commended. The second volume recounts a dialogue between "a modernist lady and an intelligent young girl." The former accuses the latter's father of keeping her imprisoned at home, as if in jail. The young girl protests that jailers keep criminals under lock and key, whereas "diamonds and gold [are kept] in a safe place. I am my father's diamond, which he keeps in this holy sanctuary [home] ... the thought of escaping does not arise in my mind ... I love the safety and peace of my home" (2:42–43). In the first volume a hadith is narrated in which women are enjoined to pay "*sadaqah* [alms] and offer repentance abundantly," as women feature more prominently in hell than men. The reason, according to another hadith, is that women are "more habituated to cursing (during conversation) and ... are ungrateful to ... husbands" (1:11). Another scholar is cited as saying that "Women who possess degrees of B.A. and M.A. cannot compete in understanding and intelligence with women who have acquired *deeni* [religious] knowledge. Yes, in deception and schemes, the western-educated women may be ahead.

But remember, that words of intelligence will come out from women of piety"
(1:41).

Mufti Saiful Islam is clearly not much impressed with Western education.
A poem entitled "The Western Youth" includes the following:

"He thought he was only twenty and was going to live to seventy.
The West taught him to be free and to acquire a useless degree.
Filled with selfishness and free, never did he perform a single deed.
When told to change and repent, he said why? I'm happy and content.
If only he knew what contentment was, he may not have made such a loss.
Satisfaction is what he chased, with disbelievers he embraced [...]" (1:24)

In conversation, however, he pointed out that in a non-Muslim context "the
law of necessity" operated. Because the community needs women teachers
and medical personnel, they would be allowed to go on to further education,
albeit properly covered.

His bimonthly magazine, *Al-Mu'min*, is a polished production. It enjoys a
circulation similar to that of *The Invitation*. It includes sections on *tafsir*
(Quranic commentary), hadith, religious and historic personalities central to
Islam, a women's section, poems, a children's corner, and a question-and-
answer page where the mufti gives fatawa on everything from clones to
contraception. Although there is a women's section, women themselves do
not seem to write for the magazine (though they do for *The Invitation*).
Moreover, there are fewer articles on contemporary political events.

However, there is no embarrassment about asking difficult questions; for
example, a questioner asks whether a man's marriage is still valid if he has
had an affair with his wife's sister. The mufti answers that the marriage
remains valid, and then points out that the prevalence of such immoral
behavior is rooted in the failure to maintain strict segregation (purdah) among
close relatives within the family. A recent issue even answered questions
about oral and anal sex. Moreover, many of the articles self-consciously seek
to connect with the world of Muslim youth by using such catchy titles as
"Designer Clothing," "Benefits and Harms of the Internet," and "Football: A
Religion?"

One innovation that Mufti Saiful Islam has pioneered is that of teaching
the '*alim* syllabus to local adults on a part-time basis—the course of study can
take up to ten years. He realized that many men wanted to take up this study
but, because of family commitments or full-time jobs, could not afford to
study full time at a seminary. Already this pattern of religious formation is
bearing fruit: one of his trainee imams, Amjad Mohammed, is already trained
as a teacher; another, Rafaqat Rashid, is a local doctor. Both are in their early
thirties and form the nucleus of a small group of fellow Muslim professionals
who established the Islamic Cultural Association (ICA) in Bradford in 2003.

The aims of the ICA are listed in their literature and on their Web site.
They include portraying a positive image of Muslims; enabling Muslims to
play a more positive role in the wider community by fostering better commu-

nity relations and working for the good of society as a whole; facilitating a two-way communication between Muslims and public bodies and addressing educational and health deficits in the community; and seeking to eradicate the discrimination and disadvantages faced by Muslims. They stress that the ICA "consists of professionals who have been raised in England" and who have "a training in the classical sciences from qualified teachers and sources."

Their Web site has a range of helpful articles on Islamic beliefs. Many are self-critical, such as one entitled "Male Chauvinism and the Muslim World," in which they criticize as incompatible with Islamic law such abuses as female mutilation, honor killings, and forced marriage. They have a chatroom where contemporary local issues are discussed, such as "Are our Muslim parents playing a proactive role in the education of their children?" and "What should the government do to promote social inclusion of Muslims?" Non-Muslims also take part.

The vice chair of the ICA, Amjad Mohamed, produced an illuminating article on their Web site entitled "British Muslims—Where From, Where To, Where Now?" In it he noted:

"Today, the Muslim community in Britain is a relatively settled community [...] [which has] established a diversity of Islamic organizations. [...] However, occurrences like *The Satanic Verses*, for example, are perceived as a conspiracy against Muslims. Also, external factors such as problems in the Holy Land (Palestine), the massacre of Muslims in Bosnia, and [...] [lately] the wars in Afghanistan and Iraq, not forgetting the controversial French ban on the headscarf, unsettle the resident British Muslims. [...] The Muslim community had decided, possibly unconsciously, that rather than defend their religion, it would be better to isolate [themselves] from the wider society and, therefore, not attract attention. However, events over the last few years have changed that position. British Muslims can no longer hope not to be seen nor questioned. *Events outside of their hands have dragged them from seclusion into the questioning eye of the general public.* British Muslims have [...] to decide whether [or not] to 'open their doors' to the wider community [...] [and thereby] dispel myths, misconceptions made against the religion of Islam." (italics mine; see www.ica-online.org)

The activist thrust of their work is evident in the Quranic text that adorns their literature: "[...] mankind can have nothing except what it strives for" (Surah An-Najm 53:39). Thus far they have organized or participated in a number of local conferences. In June 2004 they ran a drugs-in-community project in cooperation with the police. Dr. Rashid has organized gender-specific workshops on diet and diabetes issues in three mosques. More recently they have been working with Muslim youth workers by mentoring vulnerable youngsters.

The ICA is a welcome development in an area of the city with high levels of educational underachievement—in one ward 46 % of the community is without qualifications—unemployment, and youth disaffection spilling over into antisocial behavior and drugs. Amjad Mohamed is frank about the difficulties in encouraging cross-community relations in the present climate, with "white faced British soldiers killing brown faced Muslims in Iraq ... brown faced Muslims doing nasty things to white [hostages] ... In all, it is difficult for Jones to feel comfortable with Ali and vice versa." Moreover, unlike the Indian Gujarati communities of Batley or Leicester, which are used to living as a minority in India or East Africa, the large Pakistani communities in Bradford feel comfortable in their Muslim enclaves, where they are now the majority. The British National Party and far-right activity also make them reluctant to move too far outside the substantial Muslim quarters of the city.

Jihad to Engage Journalists

Sheikh Ibrahim Mogra, a Gujarati in his mid-thirties, is based in Leicester in the East Midlands. Originally from Malawi, he was sent to the United Kingdom to train as a doctor, but decided to become an *'alim* instead. His educational formation includes Bury, al-Azhar, and an MA at the School of Oriental and African Studies in London. Mogra has worked part time in mosques, taught in one of the three Islamic seminaries in the city, and now runs his own mosque school. In addition to these traditional roles, he has pioneered work in the wider community, not least with local interfaith groups. He has organized joint Christian-Muslim fundraising for hospitals in Kosovo and Gaza. He has been part of a joint Christian-Muslim group setting up and delivering an innovative chaplaincy course for Muslims at a local Islamic institute. He runs the Leicester-wide Radio Ramadan, which, like two dozen similar ventures across the country, is granted a license for the period of Ramadan. Mogra realized that if a traditional imam has a congregation of some two hundred on Friday, Radio Ramadan would give him a constituency of thousands for his teaching and preaching. He consciously invites imams from all traditions to participate. He is active in the three local universities, where he delivers the Friday *khutba* on consecutive weeks and takes part in the annual conference of the Federation of Student Societies. The 2004 conference, with its seven hundred students, was covered in the *Guardian* newspaper. Sheikh Ibrahim Mogra, "a leading young imam," was said to call on

"Muslim students to reach out to their peers. Urging them to be more integrationist, he said: 'That is where the struggle lies. If we reach out we can win the hearts of this country.'" (*Guardian*, June 19, 2004)

Mogra has frequently insisted to me that he did not want to be limited to the traditional role of imam. He preferred to work part time in his own mosque school rather than serve as a full-time imam and thus be constrained within the role envisaged by a majority of mosque committees. His local community work has won him a measure of national recognition. He has been appointed as an area representative for the MCB and chairs their mosque and community committee, for which he was reselected in May 2004 for a further two years. The MCB has very few active 'ulama as members, and of these Mogra is the first *'alim* of his generation who was educated in a British seminary. In October 2004 he helped open the first regional office for the MCB outside London, based in Leicester. He is grateful to the MCB for giving him a national platform for his gifts—as well as for enhancing his skills with leadership training.

Ibrahim Mogra passionately believes that post-9/11 Muslims must engage the media to correct misunderstandings and that mosques must open their doors to the public in order to show that they have nothing to hide. As part of his own efforts in this respect, he was profiled in a radio documentary entitled "Rookie Imams," for which he negotiated access to a Deobandi seminary.[14] His personal jihad, he told me recently, was to engage journalists. He is unusual in that he is prepared to talk to and work with the local and national media. Imam training does not, historically, include communications skills necessary for a public and civic role, as such a role simply is not envisaged.[15] He was prepared to appear on a recent hard-hitting television program, *Some of My Best Friends Are Muslim*, broadcast on Channel 4 (August 17, 2003) and produced by Yasmin Alibahi-Brown, a columnist for the national broadsheet *The Independent*. Here Alibahi-Brown spoke openly about her worries about increasing intolerance in the community and about her own experience of receiving death threats and hate mail because, as an Ismaili, she is not considered an Orthodox Muslim—her sin compounded by the fact that she has married a Christian.

Through his work with the MCB, as well as local and national interfaith contacts, he is clearly developing a national profile: he was one of six British imams to appear in a British television series entitled *Shariah TV*. The series consisted of six weekly, hour-long programs screened for Channel 4 in May and June of 2004. In many ways it indicated the coming of age of Islam in Britain. A Muslim was the head of religious affairs; the series was researched by Muslim consultants and fronted by a young mainstream television presenter, So Rehman, who is himself a Muslim. The aim of the programs was to provide an opportunity for young British Muslims to pose a range of questions to specialists on Islamic law and other experts. So Rehman made clear in his introduction to each program that there are different interpretations on a range of issues.

What was refreshing was a context in which imams could be quizzed on a range of controversial issues by a cross section of young Muslim profession-

---

14 Access to such institutions remains very difficult; see S. Gilliat-Ray (2005).

15 Tim Winter, an English Muslim who lectures on Islam at Cambridge University and who often appears in the media, recently wrote that "[...] we need to be more frank in blaming our own Muslim communities for failing to engage in more successful and sophisticated public relations [...]. Major mosques and organisations have little or no public relations expertise. To accuse the West of misrepresentation [of Islam] is sometimes proper, but all too often reflects a hermeneutic of suspicion rooted in zealot attitudes to the Other" (Seddon 2003, 13).

als, male and female, with and without the hijab. Most were in their twenties and thirties and clearly were located along the complete spectrum of Muslims, from cultural Muslim to traditionalist and radical. They were respectful of the imams, without being deferential. The series touched on a full range of issues, from domestic to civic and political, from homosexuality to mortgages to citizenship and interfaith relations. The program in which Mogra appeared touched on "consumerism and lifestyle" issues: Could a Muslim barrister-in-training attend meetings in pubs if she did not herself drink? Should students apply for student loans? Was it halal to take out house mortgages? Could a Muslim doctor recommend abortion in the case of fetal abnormalities? Was it acceptable to run a sports club for young Somali Muslim women? Was there a place for cosmetic surgery, or was this prohibited? What was the status of organ transplants? Could a Muslim with Christian relatives attend a christening service or a Christmas party?

The Politics of Visibility: Conclusion

It will be clear that the "politics of visibility" refers to a number of issues: the extent to which the state encourages religious actors to engage in civic society; whether even British-educated 'ulama have the skills, competence, desire, and freedom to capitalize on such opportunities; and whether mosque committees, citywide councils of mosques, and national umbrella bodies—traditionally run by Muslim businessmen and professionals—actually want to make space for a contribution by these 'ulama.

We can conclude that, notwithstanding the events of 9/11, both state and local government, as well as public services, have sought to work with Muslim communities in general, and 'ulama in particular, on a range of issues. They are especially alert to the need to connect with British Muslim youth and welcome religious leaders who are willing to act as mediators in this process.

Surprisingly, perhaps, 9/11 has not proved an unmitigated disaster for Muslim communities. Some 'ulama have seen it as a wake-up call for Muslims to venture out from their comfort zones and relatively closed communities. They view it as an opportunity to explain themselves to the media and to engage with professionals in wider society—whether clergy, teachers, social workers, or the police—in order to address youth disaffection and help raise the worryingly low educational standards among sections of Muslim youth.

The 'ulama presented in this chapter are all exceptionally able and have successfully negotiated multiple linguistic, educational, and cultural worlds. However, even they fall into two categories: one "cosmopolitan," the other "transnational."[16] The latter, in contrast with the former, are "rarely heard and

---

16 This useful distinction is developed by Pnina Werbner (2002) in her studies of Manchester Muslims.

even more rarely recognised and listened to beyond their own communities. They speak a foreign language or enunciate alien, widely unacceptable sentiments" (Werbner 2002, 6–7). It is clear that two of the 'ulama discussed could probably be characterized as transnational in this sense. Both were trained and socialized in a relatively closed Islamic environment; neither have had direct exposure as the others have to Western tertiary education. Nor have they taken up social roles as chaplains, for which they would have to develop new social and intellectual skills—most often referred to in shorthand as the need for "professionalism." However, in the case of Mufti Saiful Islam it will be interesting to see whether his training of 'ulama locally, of men who are already "professionals"—teachers and doctors—forces him to engage vicariously with such complex social and intellectual worlds, the sine qua non of any mufti working in Britain.

It is also evident that if more British-educated 'ulama are to follow these pioneers in seeking to access and influence civic and public life, certain structural weaknesses will have to be addressed in both mosque culture and the seminary. All of the 'ulama discussed have felt the need either to set up independent institutions or to maintain their economic independence of mosque committees. Ironically, working part time as a chaplain can generate a salary larger than what one would earn as an imam in a mosque. However able, an imam in a mosque usually is poorly remunerated and lacks contractual security. Further, if mosque committees are to attract the better educated who can connect with British Muslims, they will have to provide not just a living wage but also resources and opportunities for imams to develop professionalism.

Clearly, seminary formation will have to include new intellectual, social, and communication skills. At the moment, it can take as much as ten years for the most able products of these seminaries to feel at ease in wider society. If these issues are not addressed, there is a danger that a two-tier system of 'ulama will be created: those least able to understand and connect with the concerns of British Muslims will find employment inside the mosque, whereas those most able to connect will find employment outside it.

What is also clear from these snapshots of the world of British 'ulama is a willingness to work with Muslims outside their own sectarian tradition. Dr. Hussian's visit to Iraq is a spectacular example of this: because he is a Sufi, one might have expected him to have little in common with the member of the Muslim Brotherhood who accompanied him; yet they worked well as a team. Increasingly, there are examples of Islamists and 'ulama working together. Arguably, the MCB is—in origin and ethos—Islamist, yet it has begun to enlist a few able 'ulama into its ranks. Such active collaboration across sectarian divides bodes well for the future.

References

Ansari, H. 2002. Muslims in Britain. London: Minority Rights Group International.

———. 2004. "The infidel within": Muslims in Britain since 1800. London: Hurst.

Birt, J. 2005. Wahhabism in the United Kingdom: Manifestations and reactions. In Transnational connections: The Arab Gulf and beyond, ed. M. al-Rasheed, 168–184. London: Routledge Curzon.

Birt, J., and P. Lewis. Forthcoming. The pattern of Islamic reform in Britain: The Deobandis between intra-Muslim sectarianism and engagement with wider society. In Producing Islamic knowledge: Transmission and dissemination in Western Europe, ed. S. Allievi and M. van Bruinessen. London: Routledge.

Commission on British Muslims and Islamophobia. 1997. Islamophobia: A challenge for us all. London: Runnymede Trust.

Farnell, R., R. Furbey, S. Shams al Haqq Hills, M. Macey, and G. Smith, eds. 2003. Faith in urban regeneration? Engaging faith communities in urban regeneration. Bristol, UK: Policy Press.

Fetzer, J. S., and J. C. Soper. 2005. Muslims and the state in Britain, France and Germany. Cambridge, UK: Cambridge University Press.

Gilliat-Ray, S. 2005. Closed worlds: (Not) Accessing Deobandi dar ul-uloom in Britain. Fieldwork in Religion 1 (1): 7–33.

———. Forthcoming. Educating the 'ulama: Centres of Islamic religious training in Britain. Islam and Christian-Muslim Relations (January 2006).

Home Office Faith Communities Unit. 2004. Working together: Co-operation between government and faith communities. London: Home Office Faith Communities Unit.

Inter Faith Network for the UK. 2003. Local inter faith activity in the UK: A survey. London: Inter Faith Network for the UK.

Islam, S. 2001. Pearls of wisdom. Bradford, UK: Jaamiah Khaatamun Nabiyeen.

———. 2002. Pearls of wisdom 2. Bradford, UK: Jaamiah Khaatamun Nabiyeen.

Lewis, P. 2002. Islamic Britain, religion, politics and identity among British Muslims. London: I. B. Tauris.

Richardson, R., ed. 2004. Islamophobia: Issues, challenges and action. Stoke-on-Trent, UK: Trentham Books.

Sardar, Ziauddin. 2004. Desperately seeking paradise: Journeys of a sceptical Muslim. London: Granta.

Seddon, M. S., D. Hussain, and N. Malik, eds. 2003. British Muslims, loyalty and belonging. Markfield, UK: The Islamic Foundation & The Citizen Organising Foundation.

Werbner, P. 2002. Imagined diasporas among Manchester Muslims: The public performance of Pakistani transnational identity politics. Oxford, UK: James Curry.

Hamed Abdel-Samad

ALIENATION AND RADICALIZATION:
YOUNG MUSLIMS IN GERMANY

"I want to call myself 'a Muslim' whenever I want, but I do not want to be called 'a Muslim' by 'the others' whenever they want. It is like when you call yourself 'a farmer': you mean that you are reliable, steadfast, and generous. But when others call you a farmer, they might have rather negative connotations, like being dirty and uncivilized." (Algerian, 32 years old)

These are the words of an Arabic student whom I interviewed in 2002 in Augsburg, Germany. He did not want to be viewed as a Muslim in Germany and refused the German media's frequent demands that Muslims should organize demonstrations in order to distance themselves from violence and terrorism:

"Why should I go out and excuse myself for the terror attacks on New York, when I am not personally responsible for them? Why do I not expect every Christian to come to me and excuse himself for the massacre of Muslims by Christians in Bosnia and Chechnya?"

In this chapter I examine two common assumptions in Germany. One holds that religious Muslims are more inclined to radicalization and militant ideologies than are "westernized" or "Western-oriented" Muslims. The other suggests that the established Islamic organizations in Germany are breeding grounds for terrorism and might even have relations with international terrorist organizations. I question the relation between religion and terrorism in order to determine whether or not the practice of violence as a means of visibility is a widespread phenomenon among Muslim diaspora communities.

As I examined the issue of the (in)visibility of young Muslims in public space in Europe, I observed that the majority of my interviewees were at no point willing to draw political or media attention to themselves. They did not want to be visible as individuals, though they were trying to put their "case" at the center of the political debate. That case was by no means always the same. An Arabic student has different priorities and demands than a Turkish worker does, even when both define themselves as Muslims. I was able to discern, however, a set of strategies adopted by young Muslims in their attempt to create a collective voice in their European societies. This collective voice should not be confounded with the "voices" of public violence (Guggemos and Abdel-Samad 2003; Waldmann 2003).

This chapter draws mainly from interviews with sixty-five Muslims, which I conducted in various German cities during the years 2002 and 2003.[1] Most of the interviewees were Arab students, others were members of the first generation—the so-called guest-worker generation—or second generation. The interviewees were selected according to the following criteria: age (up to 40 years old), length of stay in Germany (minimum of two years), and their willingness to be interviewed. Their political inclinations (e.g., their personal views on terrorism) did not represent a criterion, as the idea was to get to know the worldview of "normal" Muslims. While assembling the sample, however, I aimed at an equal proportion of religious and practicing Muslims and nonreligious Muslims. Personal contacts were also significant in the process of selection. When the interviews were conducted, most of the participants were between 26 and 38 years old. Twenty-five of them were Arabs (mainly from the Near East), another twenty-nine were Turks (including Germans of Turkish origin). Forty of the interviewees were students (among them, nine were women). The total number of women interviewed was fourteen. Twenty-three were active members of or sympathized with some form of Islamic organization.[2] About half of the interviewees are among those who visit Islamic associations, mosques, and other community settings on a regular basis.

I had started off by distributing questionnaires, but soon realize that this method was in many ways insufficient to represent the various worldviews of young Muslims in Germany in a realistic and differentiated way. Especially since 9/11 many young Muslims in Germany have been interrogated by the police about their living habits and political opinions; it therefore was hardly advisable to confront the interviewees with standardized questions reminiscent of officialdom. An evaluation of the questionnaires that had been filled out revealed that most had answered the questions rather reticently and sometimes evasively. Thus, the questionnaires could not fully reflect the real situation of the subjects in question. Suspicion towards the questionnaires even kept some from answering in their own handwriting, so as not produce any evidence that could be used against them. My decision to switch to qualitative interviews proved successful in many ways. During extensive conversations I gained the confidence of these individuals, who allowed me to get a more detailed look into their lives and life philosophies. Most of them, however, insisted on remaining anonymous, making it impossible to use a tape recorder or even take notes during the interview. I attempted to reconstruct the discussions immediately afterwards in as complete a form as possible. Therefore, some of the quotations in this chapter reproduce content but are not verbatim. Many interviewees insisted on keeping silent about their personal data, but at least granted me the right to mention their country of

---

1   The duration of the interviews varied between thirty minutes and six hours; most took about three hours.

2   I am aware that it is difficult to draw a clear line between an active member and a regular visitor of communal activities.

origin. Though I am aware of all these shortcomings, I had no other alternative but to finish my fieldwork under these circumstances, as others did before me in similar situations (see, e.g., Lindholm 2002).

What I intend to stress in the following is that the process of radicalization in a foreign environment always depends on the articulation of several factors. In some isolated cases these factors can evolve in a framework in which an individual opts for violence aimed at public space (Finn 2001). More often, however, violence surfaces in a closed circuit: within the individual's personality, in which some or all of these factors clash, or within the private sphere of marriage and partnership. In the first two sections I consider the web in which personality structure links up to marginalization and culture shock. In particular, I distinguish between two pathways: the first leading to isolation and the second to radicalization. In the next section I add gender conflicts in cultural transfers as a further component on the path to eventual acts of violence. In the final section, I recount the options that are open to individuals caught up in this web: to either remain invisible or to gain a visibility of their own choosing and making.

Individual Embeddedness in a Complex Web: Pathways to Isolation and Radicalization

The ways people practice Islam and live as a Muslim in a foreign environment are clearly different from the way people experience Islam in Muslim societies. In considering such difference, it is important to recognize that Islam is both a way of life and a *Weltbild* that is constitutive for identity. Within Islamic societies, Islamic belief and practice are part and parcel of everyday life, which means that Islam is automatically lived with a certain sense of commonality. Within the diaspora community, this sense of commonality often finds expression in an automatism of confrontation. Consequently, Muslims in the diaspora have no fixed strategies for (in)visibility. Rather, one's behavior as an individual or the image of a group depends on subjective interpretations as well as social and political calculations. Echoing the first quotation by the student who did not want to be called a Muslim by others, one female student tried to explain to me why "German paranoia" is responsible for disrupting the religious and social meaning of her veil.

"The original purpose of wearing the veil for a woman is to be hidden, and as a consequence to be protected in society. But when everybody—both Germans and Muslims—either attacks or defends the veil publicly, then the veil automatically becomes a means of visibility ... Why can't I simply wear my veil peacefully without German institutions or Muslim interest groups making politics out of my harmless piece of cloth?" (Turkish, 26 years old, in Munich, 2002)

The Muslim diasporas of Europe find themselves having to confront different worlds, and the challenge lies in finding a way to live within a non-Muslim

193

secular society that is subject to rapid societal change. At the same time, Muslims face the dilemma of complying with both the customs cherished by the members of the diaspora, on the one hand, and the normative regulations of a European society, on the other. Additionally, they feel compelled to clearly define their position towards their places of origin and/or home countries. Grappling with issues of continuity and preservation of cultural independence in a foreign environment often leads to an increase in the importance of religion. Moreover, in many cases the resulting fear and insecurity arising from these pressures instigate diaspora communities to turn to forms of tradition that are more radical than those commonly practiced in their home societies. In addition, many perceive their voluntary migration due to economic hardship as a form of exile and therefore mystify it. There is no shortage of examples of groups that have held on to outdated forms of religious expression, in all kinds of religious contexts: the German protestants who during the nineteenth century emigrated to southern Chile and rebuilt their rural communities in the middle of the Araucarias; the pivotal role of Catholicism among the Irish in the United States; and the role of the Talmud among the Jews in their various communities around the world until the founding of the Israeli state (Berthomière 2003).

Like many Europeans, Muslims have a rather ambivalent attitude towards the expansion of Europe. On the one hand, they see the opportunity to live as equals in a pluralistic society that guards the rights of religious minorities; on the other, they fear that European society will be unable to offer them a stable sense of identity. There is a tendency, particularly among Muslim youth, to visualize their future in terms of the *umma*, the community of all-faithful, rather than to think of themselves as part of European society. The search for and insistence on possessing and maintaining a stable "closed-corpus identity" may lead to alienation as well as social and political radicalization. It is thus essential to map the forms of radicalization that have gained prominence in various milieus of migration. They can, but must not of necessity, lead to violence (Waldmann 1974, 2003).

Mapping the Pathways to Isolation

First on the map of pathways to isolation would be *archaic conservatism*, a tendency common among groups of migrants that come from rural, patriarchal regions where only a low level of education is available and tribal law is applied. This form does not necessarily rest on religious attitudes, yet religion is often instrumental in its legitimization of various forms of action. The violence that is generated within this atmosphere is usually not directed at the society of the host country. Rather, the "apostates" of the diaspora community become the victims of this violence, because they are charged with endangering the stability and integrity of the entire group. This form of radicalization is exemplified in cases of honor killings and forced marriage, which various

European governments are currently targeting as a new kind of public problem. In Germany, for example, the norms and behavioral attitudes among certain groups of Turkish migrants have long been outdated in Turkey itself. Yet the existence of the virtual community in the diaspora is thought to be— at least according to my research—dependent on the moral conduct of its members. Not only are blasphemous acts and apostasy severely sanctioned, so too are any kinds of liberal thinking or Western-oriented action. Characteristic for such milieus is the demand for unconditional solidarity as well as strong social and moral surveillance.

Young people who grow up with weak social structures are especially open to a form of radicalization that I call *escapism*. To them, neither their own families nor the host society can offer any kind of useful guidance in life. Frustration and a lack of substantial, positive perspectives for their future push these members of the second and third generations and young people with a migrant background to form so-called Turkish gangs and to direct outbreaks of violence against others in the migrant community. In the district of Mülheim in Cologne, cases of street-fighting between Turks and Arabs are common, despite the fact that they are coreligionists.

Religious avant-gardism can be found in the biographies of certain radical individuals. They generally refrain from traditional forms of Islam by steering clear of the conservative centers of so-called mainstream Islam in Europe. Religious solipsism, a tendency towards autodidactic methods, intergenerational tensions, dissolution and/or rejection of any kind of family-based authority, a minimum of socialization within one's own ethnic and religious communities: all are as characteristic for these individuals as their strong orientation towards the *umma*—conceptualized in the form of an ahistorical, abstract, and falsely heroic model of Islam.

These three pathways often produce isolated individuals. Once alienated from their milieus of origin, they rarely become integrated into the host society and consequently suffer a double marginalization. Lack of integration is especially critical among second-generation Muslims. It is thus especially alarming that members of the second generation—in particular those with an academic education—set the tone within the radicalization process. One example is the conduct of the Kaplan community, whose leaders explicitly aim at an "Islamic revolution" (Schiffauer 2000). Yet members of the first generation do not seem to be immune to radicalization. A closer look at the biographies of the perpetrators of the terrorist acts in New York and Madrid reveals that these individuals initially arrived in Europe as ambitious students oriented to the West, who then became radicalized during their stay in the "Occident." One should therefore recognize that the anxieties caused by an identity conflict and the unsuccessful pursuit of a sense of security may also become reasons for a turn to radical Islamic organizations.

195

Pathways to Radicalization

A closer examination of the relationship between religion and terrorism can clarify this. It is a common (mis-)conception in the West that a potential for violence is inherent in Islam, and that, as a result, faithful Muslims are more open to intolerance and radicalism than are their more "liberal," Western-oriented coreligionists. Most Muslims, however, are eager to stress that Islam literally means "peace" and hence has nothing to do with violence and terror. Certainly there is in Islam, as in any other religion, a potential for peace and charity as well as war and division. Whereas the West nourishes the commonplace notion of an "Islam on the move," in which Muslims increasingly turn to their postulates of faith for guidance, Muslims feel rather defensive about their faith and complain about a general decline of religiosity within Muslim societies. In fact "Islam on the move" is nothing more than a drifting from mainstream Islam. The jihad Muslims believe that they are living in an emergency situation and therefore try to reconstruct an "emergency Islam" in which they search for angry answers to their geopolitical situation. Needless to say, when it comes to Islamic terrorism, religion constitutes the central factor in the mobilization of zealots and the legitimization of violence, as it remains the most important source of identity.

An examination of the biographies of the alleged perpetrators of the 9/11 attacks shows that, against all appearances, the majority of them did not visit Quranic schools in their childhood. They did, however, belong to those Muslims who are decisively familiar with the West: "They all pursued modern ways of life common to the secular middle and upper classes in the West, their lives marked only later by experiences of conversion" (Kermani 2002, 27). Such biographies make it clear that we are not dealing here with poor, underprivileged, barely educated, and naive individuals who spent their lives in religious isolation. Rather, these people have had a rich experience of life and have been commuting between the East and the West. Under the pressure of their insecurity and isolation in the West, they turned to radical organizations, but they had envisaged other aims in life before turning to the career of a terrorist. Religion, then, was not the driving motive behind their terrorist activities; it rather became the legitimization of their actions. To a great extent, these were converts discovering their religion for the first time or rediscovering it after a period of "drifting." They were not socialized in these religious structures to any considerable degree; rather, religion became more important later in their lives, offering them much-needed shelter from disappointment and social stress. Converts and reconverts seem to be especially susceptible to extreme forms of religiosity and moral purism.[3]

---

3   In this context it is of particular interest that the life of the current U.S. president, George W. Bush, also has a biographical turn of a religious nature. After a "sinful" life of indulging in the consumption of alcohol and the like, he experienced a Christian conversion that changed his life radically. Now, as a president, he does

Yet one cannot conceive of a direct link between religiosity and radicalism (Roy 2004). Instead, one might consider the nexus that forms when a certain personality structure hits upon the double process of marginalization, the identity conflicts that are specific to migration, and the proximity of a radical group. A few lines will suffice to typify each of these strands.

The *personality structure* matters. A sensibility for social issues and low frustration-tolerance are characteristic for individuals involved in extremist groups. Often they are people who want to change the world radically but do not have enough patience with it. They suffer from the paradoxical combination of an inferiority complex and dreams of omnipotence. This explosive combination explains how these people can both lead a schizophrenic way of life and perpetrate inhumane, deadly acts of terror. *Marginalization* touches upon the dual experience of alienation and marginality. It is "characterized by close relationships entertained by persons of diverse groups, while the issue of belonging remains unclear" (Heckmann 2002, 7). There is much to back the hypothesis that emotional and social isolation facilitate the bonding of individuals with radical groups. The most important forms of isolation are (a) self-isolation, (b) isolation resulting from discrimination, and (c) marginalization, or the isolation of entire groups. *Culture shock* results from a range of identity conflicts specific to migration—the problems of alienation among Muslim migrants among them. The term culture shock is actually too simplistic to adequately describe the complex processes that a young Muslim undergoes in a foreign society. There is more at stake than merely coming to terms with two very different cultures. Questions of origin, cultural identity, and positioning one's self become especially salient when the decision to live in a foreign environment is made. Finally, *radical proximity* can take several forms, including growing up within a fundamentalist infrastructure and proximity to a radical (peer) group or radical preacher. It seems that when young Muslims turn to extremist organizations, it is mainly due to a lack of self-esteem and a feeling of abandonment. Initially these organizations offer youth a way to re-establish self-esteem, while empowering them as emancipated social actors. Soon, though, the organizations demand full commitment. This newly acquired membership status helps compensate for numerous frustrating experiences in both the family network and the host society at large.

Culture Shock, Male Pride, and the Concept of "Sin"

There are roughly four groups that account for the presence of people with different religious and social backgrounds in Germany today: the so-called guest workers (*Gastarbeiter*), fugitives who seek asylum, academics and

---

not seem to be willing to accept "evil" in the world, pursuing his goal to free the world of its "villains."

other intellectuals pursuing an education, and persons who marry a German.[4] Putting the category of guest workers aside, we are looking at persons who seem in principle to be willing to dispose of their old shared social structures by adjusting themselves to new conditions in order to work towards political, economic, and/or personal fulfillment. To a large extent they are capable of and willing to take risks, such as the danger of losing contact with their homeland or, worse, the danger of sacrificing part of their cultural identity. They are emotionally prepared to confront something new, and they approach the prospect of being intellectually and culturally challenged with curiosity and eagerness.

The problems that develop in the process are specific to each group. The guest workers conceive of themselves as migrants, whereas their children usually view themselves as part of the host society. In other words, what is "home" to the first generation is myth to their children. On the other hand, what is "home" to these children remains an alien environment to their parents. The children often cannot afford to limit their social activities to diaspora circles: the host society has certain expectations of them, and often they have no choice but to conform (e.g., learning the language of the host country). Whereas this participation is crucial to the development of the children, it was less central to their parents' concerns. On the other hand, a new factor for the second generation is an inescapable friction with the country of origin. For many, their own families appear to be rather conservative, yet the seemingly more liberal host society appears to be exclusive and difficult to approach. According to a young Turkish Muslim male, many feel pressured and hindered by both their family and the host society. Nevertheless, the second generation finds new and more creative ways to deal with the issues of discrimination and marginalization, perhaps because members of this generation have proceeded further on the path of assimilation and have been socialized to some extent according to the norms of the host society. As one Turkish male interviewee told me, "Since kindergarten we have been learning to make ourselves heard ... but we certainly have gained more than just bad experiences" (Augsburg, 2003). In contrast to the first generation—and many other migrant groups—the second generation has advanced German language skills and identifies to an extent with Germany. Germany has become, by necessity, the center of their lives. In fact, although a conscious adoption of a German identity might still be problematic for some, a self-understanding in terms of regional or urban belonging—for example as an "Augsburger" or a "Kölner"—is more easily accepted.

The situation for refugees is far more problematic. Unlike other migrant groups, refugees do not have a choice between two or more societies while "relocating" their identity. The factors that force them to leave their countries essentially make them dependent on the protection of the society of refuge.

---

4 This list is not exhaustive. There are many other ways to enter Germany legally (e.g., as a tourist) or illegally (e.g., clandestine migration).

Indicative of the complex emotional implications that result from this relation of dependence is the fact that many traumatic processes are projected onto the host society. Marginalization and discrimination levels are, it seems, at their highest when it comes to refugees. The paradox of their situation—being excluded from the very society that simultaneously welcomes them as a place of refuge—generates a kind of "love/hate relationship." This ambiguous sentiment can be observed among all migrant groups but is strongest among refugees, in part because complex problems originating from their socially and politically charged places of origin continue in exile. Often the refugee has been politically active in the home country, in some cases within fundamentalist circles. In the latter case, neither the authority of their home country nor the principles of the host society can have much of an impact when competing against their own ideologies. Consequently, the options for social ascension that are open to refugees—including the illegal ones—are rather few and far between, to say the least. As one refugee put it, "I thought I would come here and after one or two years I would be financially independent. But never in my life have I been more dependent than I am today" (male Iraqi refugee, 37 years old, in Cologne, 2002).

Inappropriate treatment by public agencies and institutions leave many refugees in doubt about the alleged principles of freedom and equality in Germany. "I have the impression that the institutions are punishing us because we chose Germany as a place of refuge … Human rights and dignity in this place are reserved for Germans" (male Iraqi refugee, 37 years old). Under these circumstances, religious frameworks offer ultimate protection in the face of humiliation and discrimination. One of the positive dynamics of religious socialization circles is the integrative power they exert on many young and insecure persons, who often stand on the verge to criminality. One student told me:

"If there is still blood running in your veins [i.e., if you still have pride and emotions], you'll lose control several times a day. They [the institutions] don't leave a single door open for us and humiliate us intentionally. If I wasn't a believer, I would already have a criminal record." (Iraqi, 28 years old, in Augsburg, 2002)

Last but not least, the so-called illegal migrants pose a rather obvious problem, as much for themselves as for the "alien" host society. An illegal migrant from the Muslim world is very much in need of support from those he meets and can trust. Hiding and keeping a low profile is a constant necessity that requires help from fellow Muslims who are familiar with the host country and who can provide offers of work on the black market. These people look for such help in the mosques and are completely dependent on whoever can offer it. Once they land in the wrong hands, they are easily manipulated and led astray.

The attraction of religious identification can enhance the resentments and frustration that young people entertain towards a society that offers them almost no perspective. The normative standards set by a "consumer and

199

hedonistic culture," widely accepted in Germany, are perceived by young Muslim men as a kind of "cultural hostility," against which they feel defenseless. The ensuing contradictions and tensions that young Muslims, in particular, have to deal with are felt more intensely in a foreign environment. In this setting religion often becomes an alternative to an imposing Western civilization and to a "God is dead" attitude. To many Muslims, freedom in a foreign environment proves to be nothing more than a fata morgana, either unattainable or simply threatening. Freedom is understood as a way to define the self and the right to participate. Yet this often remains only partly achievable. When one looks on from the outside, it is hard to grasp the psychological strain on the ambitious newcomer, who experiences rejection and disappointment once he sees his cultural identity and moral standards excluded.

In contrast to people back home, who face conflicts in a rational and practical manner, diaspora communities tend to approach conflicts in their home societies with a dogmatic spirit and largely infeasible purism. With respect to the Near East conflict, for example, the Muslim and Jewish communities in the United States and Europe usually take extremist positions. Whereas people in the affected regions try to reach a practicable solution through negotiations, the diaspora hardly ever sees options for a rational compromise. When I asked Avi Primor, the former Israeli consul in Germany, why the diaspora appears to be much more emotional and less willing to compromise, he explained, "The diaspora cultivates a bad conscience. People say, 'We are happy here. We are in no position to tell people in Israel what to do, we should simply support them'" (Augsburg, 2003).

Indeed, people abroad often judge conflicts with a sense of detachment from the real conditions, taking up an emotionally charged and dogmatic stance. This stance is often accompanied by fierce religiosity, which can be interpreted as a kind of "symbolic return to one's roots," or even a kind of "making up" with one's home country and the family one left behind. Migrants often arrive in a host country with certain "life projects" in mind and little interest for the conditions they find there. In the same sense, there is little interest on the part of the host society in the "life project" of the newcomers. All that is expected of them is a certain amount of loyalty and fulfillment of the duties that the conditions for their entry state or imply. Yet many of the hopes that drive people to emigrate in the first place remain unfulfilled, even after a long period in the new environment. Desires for wealth, freedom, independence, and the right to participate in society hardly ever are realized. Poor migrants do not really see the relation of poverty and wealth change, for even if migrants experience a slight economic improvement in comparison to their situation back home, they continue to be among the poorer, in their new environment as well.

Within a foreign environment, most migrants belong to an underprivileged minority. Various forms of dependency on the host society—for the right to asylum, employee status, or financial support from the state or even a German spouse, just to name a few—determine the situation of the foreigner in Germany to a substantial degree. These dependencies affect the self-esteem and pride of a "man from the Orient." Interestingly, one could replace "pride" with "masculinity," as the words "man" and "pride" are semantically linked in the Arab language. Maintaining a "culture of honor" in a society in which the notion of honor is rather relative and ambivalent can lead to an outbreak of violence against Western ways of life, as the murder of Theo Van Gogh in the Netherlands has shown. Yet autoaggression and violence against weaker members of one's own community (e.g., women and children) are often the result of an adherence to archaic understandings of honor. In the home societies, public practice of religion and adherence to moral standards help relieve life's pressures (Dupret, Berger, and Zwaini 1999). In a Western, non-Muslim environment, however, these practices can turn into obligations whose compliance proves difficult. If an individual is not embedded in a community in which religious practices are followed collectively, religious zeal can serve to isolate him or her. At times, this exaggerated holding on to religious principles leads to a disorientation of values and moral confusion.

Needless to say, the marginalized position of religion in societies like Germany and the usual "enlightened" treatment of religious symbols intimidate those who guard their sense of holiness. One of the Arab students I interviewed told me of his bewilderment when listening to a fellow German student tell a joke that involved disrespectful reference to Jesus and Mary. "How should a society," he asked, "that does not understand nor respect its own religion understand and respect our own?" The relativization of what is "holy" or even "sin" intimidates many Muslims of the diaspora. For the most part, the idea of sin has lost its implications for emancipated German society. Indeed, the concept is marginalized and robbed of its seriousness when it is applied to actions like tax fraud, petty crime, or even giving in to small indulgences such as eating too much chocolate. In Europe in general, the practice of quoting from the Holy Scripture or of interpreting life in wider religious contexts of meaning has become outdated. For a Muslim, however, the concepts of "sin," the "devil," and "divine punishment" are omnipresent.

When one "reads between the lines" when talking to young Muslims, it becomes quite clear that insecurity about their identity is at the core of a host of problems that these young migrants face. The friction between imported ideals of social conduct and the norms of Western societies—all accompanied by a sense of ambivalence and relativity—proves much harder to deal with than the daily experiences of discrimination and social inequality. In the West the young Muslim man lacks a certain "absolute" that functions at the center of his life. This estrangement manifests itself even in everyday language. In a way, the German use of the conditional—such as "it could be the case, but not necessarily"—makes it difficult for young Muslims to adjust and make decisions. The "lack of a center" and the "end of metaphysics" foster their fears that the line between the "holy" and the "profane" might dissolve. One of the interviewees tried to express this crisis as follows: "This relativity strips down young Muslims in front of themselves, only to reveal their purposefully hidden double morale, their personal duality, and the weaknesses of their culture." This, he added, is "unforgivable" (Egyptian, 33 years old, in Augsburg, 2003).

Although in Germany many young Muslims experience these problems of alienation and the consequent identity conflicts, the majority refrain from choosing a confrontational course with the host society. In a way it is not unlike the rules on haggling at an "Oriental bazaar," with which they are familiar: one must constantly evaluate one's own interests. Although they seldom admit it, these young people have an elastic and versatile identity. Their life practices and perspectives are constantly renegotiated while they choose from a range of values offered to them from both their families and the host society. To some extent this process of constructing a hybrid identity that can respond to specific situations unfolds as a conscious act of choosing among values. Yet most processes of adoption or rejection of the components that add up to hybrid identities take place subconsciously; the individual is seldom aware of them. Those who shy away from the idea of "contaminating" what they understand to be their "pure cultural identity," or who are incapable of coming to terms with foreign values, tend to retreat into a parallel society. Within this confined social space the forces of assimilation increasingly weaken as confrontation with everyday German society becomes less frequent. Yet the social tensions remain the same. Because of their inability to reduce or avoid the increasing pressures and expectations, some individuals project the conflicts that emerge from a hybridization of their identity onto the world around them. A reconstructed, unrealistic, and falsely heroic Islam provides them with an "angry answer" to modernity, to the geopolitical situation that they hold responsible for their situation. What these angry answers can look like can be clearly seen in the recent attacks on New York, Madrid, and London. The longing for a "sense of home," for tolerance and security, shifts the focus to the question of ethnic and religious belonging.

Gender and Class Issues in Cultural Transfers

When thinking about another migrant group in Germany, namely, those who pursue academic and other kinds of education in this country, one hardly considers them to be at all problematic. The image of an academic person lends an aura of sincerity, reinforcing their reputation as studious and—above all—temporary residents of the country. Yet since 9/11 these commonplace assumptions have been proved wrong, if not dangerous. Although a revision of the common understanding of this migrant group is in order, one should not jump to conclusions by conceiving a "sleeper theory" or regard them as typical suspects. Many Germans are not aware of the difficulties that non-European students face in Germany, let alone can sympathize with them. Their stay in Germany is complicated by extensive bureaucratic requirements, which demand from them constant attention to matters of administration. In order to prolong their visa for one year, for example, it is necessary to give proof of relative financial independence—namely, €6,000 or more in a bank account and an income—or provision from home—of €600 per month. In addition, their work allowance is limited to 90 days or 180 half-days per year. Understandably, many feel cheated and ripped off by the institutions, and this perception weighs heavily on their emotional and intellectual ties to the host society. As one Arab student lamented, "My father earns less than €150 a month. How can I possibly have €6,000 in one go? Only terrorists can meet these standards, because only they have so much money" (Egyptian, 33 years old, in Augsburg, 2003).

Students are known to be, in the best case, ambitious, curious, and critical idealists—some want to change the world. Yet, they often also are impatient and do not tolerate frustration well. None of these qualities protects a young and angry person from turning to radical organizations once he sees no other perspectives open to him. Students of the natural sciences, engineering, or economics usually do not encounter situations in which they can familiarize themselves with the outlooks and values of the host society, as do students of the humanities. For the most part, the actors involved in the terrorist attacks of 9/11 were students of the natural sciences. Yet neither quarrels with the bureaucracy nor financial burdens seem to have stood in the way of their radicalization. Rather, it seems alienation and identity conflicts played a major role.

Binational marriages provide a good opportunity and basis for integration, though at times they do become a platform for intercultural and interreligious conflict. In many cases, the foreign male depends on the woman financially and legally. This circumstance encourages the development of the love/hate relationship mentioned above, creating feelings of gratitude and at the same time nourishing general dissatisfaction. It is a constellation that primarily affects Arab men who have been socialized with a strong sense of pride. Individual conflicts often get blown out of proportion. One Arab man I interviewed told me of his marriage: "a German woman together with an Arab man equals hell." Usually it is the German woman who takes on the daily work that back home is traditionally left to men, such as caring for the material well-being of the family or dealing with administrative institutions. This situation proves harmful for the husband's pride and puts his role as paterfamilias into question.

The potential for conflict emerges with the birth of the first child. Even a moderately religious person will insist on granting his child a Muslim educa-tion. He starts to familiarize himself with the principles of Islam, often in order to sustain the upper hand in negotiations with his wife. Yet the fact that the child spends the greatest part of his or her early years with the mother is in many ways troublesome for the husband. A divorced man named one of the reasons for his divorce from his German wife: "Whenever I left the house, I feared my ex-wife would talk to my daughter about Christianity and speak disrespectfully about Islam" (Moroccan, 39 years old, in Augsburg, 2002).

Especially with regard to their daughters, Muslim fathers tend to be over-protective: "I don't want to sit and wait to see my daughter coming home with a boy at the age of fourteen." Marriage to a German woman nevertheless can help Muslim men in many respects, enabling their detachment from religion and old traditions while furthering their integration into the host society. Yet only very few continue on this path.

"My wife and I had decided to raise our children without coercion or fear. We always went around naked in the house and on the beach. But at one point I realized that my children, as they were growing up, tended to be ashamed. I tried to convince them that being naked means being free, but I had to understand that I actually did exercise coercion on my children, by forcing them to act against nature. It is in the nature of man to be ashamed, but we in the West try to rid ourselves of any sense of shame and call that free and natural ... When Adam turned from animal to human, he was looking for leaves to cover himself ... The West tries to wake up the animal in us, but Islam tries to domesticate it. Islam attempts to protect man from his own weaknesses, yet the West tries to use these weaknesses to increase consumerism, and disguises it in the cloak of freedom." (Syrian, 62 years old, in Augsburg, 2002)

The 62-year-old Arab male who made this statement has been living in Germany for forty-three years; he is now divorced from his wife. He found his way back to religion because he tried

"many ways that led me nowhere ... Freedom over here is not real freedom. While nobody would tell you not to 'do this or that,' often you would get to hear: 'What? You didn't do it?' They exercise a certain power—not with orders and command-ments, but with deals and offers!"

Young men who are married to older women in Germany—a phenomenon that can be observed among those who come from countries that are tourist destinations—often are looked down upon by fellow nationals and coreligion-ists. Within the mosques and Muslim community these men feel obliged to show ever more faithfulness and activism in order to rid themselves of the outsider role. Many avoid the places where their fellow nationals gather. Moreover, many marriages break up as soon as the husband acquires German citizenship, even if the marriage initially did not serve this single purpose. After divorce many turn back to the Muslim diaspora community and invest their time and efforts there.

Options for (In)Visibility

On the basis of my research I have concluded that Muslims in Germany choose between the following options when negotiating their relationships to the host society, religion, and the homeland:
1. The individual follows a predetermined path, sticking to the family perspective and goals or following the principles of society: for example,

a student who comes to Germany from an Arab country in order to study at a German university and then returns home after a couple of years and marries within the wider circle of relatives. Those who achieve this option usually prove to be mentally strong and quite flexible. They prefer to have things unfold according to plan. Their social backgrounds and their cultural identity serve as a protective layer between them and the influences of the host society. They seek out familiar structures within the Muslim community and/or the mosque. Because these individuals do not entertain any clear perspective during their stay in the host country and plan to return to their home country, one might expect them to be harmless. This is only the case, however, as long as aggravations from local society keep within certain limits and bonds with the family and community stay intact. One could view this relationship as a kind of "noninterventionist" agreement between the migrant and the host society, amounting to a mutual policy of "live and let live." Yet this agreement remains, at best, imaginary. For a conservative migrant to be able to reintegrate into his home society after his stay in a Western country, three factors must come into play. First, the host society does not provoke him too much; second, the bonds to his family back home remain strong over this period; and third, the migrant encounters supportive structures in the respective migrant milieu. It is commonly assumed that conservative and religious persons are more isolated and feel a stronger aversion towards the host society. Yet the research presented in this chapter has offered a slightly different picture. Through long conversations with members of migrant groups and an discourse analysis, I came to the conclusion that religious persons who stand firmly by their beliefs encounter fewer problems because they internalize a fundamental respect for hegemony through their belief system.

2. The migrant succumbs to new influences and starts to stray off the path. He becomes acquainted with new Western lifestyles and adopts them as an alternative. He may risk damaging his reputation and losing respect within traditional circles of the diaspora and homeland, but some manage to ascend socially and assimilate themselves into the host society through "westernization." An improvement of one's social and economic situation is seen as a strong enough reason to distance oneself from tradition. Families and traditional groups in the diaspora interpret this step rather harshly, as though "the lost son had sold his soul to the devil." Regrets and a bad conscience about what often turns out to be a complete detachment from religion, tradition, and family are in many cases the consequences. If the "lost son" does not find a ready and welcoming new harbor within the host society, it is likely that he will return to old structures and be left with strong resentment and frustration towards the host country.

3. The individual changes sides frequently inhabiting and negotiating the "in-between" of the two camps—the traditional one and the "Western" one—yet without having any essential connections to the core of either of them. His belonging—to his self and to the respective camps—remains

only partially defined: he is neither fully integrated nor excluded. This situation could carry on indefinitely, as long as the pros and cons offered by both worlds maintain an equilibrium. As time goes by, the pressures arising from this polarization may result in conflicts of belonging, dual identification, or multiple personality structures. At some point the desire to break out of this situation emerges; the individual then either chooses a clear orientation along the lines of one group and detaches himself from the other, or he looks for other alternatives.

4. The migrant arrives with radical ideologies but becomes increasingly tolerant and moderate within the host society. These people arrive with an exaggerated sense of being under threat, viewing the West as inherently evil even before their departure. Through positive and personal social interactions with Germans, both their ideologies and the conception of Western societies are called into question. This process presupposes a certain amount of acceptance of criticism as well as a readiness to learn and develop. Migrants who once were persecuted in their home countries for their radical beliefs now enjoy constitutional protection in the host country while exercising their freedoms of speech, religious expression, and social conduct. As a result, some may soften their radical attitudes towards German institutions. Interestingly, the original position taken towards the policies of the regimes and institutions back home is maintained in the new environment and often is even strengthened and radicalized under the favorable conditions for freedom of expression.

5. The individual tries to find a healthy balance between his or her own cultural identity and the fundamental principles of Western lifestyles. These people often have intentionally chosen Germany as their country of immigration. A pre-existing notion of or intellectual connection with Germany provides the basis for a readiness to accept Germany as a second home. Anything encountered in the host or home society that is identity-enhancing and that communicates meaning may function as an equalizing factor between one's cultural identity and Western principles, thereby helping to keep and solidify a healthy balance between the two. Once the everyday presence of Muslim symbols loses its intimidating effect on members of the host society—as is happening through the increased number of mosques and veiled women in public spaces—Muslims also might ease up in their conduct with these symbols and refrain from politicizing them. Further steps taken by the host society, such as logistical support in the process of building new mosques, might in turn encourage Muslims to engage with local society.

6. What I did not find in my sample is the option of premeditated murder. It is conceivable that this option opens up when the factors of marginalization, culture shock, and a specific personality merge with radical company and begin a process of radicalization. What follows contains a religious element that no longer can be ignored. It seems, for instance, that the perpetrators of the terrorist attacks on New York and Washington used a

manual instructing them to follow rigorous code of ritual conduct (Kippenberg and Seidensticker 2004). However that may be, my research revealed that the overwhelming majority of Muslim youth, even when they experience culture shock, isolation, radical ideologies, and loss of identity, nonetheless rejected this option.

Conclusions

It is difficult to conceive of the members of the second generation committing a terrorist act in the country that to a certain extent is their second "home country." Though many children of immigrants distance themselves from Germans when describing their experiences of discrimination and racism, they still speak of their strong bonds to Germany. Most of them view themselves as Germans, but they identify primarily with the cities in which they were brought up. Newcomers, on the other hand, seldom identify with their country of immigration. Because they do not have a history in Germany, it is easier for them to identify and label the country with terms such as "the West," "capitalism," or even "the devil." In contrast, children of the second generation have been socialized in German schools; they are reluctant, despite all difficulties, to describe their country in such vague and abstract terms.

However, against the odds there is some evidence to support the hypothesis that second-generation children are more resistant to militant ideologies and terrorism than are newcomers. They are very unlikely candidates for calculated terrorist violence. Still, it is possible that they may react to daily discrimination through spontaneous violence, anger, and frustration. Of course, one should not outright exclude the possibility that the second generation could make contacts with terrorist groups. The latest attacks in London have been terrible proof of that possibility. Yet it is difficult to compare German and British policies on immigration, for it is difficult to draw parallels between the Pakistani and the Turkish communities. It therefore seems hardly probable that a group recruiting exclusively from the second generation would perform terrorist acts on their own initiative. However, under the effects of social stress, discrimination, and identity conflicts, violence could erupt among the children of migrants as well. Typical for this group, however, is escapism or violence committed by individuals, not violence in the form of organized terrorism.

It is important to distinguish between tendencies to violence as a means of conveying a political or social message and the tendency to use violent rhetoric as a means to gain attention or publicity. Most of the time the loud paroles of violence and the conspicuous Islamic clothes are nothing more than a message aimed at both German society and Turkish communities: We are different; we are here. Though these groups wish to stress their self-made identity and to reconstruct their religion, they are in fact still willing to address their surroundings. Their clothes and rhetoric could therefore be seen as a strategy of communication. Rhetoric often is the weapon used by those who have no other weapons: those who feel helpless, unheard, and humiliated. It can be seen as an outlet or as a means of channeling frustration and social stress. A person who is seriously planning to burn the world down does not announce it in advance. The perpetrators of the 9/11 attacks chose to be "invisible" up to the actual attacks. In accounts made to the press, they were frequently described by those who had known them as "polite," "restrained," and "helpful."

Some Muslim organizations nevertheless use violent rhetoric occasionally as a strategy to keep their own members or gain new supporters. When such groups talk about their aims, they do not claim to behave like good citizens— at least not as the concept is commonly understood. Rather, they wish to give their supporters the feeling that they are part of a great avant-garde mission, one that "liberates the world from injustice," "leads the world to the path of Islam," or "sends the unbelievers to hell." Undoubtedly, such statements work against peace and integration, but there is not always a readiness for violence behind them. Such statements are made primarily to legitimate the existence of the club or organization and to increase the likelihood of receiving more donations. Nevertheless, one should not underestimate the effects of the rhetoric of violence. Many young people begin their radical career after listening to a charismatic leader using precisely such rhetoric. Since the latest wave of violence in the name of Islam, many members of Islamic organizations seem to understand that they cannot maintain the split between democratic structures and militant rhetoric for much longer. Yet there are still some among them who believe that following the ideology of jihad is a better investment.

Finally, there are ways to counteract these processes within the migrant context, so that political radicalism will remain the exception and not become the norm. The classic candidate for such radicalism is the socially isolated individual—the biographies of the 9/11 perpetrators and the members of the Kaplan community have made this clear. To them the attractiveness of radical organizations and their charismatic leaders lies in the promise of "community" and "security." Further conclusions can be summarized as follows:

1. The diaspora does not nourish the tendency to violence; rather, it creates conditions for political calm and conservatism.
2. Those who feel grounded in their faith tend less towards radicalism than do "converted" or "reconverted" former liberals. This claim is supported by the biographies of the 9/11 perpetrators and by analysis of the interviews conducted for my research.
3. Individuals who are not fully integrated into a religious or ethnic community or into the host society may be more open to terrorism.
4. In the diaspora community, Islam is understood to be the main source of ethnic self-understanding and continuity with the past. Therefore, the ethnic community and the religious community are considered to be identical.

5. There is reason to believe that integration into the migrant milieu (i.e., internal integration) can neutralize tendencies towards political radicalization.

References

Berthomière, W. 2003. Integration and the social dynamic of ethnic migration: The Jews from the former Soviet Union. In Diasporas and ethnic migrants: Germany, Israel and Russia in comparative perspective, ed. R. Münz and R. Ohliger. London: Frank Cass.

Dupret, B., M. Berger, and L. al-Zwaini, eds. 1999. Legal pluralism in the Arab world. The Hague: Kluwer Law International.

Finn, P. 2001. A fanatic's quiet path to terror: Rage was born in Egypt, nurtured in Germany, inflicted on U.S. Washington Post Foreign Service, 22 September.

Guggemos, P., and H. Abdel-Samad. 2003. Räumliche Dimension des Terrorismus. Internal paper, Universität Augsburg, Germany.

Heckmann, F. 2002. Islamische Milieus: Rekrutierungsfeld für islamische Organisationen? Paper presented at "Politischer Extremismus in der Ära der Globalisierung," a symposium of the Bundesamtes für Verfassungsschutz, Cologne, Germany.

Kermani, N. 2002. Dynamit des Geistes. Martyrium, Islam und Nihilismus. Göttingen, Germany: Wallstein Verlag.

Kippenberg, H. G., and T. Seidensticker, eds. 2004. Terror im Dienste Gottes. Die "geistliche Anleitung" der Attentäter des 11. September 2001. Frankfurt: Campus Verlag.

Lindholm, C. 2002. Kissing cousins: Anthropologists on Islam. In Interpreting Islam, ed. D. Hastings, 110–130. London: Sage.

Roy, O. 2004. Globalised Islam: The search for a new ummah. London: Hurst.

Schiffauer, W. 2000. Die Gottesmänner. Türkische Islamisten in Deutschland. Frankfurt: Suhrkamp.

Waldmann, P. 1974. Der Begriff der Marginalität in der neueren Soziologie. Civitas. Jahrbuch für Sozialwissenschaften 13: 127–148.

———. 2003. Deutschland—Nährboden für den radikalen Islamismus? Speech given at Universität Augsburg, Germany, 28 January.

APPENDIX

ABBREVIATIONS

ACEI	Associazione per la Cultura e l'Educazione Islamiche (Association for Islamic Culture and Education) (I)
ACLI	Associazione Cristiane Lavoratori Italiani (Association of Italian Catholic Workers) (I)
AEL	Arab European League (B)
AMS	Association of Muslim Schools (UK)
BTBTM	Berlin Türk Bilim ve Teknoloji Merkezi (Turkish Science and Technology Center Berlin) (GER)
CDU	Christlich-Demokratische Union (Christian Democratic Union) (GER)
CFCM	Conseil Français du Culte Musulman (French Council for Muslim Worship) (F)
CSU	Christlich-Soziale Union (Christian Social Union) (GER)
FUCI	Federazione Universitaria dei Cattolici Italiani (University Federation of Italian Catholics) (I)
GMI	Giovani Musulmani Italiani (Association of Young Italian Muslims) (I)
ICA	Islamic Cultural Association (UK)
IUR	Islamic University of Rotterdam (NL)
MCB	Muslim Council of Britain (UK)
SPD	Sozialdemokratische Partei Deutschlands (Social Democratic Party of Germany) (GER)
TBB	Türkischer Bund in Berlin-Brandenburg (Turkish Union in Berlin-Brandenburg) (GER)
UCOII	Unione delle Comunità e Organizzazione Islamiche in Italia (Union of Islamic Communities and Organizations in Italy) (I)
UGEI	Unione dei Giovani Ebrei in Italia (Union of Young Italian Jews) (I)
UMIVA	Unie van de Moskeeën en Islamitische Verenigingen van Antwerpen (Union of Mosque and Islamic Organisations of Antwerp) (B)
UMP	Union pour un Mouvement Populaire (Union for a Popular Movement) (F)
WIM	World Islamic Mission (NL)

Hamed Abdel-Samad (Giza, 1970), BA at Ain Sams University (Cairo) in English and French; MA at Augsburg University (Germany) in Political Science, English Literature, and English Linguistics; studies at Kwansei Gakuin University (Japan); a DAAD German Exchange Service Award for excellent achievements; affiliated with the UNESCO-IBE International Bureau of Education, Geneva. He is currently a research assistant at Erfurt University (Germany). Title of PhD project: The Relation between Early Islam and the Eastern Church (2007). His publications include "Radikalisierung in der Fremde" (in Determinanten des Terrorismus, ed. P. Waldmann, 2005, Velbrück Verlag). E-mail: hamed.abdel-samad@uni-erfurt.de.

Valérie Amiraux (Paris, 1969), PhD at the Institut d'études Politiques (Paris). She is a permanent senior research fellow in sociology at the CNRS in Amiens (CURAPP, University of Picardie) and currently a Marie Curie Fellow at the Robert Schuman Centre for Advanced Studies (EUI) in Florence (2005–2006). Studies in Muslim minorities and religious discrimination in the European Union. Her publications include Acteurs de l'islam entre Allemagne et Turquie: Parcours militants et expériences religieuses (2001, Paris: L'Harmattan), Musulmanes, musulmans au Caire, à Téhéran, Istanbul, Paris, Dakar (ed. with O. Roy, 2004, Marseille: Indigène), "Les risques du métier" (in Cultures et conflits, ed. with D. Cefaï, 2002, Paris: L'Harmattan). E-mail: amiraux@iue.it.

Welmoet Boender (Rotterdam, 1974) is currently affiliated with the International Institute for the Study of Islam in the Modern World (ISIM), Leiden (NL). Title of PhD project: Imams in the Netherlands: Role, Authority and Binding in a Secularising Society (2006). Her publications include Nederlandse moslims: Van migrant tot burger (ed. with D. Douwes and M. de Koning, 2005, Amsterdam), "Imams in the Netherlands and Islam Teachers in Flanders," with Meryem Kanmaz (in Intercultural Relations and Religious Authorities: Muslims in the European Union, eds. W. A. R. Shadid and P. S. van Koningsveld, 2002, Leuven: Peeters). E-mail: welmoetboender@yahoo.com.

Nadia Fadil (Antwerp, 1978) is currently a research assistant for the Fund of Scientific Research of Belgium (FWO-Vlaanderen) and affiliated with the Centre for Sociology of Culture at Leuven University. Title of PhD project: Processes of Religious Individualisation and Privatisation among Secular and Religious Second-Generation Maghrebi Muslims in Belgium (2007). Her publications include "Muslim Girls in Belgium: Individual Freedom through Religion?" (ISIM Newsletter, 2003), "Individualising Faith, Individualising Identity: Islam and Young Muslim Women in Belgium" (in European Muslims and the Secular State, eds. J. Cesari and S. McLoughlin, 2005, London: Ashgate). E-mail: nadia.fadil@soc.kuleuven.be.

Annalisa Frisina (Bergamo, 1973), PhD at Padua University. She is currently affiliated with the Department of Sociology of Padua. Studies in (Italian) citizenship, children of immigrants, high-school students. Title of PhD project: Difference as an Opportunity? Young Italian Muslims and Citizenship Requests. Her publications include "Musulmani e italiani, tra le altre cose. Tattiche e strategie identitarie di giovani figli di immigrati" and "Giovani musulmani d'Italia: Trasformazioni socioculturali e domande di cittadinanza" (in Giovani musulmani in Europa, eds. A. Pacini and J. Cesari, 2005, Turin). E-mail: annalisa.frisina@unipd.it.

Gerdien Jonker (Amsterdam, 1951), PhD at Groningen University (NL). She is currently affiliated with the Georg Eckert Institute for International Text-book Research, Braunschweig (Germany). Studies in Muslim minorities in the European Union, religious history and memory, conflict and gendered communication. Her publications include The Topography of Remembrance: The Dead, Tradition and Collective Memory in Mesopotamia (1995, Leiden: Brill), Eine Wellenlänge zu Gott: Der Verband der islamischen Kulturzentren in Europa (2002, Bielefeld: transcript). E-mail: jonker@gei.de.

Philip Lewis (London, 1949), PhD at London University. He currently lectures in the Department of Peace Studies, Bradford University, and is Inter-Faith Adviser to the Anglican Bishop of Bradford. His publications include Pirs, Shrines and Pakistani Islam (1985, Pakistan: CSC Publications), Islamic Britain: Religion, Politics and Identity amongst British Muslims (1994/2002, London: I. B. Tauris), "Muslims in Europe: Managing Multiple Identities and Learning Shared Citizenship" (2005, Political Theology 6:3). E-mail: p.lewis@bradford.ac.uk.

Gökçe Yurdakul (Istanbul, 1974), PhD at Toronto University. Studies in sociology (Istanbul) and gender and women's studies (Ankara). Title of PhD project: Immigrant Mobilization and Political Representation in Germany. Studies in migration, citizenship, race and ethnicity, gender and women. Her publications include Migration, Citizenship, Ethnos (ed. with M. Bodemann, 2006, New York: Palgrave Macmillan). E-mail: gyurdaku@chass.utoronto.ca.

INDEX

Die Titel dieser Reihe

**Leseproben und weitere Informationen finden Sie unter:
www.transcript-verlag.de**

Die Titel dieser Reihe

Leseproben und weitere Informationen finden Sie unter:
www.transcript-verlag.de